The Amateur's Guide to Death and Dying:

Enhancing the End of Life

First Edition

Here's to a good death!

Richard Wagner, Ph.D., ACS

ISBN: 978-1-61098-199-6
Ebook ISBN: 978-1-61098-200-9

Published by

The Nazca Plains Corporation ®
4640 Paradise Rd, Suite 141
Las Vegas, NV 89109-8000
© 2012 by The Nazca Plains Corporation. All rights reserved.

Cover Photo, xefstock
Author's Photo, Michael Henry
Art Direction, Blake Stephens

The Amateur's Guide to Death and Dying:

Enhancing the End of Life

First Edition

Published by The Nazca Plains Corporation
Las Vegas, Nevada
2012

Dedication

Brian Friedman, M.D.

March 20, 1955 - July 18, 2010

Acknowledgements

I want to thank Joann Lee, my editor, and Michael Strickland and Steven Webb, who helped proofread the book.

I am grateful for the generosity of the following good friends and colleagues who helped as presenters to PARADIGM groups and in writing this book:

James ("Jay") B. Creighton, Esq. He practices law in San Francisco and San Mateo, CA.

Emmett Giurlani, Esq. He practices law in San Francisco, CA.

Steve Susoyev, Esq. He practices law in San Francisco, CA.

Reverend David Pettee, MSW. He served as a hospice social worker from 1993 to 2002. He is now the Director of Ministerial Credentialing for the Unitarian/ Universalist Church.

Dr. Cheryl Cohen Greene, DHS. She is a clinical sexologist and surrogate partner therapist. Her practice is in Berkeley, CA.

Dr. Brian Friedman, MD. He was the director of the Emergency Department at Davies Medical Center, San Francisco, CA until his sudden and unexpected death in 2010.

Table of Contents

Getting Started   1
Introduction to the Basic Principles and Tools

Chapter One   19
Week 1: This Silence Isn't Golden

Chapter Two   51
Week 2: Picking Up the Pace

Chapter Three   75
Week 3: Unfinished Business

Chapter Four   115
Week 4: Details, Details, Details

Chapter Five   153
Week 5: Going Home

Chapter Six   179
Week 6: Don't Stop

Contents continued...

Chapter Seven   **215**
Week 7: Charting a Course

Chapter Eight   **249**
Week 8: Approaching The Exit

Chapter Nine   **283**
Week 9: With a Little Help From My Friends

Chapter Ten   **319**
Week 10: Closing the Circle

About the Author   **343**

"All goes onward and outward
Nothing collapses.
And to die is different from
What anyone supposes,
And luckier."

Walt Whitman

Getting Started

Introduction to
the Basic Principles and Tools

*J*ust a guess, but I'll bet you have mixed feelings about tackling this workbook. That's understandable. For most of us, coming to grips with the end of life is not on our top ten list of things to do. Lounging on a boat bound for Tahiti, eating a chocolate sundae, or watching a marathon of I Love Lucy reruns — now there's a good time. But dying? Well, it doesn't have quite the same appeal. After all, when it comes to death, we're all just a bunch of amateurs.

It's too bad facing our mortality isn't seen as the great adventure it can be.

Talk of death makes most people squeamish. The slightly less timid among us might consider picking up a book and sitting quietly reading words of comfort about "passing on" from sensitive professional types. But both of these responses only increase the passivity and isolation that create our "patient" role. They make us more dependent and rob us of our dignity. After all, you didn't consider living your life this way, so why would you want to live your dying this way?

I think we need something radically different. We need a way to access information, explore our feelings, and learn from others similarly challenged.

Here is your chance to confront your mortality in a truly adventurous way. I am inviting you to jump into this interactive environment and become a member of our on-the-page support group.

Each of the following chapters involves you in a group meeting. You'll get to know and identify with the issues and concerns of the other group members. You'll be able to participate fully in all the discussions, weekly exercises, and homework. You'll be challenged by a host of speakers offering valuable information on timely issues such as spirituality, sexuality and intimacy, legal concerns, final stages and assisted dying. You'll receive the encouragement you need to design your own practical solutions to end-of-life problems and develop a strategy for successfully navigating your final life passage. You may even find yourself celebrating your newly found identity as a mortal.

The best part is that you can do it all at your own pace. You won't have to tear through your closet looking for something to wear, fight traffic, search for a parking space or rush to get here on time. You can just "show up" by getting comfortable wherever you are.

Let's make one thing crystal clear from the start. There's no one way of dying well. However, there are some things we might want to consider if that is our goal.

- First, death isn't only a universal biological fact of life, part of the great round of nature; it's also a necessary part of what it means to be human. Everything that we value about life and living — its novelties, challenges, opportunities for development — would be impossible without death as the defining boundary of our lives.

- While it may be easy to accept death in the abstract, it's often more difficult to accept the specifics of our own death. Why must I die like this, with this disfigurement, this pain? Why must I die so young? Why must I die before completing my life's work or before providing adequately for the ones I love? These are some of the most difficult questions dying people ask themselves.

This workbook will provide you with the opportunity to find your own answers to these pressing questions.

- Living a good death begins the moment we accept our mortality as part of who we are. We've had to integrate other aspects of who we are into our daily lives – our gender, racial background, and cultural heritage, to name a few. Why not our mortality? This workbook will provide you the support you need to begin the process of acquainting yourself with death and growing empowered in your new identity as a mortal. Putting death in its proper perspective will help you regain control of your life and achieve a greater sense of balance and purpose.

- Dying can be a time of extraordinary alertness, concentration, and emotional intensity. It's possible to use the natural intensity and emotion of this final season of life to make it the culminating stage of your personal growth.

- In the process, you will pioneer new standards of a good death that the rest of us can emulate. You're in a unique position to help the rest of society desensitize death and dying. Most importantly, you'll be able to support those you love as they prepare for your death. In fact, you'll be able to join them as they begin their grieving process.

- You'll regain lost dignity by actively involving yourself in the practical preparations for your own death. Some of the things we'll be considering include negotiating pain management, choosing the appropriate care for the final stages of dying, putting your affairs in order, preparing rituals of transition, as well as learning how to say good-by and impart blessings.

- Finally, you'll learn to heed the promptings of your mind and body, allowing you to move from a struggle against dying to one of acceptance and acquiescence.

$\mathcal{P}$ersonal $\mathcal{I}$ntake $\mathcal{F}$orm

Let's begin by having you take stock of your current situation. This will give you a baseline from which to evaluate your progress throughout the program.

First, Some Things About You

Name:

_____

Nickname:

_____

Date of Birth:

_____

I was born and raised:

_____

I currently live:

_____

Religious background:

_____

Current religious practice, if any:

_____

Five significant events in my life:
1. _____
2. _____
3. _____
4. _____
5. _____

Interests, hobbies, pastimes:

_____

_____

_____

_____

Your Current Situation

Diagnosis:

_____

_____

Brief medical history, symptoms, etc.:

_____

_____

Current support system (partner, spouse, family, friends, other support groups):

_____

_____

_____

_____

Personal Growth Goals

List three things you wish to accomplish during the next ten weeks.

    1. _____

    2. _____

    3. _____

List three things you'll need help with.

    1. _____

    2. _____

    3. _____

Your Fellow Participants

Now that you've completed your intake form I'd like to offer you a sneak preview of the ten other people who will be joining you in this group. These are fictional characters, composites actually of people who have done this program before you. You'll have plenty of opportunity to formally introduce yourself once we get started, but until you get better acquainted, these thumbnail sketches will serve as a handy reference. In fact, you may even want to bookmark this page so that you can return to this section if, at first, you find all these personalities a bit confusing.

Janice, 62, has late onset diabetes and rheumatoid arthritis. She is a neatly dressed, silver haired woman with gnarled hands and feet. The thick lenses of her glasses sit heavily on her pleasant, open face. She is of medium build, and walks with the aid of a cane. She has the shy, nervous demeanor of a young girl, often absent-mindedly fidgeting with the buttons on her favorite mauve sweater. She is a Red Cross volunteer

and a recent widow. She was raised a Methodist in Alton, Illinois, a small town just across the Mississippi River from St. Louis, but she currently has no religious affiliation. "I miss not having a church to attend. At least the social part of it."

Her husband Albert died in the hospital of congestive heart failure 18 months ago. Albert's sudden death dramatically changed her life. She was forced to give up the comfortable home they shared for nearly 30 years and now lives alone in a modest apartment in a subsidized senior housing complex.

She says she is often alone and lost in her profound grief. "Our marriage was a traditional one, the kind that was popular fifty years ago. Albert was solely responsible for the family finances. He shared little of the intricacies of these things with me. I'm afraid that he kept me completely in the dark about all of it." Albert withheld their troubled financial situation from her in order to shield her from the unpleasantness. He died without a will or an estate plan, leaving Janice completely lost and befuddled.

Albert died in intensive care and Janice was unable to be with him when he died. She has a great deal of guilt about this. She claims that her biggest fear is "dying alone in some awful hospital, hooked up to a bunch of beeping machines." However, she's just as anxious about becoming dependent on strangers. "You see, I'm losing my eyesight to the diabetes."

Michael, 52, was diagnosed with multiple sclerosis four years ago. Two years ago his disease process escalated to the point where he was confined to a motorized wheelchair. This past year he has had several MS-related setbacks that have kept him bedridden for several weeks at a time.

Things have become so difficult that two months ago he was forced to sell his once-thriving law practice. The few hours of work he can manage a week at his old firm are more frustrating than fulfilling for him.

Mike is often depressed. He continually repeats his self-defeating mantra: "I'm not half the man I used to be." The superhuman support of his second wife Maryanne and his son Kyle along with his beloved Oakland Raiders are the only things that keep him from killing himself.

An exasperated Maryanne accompanied Mike to his intake interview. She tearfully reported how Mike's smoldering rage and bouts of sullenness terrorize the family. "I love him, but he's gotta get off his pity-pot or I'm gonna walk, and take Kyle with me." Mike sheepishly acknowledges his disruptive behavior. His ruggedly handsome face distorts with shame. "It's not me. It's this damn MS. I just can't seem to get it together. I feel like such a failure."

Even though he thinks participating in the group is an admission of defeat, he promises his wife that he will give it his best shot. This soothes Maryanne. She hugs him and promises to help in any way she can. "We're in this together, babe."

Holly, 43, is a breast cancer survivor. She has been cancer-free for three years. She's a graphic artist, shares a home with her partner of ten years, Jean, and their teenage daughter Annie.

Holly is a splendid figure, nearly six feet tall, weighing over 200 pounds. She is as soft-spoken as she is imposing. A beautiful smile radiates from her full face. Oodles of thick jet-black braids spring from her head as from a fountain gone mad. She is forever brushing one or another of them from her face as she speaks. Her frequent laughter is like music, making her whole body dance and shake, but her levity masks a somberness and apprehension that is very troubling to her.

"I often become consumed with worries about getting sick again. My fears can turn into a paralyzing dread that takes days and sometimes weeks to shake. I know that until I can accept the possibility of my own death, I'll never be able to embrace all the great things that are right in front of me."

For therapy, she spends hours tending ten different varieties of roses in her immaculate garden. "I lose myself there. The rich earth soothes my troubled soul."

Her church is a second home for Holly. It always has been. "I was raised in rural Georgia. As a child, my momma took me to this little makeshift church in the woods near the river. It had no heat in the winter, and come summer, why honey, you'd about roast. The Oakland church I attend now has both heat and air conditioning, but child, the singing and preaching still can raise a cold sweat on me."

Raymond, 50, is a social worker employed by a home health care agency in San Francisco. He is thinking about applying for a position in the agency's hospice program, but he's not quite sure he's ready for the responsibility. "I need to better understand my own feelings about death and dying before I can hope to assist anyone else." He hopes this group will help him do this. "If I'm going to do this work, I want to do it well."

Raymond's mother died of ovarian cancer when he was seven years old, but he never really processed the loss. Now a dear friend of long standing, Joann, is also dying of cancer. Joann's imminent death has opened the floodgates of his unresolved grief associated with his mother's death. "I'm both drawn to Joann and repulsed by her all at the same time. And she knows it. It's so crazy. You should see me. I'm confused and disoriented, which is not at all like me."

Raymond says that his interest in this group is strictly professional. "I don't have a life threatening illness myself." But upon further investigation, Raymond reveals that a recent visit to his doctor disclosed that he is at high risk for heart disease. Raymond is considerably overweight. "I guess I've pretty much let myself go to seed. I've always been a big guy, big-boned, as my mother would say, but now I'm just Fat with a capital 'F'". The heart disease news, while shocking, didn't come as much of a surprise.

Three years ago Raymond went through a very acrimonious divorce. "My life shattered before my eyes." His three children, two girls and a boy, live with his ex-wife in another state. He gets to see the kids only on holidays and for a month during the summer. "After the divorce, I just didn't care if I lived or died. I ballooned. I put on over a hundred pounds in a matter of months. Hey, wait a minute. Maybe that's why I'm considering this hospice move, and why I'm so ambivalent about Joann, and why I want to do this group. Maybe I need to recover a sense of meaning for my life."

Clare, 73, and her husband, Charley, have been married for fifty-three years. They have four children, nine grandchildren, and five great-grandchildren. Clare's leukemia, which was in remission for over ten years, has recurred. This time it is considered untreatable. She has decided to forego any of the heroic, life-sustaining measures for which modern medicine is

so famous. She and her doctors agree that hospice is her best option. "I've done my homework. I've shopped around. I interviewed all the hospices in town and have chosen the one I feel will honor my wishes for the kind of end-of-life care I want."

Clare has lived a rich and full life. "I was a career woman long before there was such a thing as a career woman. I've always been a take-charge kind of gal. This leukemia may very well kill me, but it will never get the best of me." Her illness has made her very frail. Her skin is almost translucent. She has an otherworldly look about her, but there is no mistaking her remarkably robust spirit.

Her youngest son Stan, her one and only ally in the family, brought her to the interview and will see that she makes it to each meeting. Stan says, "Oh yeah, she's feisty all right. There's no flies on her, and the ones that are there are paying rent."

Clare's an avid pantheist. "God is everywhere and in everything. I have always had a close and abiding relationship with God." Her faith has sustained and comforted her all of her life and she is at peace.

Clare's biggest concern is her family. They are pressuring her to fight against death even though she doesn't want to. She wishes that they would join her in preparing for her death rather than denying the inevitable. "I worry about how they will manage when I'm gone. And even though I'm ready to die, I feel as though I need their permission before I can take my leave."

*K*evin, 39, is living with HIV. He tested positive twelve years ago. Luckily he continues to be asymptomatic.

Kevin's a music teacher and member of a jazz quartet. He is currently single and shares his house with two roommates.

His lover, Doug, died five years ago just one month shy of their tenth anniversary together. Kevin is trim and buffed. He works out at a local gym four days a week. He is boyishly handsome with tousled red hair. He rides a motorcycle and is a wicked pool player.

"Even though I've had many friends die of AIDS, I still have plenty of my own death stuff to deal with."

He reports that he has recently engaged in some questionable sexual practices. "That's a sure sign that I'm

shoving a lot of this under the carpet. And I know this kind of thing could be, well, a fatal mistake!"

Kevin was born and raised a devout Roman Catholic. His Boston Irish family had high hopes that one day he would become a priest. "I know I disappointed them and I don't think they ever really got over it. Ya see, when I came out in college I left the church at the same time. It was a preemptive strike, if you want to know the truth. I wasn't about to wait around for them to throw me out just because I was gay." His inability to find a suitable spiritual home makes him sad. "Sometimes I feel lost and rudderless. I know God loves me, but the sweet and easy connection I once had with God as a younger man eludes me now."

Kevin believes it's important to ritualize the end of life, but doesn't quite know how to make that happen. "Maybe I'll get some ideas from the other people in the group."

*M*ia, 31, is a graduate student in Medieval Languages at Stanford University. Several months ago, she landed in the ICU, near death from an acute lung infection. While she was in the hospital she was diagnosed with a rare lung disorder, which was the source of the initial infection. Since that initial hospitalization, she needs to use oxygen and was advised to seriously consider a lung transplant if she expected to live past 35. Mia reluctantly uses the oxygen, but she won't consider the transplant. She has chosen a different path.

Mia regularly consults a doctor of traditional Chinese medicine, which is consistent with her cultural heritage. She uses a wide array of other modalities, including vitamins, acupuncture, meditation, yoga, massage and biofeedback. "This is the way I want it. These things make me feel involved and empowered, and that's more important than anything else."

Although she likes her American doctor, western medicine leaves her feeling cold and disconnected. She felt robbed of her dignity in the hospital. "They didn't see me, they just saw my disease."

Mia was born in Hong Kong, the only daughter of socially prominent and professionally successful parents. She's lived a charmed and pampered life, but now she knows the downside of living a life of privilege. "Nothing in life prepared me for this kind of adversity."

Despite her frailty, she has a decidedly tomboyish appearance. She is lively and animated when she speaks. Sometimes she even gets tangled in the plastic tubing that runs from the ever-present oxygen canister to her face. "I haven't got the hang of this yet. Can you tell?"

The pulse and spritzing sound of the oxygen keeps time with her labored breathing. "I once felt immortal, which now seems weird because I'm starting to realize I could be quite dead in a year." She has an overriding dread of her final days. "I can't even imagine what it will be like. I'm sure it'll be just horrible. I panic when I have to struggle for a breath now. What will it be like then? I sometimes get so frightened I cry."

Raul, 18, was born with a genetic kidney disorder. He has had countless hospitalizations and surgeries. He has been on dialysis for many years. He had a kidney transplant three years ago, but his body rejected it. Within three months of the transplant he was back on dialysis. "Man, I am so tired of living in a body that never works right."

Raul is as thin as a reed and his skin has the ashen pallor of one who is near death. His chronic pain has aged him far beyond his years. During his interview, Raul is having difficulty making himself comfortable. "I'm havin' a bad day. The pain is real bitchin'. It ain't like there's some days when there's no pain, only most of the time it ain't this bad."

Raul is exhausted and exasperated. Many family concerns weigh upon him, adding anxiety to his already difficult life. "My parents are heavy into the church. I am too, but not like them. They keep telling me it would be a sin to give up. But hey, man, how can it be a sin to wish this shit would end? It's not like I haven't tried. I've been in the hospital so many times I can't even count 'em."

Raul's anger and frustration are written all over him, but his machismo prevents him from revealing too much of his inner struggle. His teeth clench against the pain, but then his eyes brighten for a moment. "Hey, ya know there's this real hot babe in my school. She's so fine. I try to talk to her, but she don't like talking to me. I think she's afraid I'll give her some kind of sickness or something." Raul has never had a girlfriend. "I never even kissed a girl, 'cept my sister, and she don't count. What if I die before I get some lovin'? That would really top off this crummy life."

Only one of his sisters knows that he wants to do this group. "Amelia is the only one who tells me it's okay to feel the way I do." Raul is looking for some support for expressing his feelings. He hopes this group will provide that. "I want to be able to talk about dying with my family, but I don't know how. We're all real messed up, I guess."

Robin, 25, is in recovery and has been for four years. She ran away from home at 16 and lived on the street until she was 19. She was a big-time heroin addict who turned tricks to pay for her habit. "It was a crummy life. I had this total death wish. I shared needles, had unprotected sex, you name it. How or why I survived, I'll never know. I've been raped, beaten, and robbed, each more than once."

Only after being hospitalized for a severe case of pneumonia and testing positive for HIV did Robin begin to turn her life around. "Is it okay to say that HIV is the best thing that ever happened to me?"

After a year of rehab, she got a job at Safeway and moved into a small flat with her boyfriend Bobby. "We met at an AA meeting. He's in recovery too." Her life was finally coming together.

"The new HIV drug cocktail I'm on has worked miracles. My viral load went from 700,000 to an undetectable level. I applied to journalism school and am supposed to start in the fall."

But she's had to put everything on hold. Bobby wasn't as lucky. No combination of drugs halted the ravages of AIDS for him. Now 27, he is actively dying. It's not likely he'll live out the month.

Despite Bobby's bad luck, Robin is trying to stay upbeat. "I've been through so much to get to this point. I can't let this setback pull me down again. Bobby would never forgive me."

She says that watching the man she loves slowly die is the hardest thing she's ever had to do. "Getting clean and sober was a cakewalk compared to this." She's emotionally drained. "It feels like something in me is dying." Tears well up in her green eyes.

Her moussed platinum hair is scattered wildly on her head. One simple nose ring is all that remains of the dozen or so body piercings she once brandished. A poorly designed tattoo on her upper right forearm peeks out from under her baggy sweatshirt. "I don't even know how I got this. I was strung

out most of the time. Let's face it, I was a total freak."

Max, 86, is a retired salesman. He is 5'7" with a stocky build. He has the spry demeanor of a man twenty years his junior. He sports a full head of unusually black hair. "Comes right out of a bottle. Gray hair is for old guys."

He is quick with a joke and has an infectious Cheshire cat grin. Max had bypass surgery several years ago, and until recently has been healthy and active.

Six months ago he began to complain of stomach pain and noticed that he was losing weight. The doctors found cancer in eighty percent of his stomach. Surgery was out of the question, because at his age it would be too risky. When pushed, his doctors finally conceded that, at best, he might have a year to live. "The news hit me like a ton of bricks. It's not me I'm worried about, it's my Sylvia."

Max is the primary caregiver for his wife of sixty-five years, Sylvia, who recently has had a series of small strokes. Max's three sons and other family members have been trying to buoy his spirits by reminding him that he is a fighter. "You'll beat this too, dad. You'll live to be a hundred."

Sylvia is also in denial about Max's condition. She claims he is fine and assures everyone that they are managing just as before. However, when their youngest son came to visit the other day, he found no food in the house and discovered his parents had not eaten in over twenty-four hours. Sylvia broke down and tearfully admitted she had been rejecting relatives' offers to shop and cook because they were too ashamed to admit they couldn't care for themselves.

Max was raised a pious Jew in Poland, but now he says he's an agnostic. "How could there be a God when there is so much pain and sorrow in the world?" Max concedes that instead of planning for his death, he is frozen in a panic about what will happen to Sylvia after he dies. "I know this isn't helping matters any, but I don't know what else to do."

USING THIS WORKBOOK

If you are reading this book you already know that our society has an enormous death taboo and that few opportunities exist for sick, elder and dying people to connect with others in a purposeful way. You probably also know that instead of taking a lead role in orchestrating our finales, we are expected to be unobtrusive, dependent on the care of others and wait *passive-ly* and *patient-ly* for the curtain to fall.

Well, you can kiss that unhealthy mentality goodbye right now. *The Amateur's Guide to Death and Dying* is, as its title suggests, an interactive workbook for enhancing the end of life. It is designed to help you reclaim your dignity and dispel the myth that sick, elder, and dying people are unable to take charge during their final season of life.

The Amateur's Guide to Death and Dying offers you a way to face your mortality within a framework of honesty, activity, alliance, support, and humor. And most importantly, instead of having some well-meaning "expert" lecture you on how to think and feel, you'll be learning how to navigate through this new territory from the best possible teachers available – other people just like you.

The most exceptional aspect of this workbook is its format. *The Amateur's Guide to Death and Dying* is modeled on a remarkably successful 10-week program developed by PARADIGM

Programs Inc., a nonprofit organization in San Francisco. You will be included in an on-the-page support group, which simulates participation in an actual PARADIGM group.

The Amateur's Guide to Death and Dying offers practical information on the nuts and bolts of successfully living one's dying. As in our real-life groups, you will be exposed to authentic life situations that arise when people consciously face their mortality in our death-negative society.

You will gain insight and perspective into a myriad of issues related to dying in this modern age. In addition, six dynamic speakers will present you with important and timely information that is full of humor and compassion.

All of this is designed to help make the end of life less of an intimidating process and more of a rich, poignant transition.

You'll find everything you need, right here, to be an active participant in this process.

My Check-In

Each week our group session begins with an opportunity to check-in. This provides each participant a chance to share his or her weekly progress with

the rest of us. In the "My Check-In" section that follows, you'll be offered that same opportunity. You'll also be able to respond to the previous week's issues and talk about key events of your past week.

My Turn

Each week we'll tackle a specific issue: spirituality, legal concerns, early messages about death, etc. You'll sample the discussion of your fellow participants as they come to grips with their own fears and anxieties. In the "My Turn" section that follows, you'll be offered an opportunity to join the discussion. You'll have plenty of opportunity to detail your thoughts and inner dialogue, and respond to the other group members and to our speakers.

Exercises and At Home Work

Each chapter contains creative exercises to further your involvement in the particular subject being addressed. You'll be able to join the other participants as they tackle these thought-provoking exercises right along with you.

Each chapter also contains an "At Home Work" section, where you will be presented with an activity that is designed to keep you engaged in the process all week long. It will also prepare you for the following week's topic.

Some Final Thoughts

Here are a few suggestions on how to enhance your involvement in this process. First, walk through the process step-by-step just as it's presented. A great deal of thought has gone into producing this program. It is tried and true. It moves from one topic to another in a specific order, each week building on the week before. In order for the process to work, you'll want to allow yourself plenty of time and space to not only read through each chapter, but also to complete each exercise and homework assignment.

One of the best ways to stay involved in this program is by keeping a personal journal. This will serve as your own personal compass throughout the process.

This workbook is only able to provide you with a limited amount of space for your reflections and comments, so you may want to keep an extra pad of paper handy for jotting down all your thoughts, observations, and questions that may not fit on the page provided.

If you find writing or typing on a computer keyboard difficult, you might want to consider the option of keeping an audio or video journal. Either way, by the time you complete this workbook, you will have a valuable legacy that you'll be able to share with others.

Even though *The Amateur's Guide to Death and Dying* provides you with a ten-person, on-the-page support group, there is no substitute for live human interaction. In light of this, you may wish to invite a friend or family member or maybe even a group of like-minded people to join you in this process.

If you work with a partner or a group, you'll want to read aloud the check-in and discussion portions of each chapter and then, after completing that week's exercises and homework assignments, you could share your responses with each other. This is an ideal way to break open a healthy conversation on what it means to die wisely and well.

John: Bring him some water.

Klienman: What do I need water for?

John: I assumed you were thirsty.

Klienman: Dying doesn't make you thirsty. Unless you get stabbed after eating herring.

John: Are you afraid of dying?

Klienman: It's not that I'm afraid of dying. I just don't want to be there when it happens.

From *Death*, a play by Woody Allen

Chapter One

Week 1:

This Silence Isn't Golden

Welcome and Introduction

Richard: I am so glad you are here. It is an honor to be in your company.

Before we get started, I'd like to walk you through a few ground rules.

This is a support group, not a therapy group. We're not here to fix anyone or anything. We're here simply to learn from and support one another.

Begin today by taking responsibility for this group. It's your group. The more you invest, the richer the experience will be for all of us.

I suggest that you take some time to prepare yourself for each meeting. Don't arrive cold. One of the best ways to be prepared is by keeping a journal.

Each group session will begin with a brief "round robin" check-in. This is an opportunity for you to share your weekly progress with the rest of us.

Finally, please personalize your participation. When you speak about your thoughts or feelings let us know that they are yours. Use "I" instead of "you."

Like life itself, our time together is limited. Even though ten weeks may seem like a long time to you now, I'll bet you'll be surprised at how quickly it passes.

These next weeks will be jammed with things to do and things to think about. I suggest that you pace yourself. Honor your limits, but don't be afraid to stretch. I promise that you will not break.

This process is tried and true. Hundreds of other people, just like you, have already completed what you are about to begin. In fact, those who have completed this process helped fine tune it and are proud to be part of bringing it to you now. So when the going gets tough, try to imagine all the other people who trod this same ground before you. It has been a challenge, in one way or another, for every one of them. After all, what kind of adventure would this be if there were no risks involved?

So relax. You're in good company. And welcome to our group. Everyone is dying to meet you!

Checking In

Richard: We will begin each week with a round-robin check-in. This week I'll ask you to introduce yourselves. Mention what brings you to the group and what expectations you have of our time together. Would you begin for us, Mia?

Mia: Sure! My name is Mia. I'm a grad student at Stanford. I'm completing my master's degree in medieval languages.

Why am I here? Well, a few months ago I found myself in the intensive care unit of the hospital. I couldn't breathe; I thought for sure that I was going to die. You see I had a lung infection, which upon closer inspection, turned out to be a rare lung disease. Why it decided to raise its ugly head at this moment in my life I couldn't tell you.

Six months ago I was training with a bunch of other women for a climb of Half Dome in Yosemite. Now, not only will I not be able to do that but I can't even climb a flight of stairs without nearly passing out.

My doctors are talking lung transplant. I'm thinking, you gotta be kidding. But without it, and maybe even with a transplant, I could be quite dead in a matter of two years. Gets a girl to thinking, ya know what I mean? Oh, I'm 31.

Mike: I'll go next. My name's Mike. I'm 52 and my wife and I live in Oakland. As you can see, I'm pretty much stuck here in this goddamn chair. I have multiple sclerosis. It's been four years now and I'm still not used to the fact that I can't jump up and toss the football around with my son, Kyle. By the way I'm a big Raiders fan — 'Go Raiders!'

I'm here mostly because my wife told me I have to be here. I think I'm okay, but she thinks that I'm depressed and angry all the time. She thinks that since I've been having all these medical setbacks lately, I've been impossible to live with. What do I know? I'm not convinced that I belong here. I'm not dying. But if it calms things at home I'm willing to give it a try.

Janice: Hello, My name is Janice, but my friends call me Jan. It's so good to be here. I have been looking forward to this group since I read about it in the paper some months ago. I have so much on my mind that I think I could burst.

I'm feeling pretty isolated these days. You see, I lost my husband last year and I don't have many friends. I am often alone and I feel pretty blue most of the time.

Albert, that was my husband's name, had a massive heart attack while puttering around in the garage. We rushed him to the hospital where he languished for two long weeks in coronary intensive care. You should have seen all the tubes, pumps, and other awful, awful machines that kept him from me. I couldn't even get close enough to him to give him a hug. It broke my heart to see him like that. Even though he never regained consciousness they kept him hooked up like that until I begged them to stop. It was like he died twice, once when he had the heart attack and again when they took him off life support. Dear God, I can still see him lying there. I have nightmares all the time.

I'm 62 years old, I have diabetes and, as you can see, I have terrible rheumatoid arthritis which causes me a great deal of pain. Although I don't think of myself as being close to death, I know it could happen at any time. Look what happened to poor Albert.

So all I can think about is what if I die just like him? What if I die in some impersonal hospital room hooked up to a bunch of machines surrounded by strangers? I don't want to go like that. There's got to be a better way.

Robin: Hi, I'm Robin, and you will have to excuse me if I seem a bit scattered. My best friend, Bobby, died in my arms two days ago. We meet three years ago at the local community-based HIV clinic. Bobby and I have HIV. Well, he doesn't anymore. He's dead.

I have HIV. I tested positive in the hospital four years ago after nearly dying of pneumonia. I was living on the street at the time. I had been sharing needles and having unprotected sex since I ran away from home at sixteen, so I'm actually pretty surprised I'm still here.

I met Bobby while we were both in recovery for drug addiction. We both thought we had this whole HIV thing beat. We were on the 'cocktail,' protease inhibitors that is. We were making plans to settle down, after he went back to work, and start a family, if not our own kids, then we were going to adopt. Really we were. Now he's dead and maybe things don't look so good for me either. I'm way busted.

Sorry for getting choked up like this, but it's all so fresh in my mind.

I just applied to journalism school. It starts in the fall, but now I'm having second thoughts. I'm afraid that if I start school I'll just die and all that work will be for nothing.

I'm 25 with no future. Six months ago every thing looked bright for the first time in my life. Now I'm frozen in place again. I'm lost without Bobby. I'm afraid that I won't be able to make it on my own. I'm hoping that this group will help me start to live again.

Max: I guess it's my turn. My name is Max. I'll let you in on a little secret; I'm 86 years old. I know I don't look a day over sixty, but it's true. I've seen it all in my time and I still have a great love for life.

My Sylvia isn't doing so good. Sylvia is my wife. She's had three little strokes this past year and I'm her nurse. Oy, what a job. And to top it off, six weeks ago my doctors found cancer in eighty per cent of my stomach. They think that surgery is too risky at my age. They say I have less than a year. Doctors! What the hell do they know? Besides, if I die, who would look after Sylvia? That's my job. I'm her husband, have been for over sixty-five years. I don't know what to do. But that's enough about me.

Raul: Oh, okay, my turn. Hi, I'm Raul and I'm kinda nervous. I've never done anything like this before. Hey, I just turned 18 last week. That's some big deal because I was supposed to die when I was a baby. I have polycystic kidney disease. It means my kidneys don't work on their own. I was born with it.

Oh yeah, nobody in my family knows I'm here, just my big sister Amelia, who told me about this group. Like we had this long talk right before my birthday. I was telling her how sick I was of fightin' something I can't win. Shit, man, it's not like I'm some kinda quitter. I've had eighteen years of this shit. I just need a break, that's all. Amelia's the only one in my family who understands.

My parents are really big into our church and stuff. They're always raggin' on me about how it's all in God's hands.

Yeah, right! They want me to keep praying to all these saints for some kinda stupid miracle. There are so many saints I can't even remember all their names. I asked Amelia what she thought. She said she didn't think it was a sin not to keep fighting. She said she wouldn't be able to do what I'm doin'. She was the one who told me I should come to this group.

I hope you guys can help me get some ideas on how to talk to my parents. And I hope you'll tell me it's okay to think this way. Shit, man, it's real hard tryin' to do this all this by myself. My parents think I'm having dinner with Amelia so if they find out I'm here, we'll both be in deep shit! Okay, I'm done.

Holly: Hi, I'm Holly. I'm a breast cancer survivor. It's the third anniversary of my remission next month.

What brings me here? Well, for several months now, I've been having these panic attacks when I start thinking I might get cancer again. There's no physical sign that the cancer is coming back, but I'm just so freaked about getting sick again and, of course, dying, that I'm driving myself nuts. It's a drag because my life feels pretty wonderful.

My partner Jean and I bought a house last year and our daughter just started high school. Well, maybe living with a full-blown teenager isn't so totally wonderful. (Everyone laughs.)

I'm a graphic designer and business is good. Plus I've really gotten into creating this fantastic rose garden in our backyard. It's the best therapy for me. But even though I have all of this going for me, I still plunge into panic and then depression.

I saw a flyer for this group at the women's bookstore in Oakland and thought it might be a good place to deal with and hopefully get past my fears. Oh yeah, I'm 43.

Kevin: Hello, I'm Kevin. I'll be turning the big 4-O in two months. Who woulda guessed? I've been HIV positive for eighteen years. I'm what they call a long-term survivor. I'm real proud of that.

I teach music at a high school in Oakland, and for entertainment I jam with a jazz quartet that I formed with some friends. We play for private parties and fundraisers. It's a low key, just for fun sorta thing.

Most of the time, except for when I'm taking my medications, I feel like things are humming along just fine, which is totally great. But about six months ago, I met this guy and, for some unknown reason, I didn't practice safe sex. This really blew me away. I was like totally freaked out.

Afterwards, I realized that I'm shoving a lot of this death stuff under the rug and I know that could be, well, a fatal mistake. A couple of weeks later I went to a rap group and talked with one of the counselors there. He told me about this group. I guess I'm here because I'm finally ready to deal with the possibility I could die at any time.

Raymond: Hi, my name's Raymond. I'm 50 years old and work as a medical social worker for visiting nurses here in San Francisco. I feel a little weird about being here, not having a life-threatening illness myself, but hopefully it's okay with you that I am.

The reason I want to do this group is because my best friend of twenty years is dying and I can't cope. I want to be there for her as much as I can, but sometimes I just cut and run. She actually understands all this, which is really amazing. In fact, she's the one who suggested I do this group!

Now I know this is gonna sound nuts, but I'm also seriously thinking of taking a position on the hospice team at the agency where I work. And I know that before I can do that I had better get to work on my own death and dying stuff. I'm really glad to be here.

Clare: Well, my name is Clare and I'm here because I have stage-5 chronic lymphocytic leukemia. It was in remission for over ten years, but now it has recurred and this time it's untreatable.

I don't want you to feel sorry for me, because it's okay. I've made my peace with it, thank God. Unfortunately, my family doesn't feel the same way. I guess no matter how old you are, even when you get to be seventy-three like me; your family still thinks they can tell you how to live your life.

I've been married for fifty-three years to my husband Charley, and we have four kids, nine grandchildren, and five great-grandchildren. And out of that whole bunch, I only have my son Stan to talk to. Everyone else, including my husband, won't hear a word when I start talking about planning my funeral or who will get my antique Tiffany lamp.

They just say, 'Oh, mother, stop talking like that, you'll outlive us all.'

I know they mean well. They're just scared and upset. But boy oh boy, it's really getting under my skin. I know I only have a short time left to live, so I want it to be real. I'm sick of always having to smile and pretend when I'm with them. It's about time for them to start considering my feelings for a change.

So, like Raul, I need help dealing with my family. I'm looking forward to being here very much.

Richard: Since I'm part of this group too, I'll take this opportunity to introduce myself. My name is Richard. I'm the founder of PARADIGM/Enhancing Life Near Death, the organization that brings you this workshop.

Although I've been working in this field for 30 years, I should probably say from the onset that this is not something I chose to do. It was more like this work chose me. Let me explain.

I was a Catholic priest for twenty years. Unfortunately, this wasn't a particularly happy association. My superiors thought I had a problem conforming to their expectations. And so for fifteen of those twenty years I was punished for what they considered to be my rebellious nature. That's all over now, I'm happy to report. However, when I was still in the good graces of the Church, I trained as a psychotherapist. I was pretty good at both of these professions, but I did have one truly big blind spot. I had a pathological fear of death. Even visiting sick people in the hospital made me weak in the knees. I had the worst bedside manner imaginable.

I finished my doctorate in 1981. That same year a mysterious thing began to happen. Gay men all across the country began to sicken and die from an unknown disease. Was this a diabolic plot of some kind? Perhaps it was divine retribution. Or was this simply a very serious medical emergency? The AIDS crisis had begun in earnest.

Because of my background in religion and psychology, friends turned to me for guidance. I'm afraid that I had nothing to offer them. Nothing, in all my years of schooling, had prepared me for what was happening to the people I loved. I was petrified. All my greatest fears were being realized. What did it all mean? It was a desperate time and I was powerless. I could do nothing but sit and watch the nightmare unfold.

As it turned out, sitting and watching was the best thing I could have done, because as fate would have it, this time I was to be the student, not the teacher. In time, I became less anxious. The monstrous thing I feared for so long was being transformed. I was able to sit with death and not be afraid. Death was no longer the enemy; she had become what St. Francis called her, 'Sister Death.'

Years of going from one death scene to another with hardly a break in between was exhausting but also rewarding. I began to see patterns develop. Despite the uniqueness of each death, I noticed there were two things all these deaths had in common. They were difficult and lonely affairs.

Difficult because in this culture we have a hard time recognizing when things are over, especially the things we enjoy – summer vacation, relationships, our youth and even life itself. This is a problem because being unable to acknowledge the end of something makes saying goodbye and thank you impossible.

And they were lonely affairs, because the wisdom people come to during the dying process often died with them. There simply wasn't a medium for collecting this abundant wisdom and thus it was frequently lost.

Each person faced his/her mortality in a vacuum of information and support. It was as if each person had to learn to die from scratch, as if no one had died before him or her.

I figured there had to be a better way to deal with this fundamental fact of life. That's why I'm here. I want to take a fresh look at my mortality, and do so in an interactive and positive way. I want to celebrate my belief that living well and dying well are one and the same thing. I'm not talking about adjusting deathbed pillows so that dying people can strike heroic poses for the edification of onlookers. I'm talking about achieving a good death in the context of real dying – with all its unpredictability, disfigurement, pain, and sorrow.

My Check-In

Richard: Take all the time and space you need to introduce yourself to the group. What brings you here? What are your expectations?

_____

_____

_____

_____

_____

_____

_____

_____

_____

_____

Group Process

Richard: Postponing any thoughtful consideration of our death, especially when it is close at hand, can have disastrous consequences for both us and those who survive us.

Why is dealing with death so hard for us? Early childhood messages about death sure don't help. Think spooks, skeletons, skulls and crossbones, and things that go bump in the night. From a young age, most of us have had it drilled into our heads that we should not ask questions or even talk about death because it's bad luck.

How many times has someone told you that a relative or family friend is now in heaven or asleep with the angels, the word dead being avoided like Aunt Agnes's infamous tuna surprise? Or perhaps you were told you couldn't go to the funeral of someone you loved when you were a kid because children don't belong there. It's no wonder those of us who are dying feel like we've been ordered to belt out our swan song without ever learning the tune.

Let's tackle this un-golden silence head on. I would like to ask each of you to share the early messages and memories you got about death and dying. You may wish to include what you remember seeing of death and dying in the movies or on television. Often people learn how their deepest fears spring straight from a traumatic childhood incident or misshapen belief.

What are some of your earliest associations or memories of death and dying? Holly, would like to begin?

Holly: I can remember my mamma taking me to my Uncle Harold's funeral when I was four or five years old. A lot of her people were church people and funerals were big family affairs, kids and babies included. I remember sitting in the hard wooden church pew, staring at all the women wearing beautiful black dresses and wide-brimmed hats. I can even remember their smell, like overripe mangoes. I can still see each one of them, wailing and shrieking into my uncle's coffin. I didn't understand how he could lay so still and not get woken up by all their racket.

So death wasn't hidden from me. In fact, in the poverty I grew up in, life was hard and death was a blessing.

Raul: When I was growin' up, I kept overhearing doctors say the 'D' word a lot to my parents when they were talkin' about me. They didn't think I was listening. They acted like I wasn't even there. That sucks, man.

When my parents got to take me home from the hospital, I'd ask my mother what it meant, 'Why are the doctors always talking about dyin' when they're around me?' She would always look away and tell me, 'Raulito, you are hearing things again.' Or she would change the subject, yelling at me for somethin' I didn't do. 'Clean up your room, Raulito, it's a big mess.'

So I had to find out on my own what it all meant. This wasn't easy, because nobody I talked to would tell me the truth. They would tell me not to worry my little head about such grownup things. This used to really piss me off. Why do they always treat me like such a kid?

I finally figured it out though. I had some bad shit wrong with me and that meant that I was probably gonna stop livin' from it.

Raymond: My mom died from ovarian cancer when I was seven. She'd been sick for about a year before that. My sisters and I knew something bad was happening. We had to move out of our house in Los Angeles and back to Brooklyn, to be closer to my mom's family. But no one ever talked about her dying.

I remember my dad driving us home from my grandmother's house the day my mom died. He had tears running down his cheeks and my older sister Elaine was sobbing. I knew something was wrong and when I asked why they were crying, dad said 'Mommy's in heaven now.' My little sister and I didn't know what to think. I remember we even started to laugh.

Once I figured it out, I was devastated but nobody paid attention to how I was feeling. I guess they were all caught up in their own grief about losing her. This is why I feel so freaked about my friend Joann's dying. It pushes all my abandonment buttons. I never got to deal with this stuff when my mom died.

Kevin: When I was five, my mother gave birth to a baby that was stillborn.

I remember being so excited, jumping up and down as I stood at our window watching my parents get out of the car, thinking I was about to see my new baby brother. But when they walked in, all my mom was holding was a teddy bear. When I asked her where my new baby brother was, she started crying. I thought it was my fault, that I had made her cry. I felt so bad. I couldn't figure our why my baby brother didn't come home with them. My parents couldn't talk about it for years.

I slept with that teddy bear every night. I would talk to it, thinking it would give me some answers about what had happened to my baby brother. I gave that teddy bear to my lover, Doug, for our ninth anniversary, when he was dying, and now I have it back again.

Doug's death helped me break through a lot of the confusion and shame I had about death, but it's still really hard for me to talk about.

Clare: I guess you could say I grew up with the flowery part of death. My Dad was the florist in the small New Jersey town where I grew up. He made up all the arrangements for the churches, the weddings, and the funerals. I used to work in the store with him, applying dozens of little white flowers to these huge black-ribboned wreaths that would say 'In Memory of our Dearly Beloved Whomever.' So death was all wrapped up with my Dad's business and I learned early to be pretty matter of fact about it.

I remember driving up to funeral homes or churches with our flowers in the back of our old pick-up truck, with a big tarp covering them to keep them from scattering in the wind. The hardest funerals to do were those for children; all those little pink carnations and baby's breath. It used to break my heart.

Max: My earliest memories of death are seared into my brain. No Jew my age can escape the legacy of the Holocaust. My family were merchants in Poland until the Nazis came. My parents knew there was danger, so they sent my younger sister Ruth and me to live with a family in England. Leaving my parents was the hardest thing I ever had to do. Getting out of Europe at that time was full of danger, especially for young people. I cared for my sister the best I could, but she got sick and died shortly after we arrived in England. The doctors said she died of a broken heart.

My heart was broken too, but I wouldn't die. I lived to hear that my entire family – parents, grandparents, aunts, uncles, and cousins, everyone in the town where I was born – died in Dachau.

Just think, I survived the Holocaust so I could die an old man with cancer. Oy, it's so crazy! That God up there has a real sense of humor, don't ya think? That's all I'm gonna say for now.

Mia: As strange as this sounds, I have no early memories of either death or dying. I've never been to a funeral, never seen a dead body or a casket, and never even been in a mortuary. Everyone in my family, except for me, is healthy. Even my grandparents, all four of them, are alive and in good health and in their 80's. This freaks me out because I've had no opportunities to rehearse my own dying. I hate the idea of being the first in my family to die. I feel like I'm letting everyone down by being sick.

The only thing I can relate to is what I know of dying from the movies. Isn't that bizarre? I mean, I want to go just like they do in the movies, all pretty and heroic. After I say my famous last words, things will just fade to black. Or even better, like in *Wuthering Heights*, there

will be a great big storm and those who love me will have to fight their way to my bedside, arriving just in the nick of time to see me flutter my eyelids and slip quietly away. How romantic. I love that movie.

Mike: My grandmother died when I was about five or six years old. She pretty much raised me because my mother was sick all the time. This is difficult for me to admit, but I loved my grandmother very much and miss her even now.

I was made to feel like such a sissy for crying at her funeral. When I started to cry my old man shook me real hard and told me to stop. He said men don't cry. He wasn't crying even though she was his mother. I thought to myself, how could he be so cold? Even at that age I thought he was a bastard. But his lesson must have stuck because since that day I haven't been able to cry for any reason. I never shed a tear at either my mother's funeral or my father's funeral. I think he broke something in me that day.

I don't much like talking about this.

Robin: As I said in my check-in, my best friend died in my arms two days ago. Bobby was just the latest in a series of deaths that started a couple of years ago. Before my diagnosis and getting involved in the HIV community, I didn't know anything about death. Sure, there were aged relatives who died back east, but that never really touched my life. I simply never gave death a thought. I guess I imagined that I would live forever. What young person doesn't? Nothing in my earlier life prepared me for what I'm living now.

Janice: My first remembrance of death was when my pet canary died when I was real little. I remember Tippy was so pretty and he sang so sweetly. It was my job to feed and water him every day. I remember how every night I would cover his cage to keep him warm while he slept and every morning I would wake him up when I pulled off the cover. One morning I did just that, only to find Tippy dead on the floor of the cage. I was shocked and I feared that it was somehow my fault. I remember crying and crying.

My grandpa who lived with us held me in his arms and soothed me, telling me that Tippy was old and when animals get old they get tired and die. He said it in such a nice way that it made perfectly good sense to me as I recall.

My grandpa helped me bury Tippy. I put him in a cigar box that I lined with a piece of velvet cut from one of my mother's old dresses. I remember saying a prayer while grandpa dug a hole in the garden. It was all so very nice, as I recall.

My grandfather died a year later. Before he died, he told me that he was going to see Tippy real soon and told me not to worry. 'Do you remember what I said about getting old and tired out? Good! Then you will be fine.'

My grandfather's words are still with me today. I'm grateful for that early education.

My Turn

Richard: What are your earliest memories and messages about death and dying? Which of the other group member's recollections would you like to respond to? What are the messages that have come to you from the media about death and dying?

_____

_____

_____

_____

_____

_____

_____

_____

_____

_____

Richard: Okay, let's look at what it is about death and dying that frightens us and see if we can pinpoint why we have the fears that we have. Here's a simple exercise to help us do just that.

Follow the instructions on how to complete the exercise, and when you've finished, we'll continue. Take all the time you need.

Exercise 1

This exercise is designed to help you confront your fears about dying. Identify the sources of your fears by responding to each of the following statements with a (Y) yes, (N) no, or (M) maybe. When you are finished, go through all the items marked yes and rank them in the order of their importance — #1 being the most important, etc.

1. _____ I am afraid there will be no afterlife, that death will be the end of everything.
2. _____ I fear abandoning the people who depend on me.
3. _____ I am afraid of being punished for the bad things I've done or the good things I've failed to do.
4. _____ I am afraid that death will be the end of feeling and thinking.
5. _____ I am afraid that my death will make those who love me unhappy.
6. _____ I am afraid of what will happen to my body after I'm dead.
7. _____ I am afraid of dying before I finish my life's work.
8. _____ I am afraid of dying in pain.
9. _____ I am afraid of the last judgment.
10. _____ I am afraid of losing those I care about.
11. _____ I am afraid of being helpless and having to depend completely on others.
12. _____ I am afraid of dying because I don't know what happens after death.
13. _____ I am afraid of dying before I am ready to go.
14. _____ I am afraid of taking a long time to die.
15. _____ I am afraid of dying suddenly or violently.
16. _____ I am afraid of dying alone.
17. _____ I am afraid of losing control of my bodily functions.
18. _____ I am afraid of dying before I come to terms with my mortality and face my fear of dying.

Richard: Everyone finished? Great! Let's see what this exercise uncovered for you about your fears and where they come from. Raul, can we start with you? What did you mark as your number one fear?

Raul: Let's see. I marked #9, the one that says, 'I am afraid of the last judgment.'

The priest at my church keeps sayin' that suffering is part of life, that no one can take the place of God, and that only He can decide when it's time for a person to die. So I'm afraid that if I don't keep doing dialysis or taking my medicines, and I die, like, you know it'll be a bad scene, burning in hell and Satan and all that bad shit.

I can't help it, that's what scares me when I think about stopping my treatments.

Clare: Raul, I had #9 at the top of my list too. I won't try any new treatments for my cancer. I'm ready to go. But I'm frightened that if I go against everyone else's wishes it will haunt me.

I keep thinking God expects me to honor my family. After all, I've done it

most of my life. And how it's sinful to be so selfish, following my own heart. I really think this fear is what prevents me from taking the steps I need to die the way I want to.

Richard: It never ceases to amaze me that people continue to pray to a God that abuses them. It's kind of like paying someone to beat you.

Perhaps there is another way of looking at this. I am not suggesting there are no moral or ethical norms, particularly when it comes to matters of life and death, but it seems to me that if there is divine retribution, then wouldn't that be reserved for the great evils that plague humankind?

You both mentioned you were taught that there is merit in suffering. Let's just say for the moment that there is. My question is, if there is virtue in suffering, how can suffering that makes you bitter and angry and at odds with yourself and your God be the source of merit?

Mike: This is strange, but until today I didn't think I had many fears at all. In fact, most of my friends think I'm a real daredevil, you know, fearless. I'll admit it, this exercise blows me away. Apparently I have more fears than I know what to do with.

Number 13 is my greatest fear, 'I am afraid of dying before I'm ready to go.' I'm never going to be ready to go and there's the rub, because one day I'm going to die. That means that I'll go out kicking and screaming, just the way my old man did. You talk about hell on earth. By the time that old bastard died, he hated and cursed everyone and everything around him. Everyone was so glad when he finally croaked. And to this day no one misses him.

To tell the truth, my greatest fear is that I will become like my father. I think I'd rather kill myself first. I feel so trapped by all of this.

Mia: I also marked #13 as my number one fear too. Damn, I'm only 31 years old. I'm just starting to live.

Richard, you talked about God a few minutes ago. I don't believe there is a God. And if there is, He is cruel and vengeful. I hate Him. Why would He do this to me now? I was just beginning to hit my stride. Maybe I'll be ready to go in thirty or forty years but not now.

Max, I want to live as long as you. You're in your eighties. It's easier to die when you're old, right?

Max: Mia, I may seem old to you but I'm not so old to me. Number 13 is not my greatest fear, but you better not think that just because I'm 86 I'm ready to roll over and die. There's a lot of life in me yet.

Holly: Number 13 is a big one for me too. I've had to struggle with lots of stuff in my life – poverty, racism, coming out as a lesbian, single-parenting and the like. The last thing I want to do is to die just when I feel things are finally clicking. I want to see my daughter graduate high school. I want to be there when she gets her first job, I want to attend her wedding, and be there when she gives birth. Jean and I want to be doting grandmothers one day. Damn, if I don't sound all traditional like! My mother would've loved it!

It's not so much fear as it is sadness. It's like all my happiness is floating in a giant bubble that death could burst at any time.

Mike: I'm not ready yet either! But that's the thing, especially with a disease like MS. It's like someone else is running the stopwatch.

You know what Holly was saying about her daughter? Well, my son Kyle's only nine, and it kills me to think I won't be around to cheer him on when he plays quarterback for the Raiders.

But seriously, I've always been a fighter and I'm not going till I'm damn good and ready.

Janice: Without a doubt #11 is my greatest fear – 'I am afraid of being helpless and having to depend completely on others.' I've seen too much of that in my life.

I'm ashamed to admit it, but 15 years ago, after my mother had her last stroke, Albert and I had to put her in a home. We just couldn't care for her on our own. I know that this is not what a daughter is supposed to do and I still beat myself up about it all these years later.

Anyway, at the home – I don't know why they called it a 'home' because it was nothing more than a warehouse – it was so terrible. My mother was just a shell of a human being and yet she lingered for two years. She couldn't even feed herself. She was at the mercy of strangers who didn't much care one way or the other if she ate or not.

Albert's death in the hospital was just as bad, but in a different way. I want to die at home, but I don't have anyone I can count on to be there for me. I have no children.

I'm also equally afraid of what will happen to my body after I'm dead, #6. I don't want to be put in a box, made up like a clown, and put on display like they do. What is all this baloney about 'she looks just like she's sleeping'? No she doesn't. She looks like a corpse with lipstick on.

Robin: I know what you mean, Jan. This is my number one fear too. Dying of AIDS isn't pretty. It just goes ahead and ravages your whole body, top to bottom. I've been there and I've seen it. By the time you die, you're just a little stick person laying in bed, helpless, like a baby.

As scary as that is for me, having my body waste away like that, I'm most afraid of dementia. HIV can get into your brain and make you all potty-in-the-head. It's one thing having someone wipe your butt; it's totally different when you're a vegetable. I don't know about anyone else, but I'm stockpiling drugs so I can off myself before that happens to me.

Mia: I marked #11 too. For me it's a question of dignity. If I lose my ability to care for myself I don't think I'd be a whole person.

Mike: Sorry for butting in here. I just gotta tell you that I thought the same thing some years back. Thought I'd kill myself if I ever had to use a chair. And yet here I am. There are lots of things I can't do for myself anymore. It's not my favorite way to live, not by a long shot, but I sure as hell didn't stop being a person. You know what I mean?

Richard: This issue comes up a lot for those of us who go from being healthy one day to sick and debilitated the next, this fear of not being able to take care of ourselves, having to depend completely on others. There are so many negative messages in our society attached to being dependent. It's bad to be a burden and anyone who is, is dismissed as no

longer being a whole, productive person. Sickness, aging and disability really conflict with the independent, gung-ho, do-it-yourself American image most of us were raised with.

We absolutely need to rethink this. We are not bad people or failures just because we may need help. Self-esteem and physical ability are not one and the same thing.

Max: Number 14 is my greatest fear, taking a long time to die.

Robin, you said that AIDS is a terrible way to die. Well, stomach cancer ain't so wonderful either. I know it's there, I can feel it eating at me. Already there are times when it's hard for me to keep food down. What if it takes its own sweet time? What if it slowly kills me inch by inch? What if I starve to death like all those Jews did in the death camps? Who will take care of Sylvia? Who will take care of me?

Clare: That's my fear too, Max. It's taken me a good long time to come to peace with my dying. Why should I prolong it? I agree with what you were saying.

Leukemia is no picnic. I'm no longer able to enjoy food and everyday I have more and more pain, which really scares me. I'm not suicidal. I don't see myself blowing my head off or swallowing hundreds of pills, but I do pray that my death be swift.

Kevin: Well, like Robin, I've had lots of exposure to death from AIDS. My lover took a year and a half to die, and it was both horrible and amazing all at the same time. He was an incredibly strong person and I know that's how he made it through. But when I compare myself to him, I feel like such a wimp, especially during a crisis. I don't think I'll be able to handle a long, protracted dying process.

Janice: May I add here that #8, 'I am afraid of dying in pain,' is closely linked to #14? It's dying in pain that is the real issue, right? The length of time it takes is almost beside the point.

I am all too familiar with pain, constant pain, with my arthritis. It can make hours seem like days and days seem like weeks.

Mia: I agree with Jan. Sometimes, when I have to struggle for breath, it's not only painful, but I panic and that makes things even worse. If this progresses, as I know it will, I don't know what I'll do.

Richard: A slow, painful, protracted death is just about everyone's worst nightmare. However, there are things you can do about this. I suggest each of you initiate a frank discussion with your doctor about pain management and comfort care. If you start now, you will have time to determine whether your doctor is of the same mind as you concerning these things. If you find that your doctor doesn't see eye-to-eye with you, shop around until you find one who does. The days of slavish loyalty to a doctor just because he or she has been your doctor for many years is over.

We will be dealing with this issue in depth in a few weeks when we discuss 'Final Stages.' Until then, you should know that there have been a number of important advances in the field of end of life pain management. Dying people have made great progress in sensitizing health care professionals about end-stage pain control and comfort care. The simple fact is that no one needs to die in pain.

Mike: Even though it's not my number one fear, #17 scares the shit out of me. I mean that literally. I'm afraid that I'll lose control of my bodily functions when I die. Even now, I'm having more and more trouble controlling my bowels. What if I shit the bed when I'm dying? Maybe this is just a guy thing, but that would be too damn embarrassing. I can't even believe I'm talking like this. You must really think I'm a jerk.

Max: Wait a minute; you're not a jerk for feeling like that. I feel like that too. Someone was talking about dignity a while ago. That's what's important for me. I'm a proud man. I make no apologies. I've had to be strong to face what life has thrown my way. This cancer is just the final indignity. Whoever said dying isn't for sissies knew what they were talking about.

Richard: So much of what we're talking about today has to do with control, doesn't it? But conscious dying has to do with learning how to relinquish

control before circumstances wrestle it away from us.

In many cultures detachment is an art form. In many religious traditions detachment is a virtue. Perhaps there is something here for each of us to consider. Ultimate control has little or nothing to do with being able to manipulate externals, which I'm sorry to say also includes our bodies. Ultimate control is about inner peace and well-being. And these are not dependent on being 'well' or being 'whole.'

Raymond: I wonder if I'm the only one who marked #18, 'I am afraid of dying before I come to terms with my mortality and face my fear of dying.'

Most of my life has been spent trying not to think about death and dying. That's beginning to change a little bit, but I'm still far from being comfortable with it. Now that I have to deal with Joann dying, I realize just how scared I truly am. I'm feeling pretty hopeless about ever being able to come to terms with death. I feel like I'll wind up dying as unenlightened as ever. I'll probably also be confused and depressed.

Kevin: That word 'enlightenment' really bugs me. Who's to say what constitutes enlightenment? Especially when it come to dying. Listen Ray, I think we can get ourselves all balled up with a real judgment thing when we start telling ourselves we must reach a certain state of mind or else we won't have a good death. Dying is hard enough. I don't want to add that kind of performance anxiety to everything else.

Richard: Is anyone else feeling like that? Do you feel as though you are expected to die the 'correct way'?

Clare: I think this world would be a much better place if people didn't force their beliefs on each other. My death will be right for me, whatever that is.

The hard part is really a step before that, giving myself permission to die when everybody else is pressuring me to keep on living.

Holly: Wait, I thought we were here to learn different ways of dealing with death so we can have a choice. I don't want to die in fear and denial. I agree with Ray

– dying confused, depressed, and angry would be way too distressing.

I mean, I'm hoping this group will offer me an alternative to that. There's gotta be a better way than dying all miserable and isolated.

Richard: You're right, Holly, there are alternatives to dying in isolation, fear and anger. But it is up to each of us to make that happen. We can choose how we want to live out our dying just like we've chosen the way we're living out our life.

Kevin: My biggest fear is #1, 'I am afraid there will be no afterlife, that death will be the end of everything.'

Ever since I've been a little kid, music has been my passport to happiness. I don't know why, but the idea of all sound stopping, the idea of eternal silence really drives me crazy. I already know that when I'm ready to check out, I wanna have my favorite music playing non-stop. I want to go out on the riffs of John Coltrane.

Clare: Another fear I have is #2, abandoning the people who depend on me.

I try to tell myself that my Charley will be just fine after I'm gone. After all he does have our four grown kids to look after him. But deep down, I know how lost he'll be without me. Even after all these years, he still needs me to help him find a missing sock!

Whenever I try talking to him about how he'll manage when I'm gone, he gets this awful flush across his face and starts shaking like a scared little boy. It makes me feel so terrible. I feel so bad for upsetting him like that.

I'm so confused! I want to talk to Charley about all of this. He's my husband and has been my best friend for over fifty years, but I honestly don't know how to reach him on this one.

Max: This is my main concern too. It troubles me to think that I might go before Sylvia. We've always been a team, through thick and thin. Already it's hard to keep up with all the chores. But I have to be strong no matter what.

Raul: Yeah, I feel bad too about leaving my family. I keep thinkin' that after I die my mom will just stay sad all the time, stare at my picture all day, and never leave the house. She's always sayin' I am her favorite. But then I get mad, because it's my life and I'm the one who's sick. Maybe if they knew how it felt livin' in my body, they wouldn't be like they are. Maybe they would finally get it.

It's easy for people who ain't sick to say 'keep fighting, don't give up.' I love my family a lot and I get really sad when I think about how bummed out they're gonna be when I die, but shit, man, it's gonna happen someday.

Richard: The importance of initiating and keeping an open dialogue going on about dying can't be overemphasized. Part of this means that we can't be afraid to challenge people on their denial, 'Oh, you've been claiming you've been dying for years' or 'You'll just keep beating the odds.'

But it also means not abandoning those we love when they do encounter their grief about our dying. We need to hold them when they cry and listen to them when they rage about how unfair it is. We may find that we resent having to do this all the time. 'Why should I have to deal with your feelings? Take your problems elsewhere. I'm not your therapist.'

But this, like everything else, is just part of being close. Being available for those we love to share their true feelings with us is the greatest gift we can offer those who will survive us. The more we talk about our impending death while we're alive, the less guilt we'll feel about how our survivors will handle it when we're dead. After all, this kind of openness will help nurture them through their grief.

Clare, you mentioned that you're having difficulty initiating this kind of dialogue with your husband. It might be helpful to think about getting the assistance of a counselor to facilitate the communication between the two of you. This may help pave the way for ongoing discussions.

Clare: Yes, that might help, but I wouldn't know where to start. And we're on a fixed income, so we couldn't afford to pay very much.

Holly: Clare, I know the Women's Cancer Resource Center offers free counseling to clients and their families. Jean and I had a few sessions when I was first dealing with my breast cancer. The counselors were aware of all the issues and it was really helpful to talk with Jean about my fears and what my dying might mean for her. If you want, I'll give you the number before we leave.

Clare: That would be lovely, dear. Thank you.

Kevin: I wonder, did anyone else mark #16, 'I am afraid of dying alone'? I've always been a major people person. All the things I love to do most, from teaching to performing, have to do with other people. I even prefer playing music as part of a combo rather than doing it solo. But since my lover died five years ago, I haven't been able to let myself get close to anyone else in that same way. I've got lots of good friends, but no one who feels like a primary relationship.

Also, nowadays, with these protease inhibitors and all, HIV is looking more like a manageable chronic disease like diabetes than the predictable killer it used to be. In fact, the whole death support community around HIV/AIDS has disappeared. Like they closed the AIDS hospice here a few years ago. And I guess I'm scared that when my time comes, there won't be anyone around I can really count on to go through this with me.

Raymond: I marked that one too, Kevin. As I get older, there are fewer significant people in my life and even fewer I would consider close friends. And now that my best friend is dying, I'm afraid that that will only add to the void in my life.

Having a family has always been really important to me, but since my divorce I haven't been able to find that kind of relationship again. I'm trying to get involved in more activities, to meet people, but it's very time-consuming. Sometimes I think to myself, if only I could learn how to be more comfortable with being by myself, it wouldn't matter if I died alone. I mean, dying is something that you gotta do by yourself anyway. It's not like I'll get to take a group of friends along with me to check out the other side!

Raul: Wow, that would be cool. Me and my buddies cruising heaven together, maybe looking for some good-looking death babes to pick up!

Holly: Hey Raul, in the afterlife I heard all the women finally come to their senses and become lesbians! (Everyone laughs.)

Raul: Bummer!

Holly: Sorry, Raul, I just couldn't resist!

Is it okay to switch gears? I wanted to talk about #10, being afraid of losing those I care about.

I immediately flash on my daughter Annie. We've had some talks about what my having cancer means, especially about the part where I could die. And there are always lots of tears. It tears me up thinking about how my death might affect her.

Mike: Yeah, I'm with you on that, Holly. I think a lot about that too. My son knows something's wrong, but I'm afraid to tell him the truth about my situation. What if he can't handle it?

Richard: Telling a child, or anyone else for that matter, that you may not have much longer to live is one of life's most daunting chores. Mostly because we have to use the 'D' word and say it aloud and look into their eyes as we're talking. There's bound to be tears and fears, but nothing that can't be overcome with some tenderness, patience, love and support.

When dealing with children, you may find you have to revisit the topic over and over, just as you would do with any other of life's important lessons.

My rule of thumb is to assume that children, even little ones, have a much greater capacity to deal with difficult things than we give them credit for. How one goes about telling a child is another issue.

The way one sets up the message is, most likely, how the message will be received. If you carry your hat in your hand, shuffle your feet, and present the news like it's a disaster, you can be sure that that's how the child will receive the news.

My counsel is to start out slowly. Take a walk in the park. Call attention to the ebb and flow of the natural world. Remember how comforting Jan's grandfather's words were to her. Nature makes no apologies for the way things are. Things are dying all around us all the time.

Another thing you might consider is writing out what you want to say first. You may even want to practice with another family member or friend. Ask for feedback on how you are coming across.

Remember that there is no substitute for honesty, and the longer you wait, the more difficult it will become. Why not start now?

Max: This reminds me of the story about the man who goes on vacation, leaving his house and the care of his beloved cat to a friend. Two days into the vacation the man calls home to see how things are going. His friend tells him his cat is dead. The guy is stunned, he's devastated. He yells at his friend for being so insensitive.

'That's not how you tell somebody about death. You break it to him gently over a couple of days. For example, when I called today you should've told me my cat is on the roof and that you can't get her down. Then in a day or two you could tell me the cat is off the roof, but in the hospital, recovering from its fall from the roof. After a few more days, then you tell me my cat is dead. That's how it's done.' The friend apologizes and hangs up the phone.

A couple of days later the guy on vacation calls his friend again. 'So, how is everything going?' 'Fine,' says his friend, 'except your mother is on the roof.' (Everyone laughs.)

My Turn

Richard: What did this exercise uncover for you about your fears and where they come from? What did you mark as your number one fear and why? Do you have responses to what you heard from the other participants?

_____

_____

_____

_____

_____

_____

_____

_____

_____

Richard: Sorry about interrupting this great discussion, but our time is just about up. And there's homework I want to distribute.

The following exercise will help you keep this inner dialogue going throughout the week. You may find that you would like to incorporate a partner or family member in this process. Or you may wish to keep this to yourself for now. Either way, put some time and energy into it, and when we return next week, we'll review our responses to the exercise.

Thanks so much for your lively participation. It's been great getting to know each of you a bit better. Have a good week.

AT-HOME WORK

Week 1 — A Death Anxiety Questionnaire*

Rate each of the following statements according to this scale: (1) Not true at all; (2) Not sure; (3) Somewhat true; (4) Very true.

_____ Air travel frightens me.

_____ There is too much anxiety in my life.

_____ People think I'm a hypochondriac because I'm always worried about getting sick.

_____ I would give anything to be immortal in this body.

_____ The worries I have about death are spoiling the quality of my life.

_____ I don't believe I've ever had a mystical or spiritual experience.

_____ I generally fall apart in crisis situations.

_____ I don't want to die the way some of my relatives died.

_____ I don't have a particular religion or philosophy that would help me face my mortality.

_____ I do not believe in an afterlife.

_____ I'm afraid that I might die before really experiencing much joy in life.

_____ I'm not very good at making decisions on my own.

_____ I don't get out into nature very much.

_____ I believe that thinking about dying will only hasten my death.

_____ I'm easily upset or excitable.

_____ I only have negative experiences of friends or family members dying.

_____ I don't think dying people should be told that they are dying.

_____ I have fears of dying while my children are still young.

_____ I have fears of dying before I have an opportunity to express my love to those I am close to.

_____ I don't believe in bothering others with my problems.

_____ I'm sure my family will fall apart after I die.

_____ I fear not having adequate pain control while dying.

_____ I fear there'll be no one available to actively assist me in dying.

_____ I am not comfortable expressing my emotions to others.

_____ I'm afraid that someone will try to hasten my death just to get rid of me.

_____ I'm afraid of being over-medicated and unconscious while dying.

_____ Thinking about dying makes me sad and depressed.

_____ I have fears of being declared dead when I'm really not or being buried alive.

_____ I'm afraid of getting confused while dying or not being able to follow my spiritual practices.

_____ I have fears of what may happen to my body after I'm dead.

_____ I'm afraid of dementia at the end of my life.

_____ I don't like to think about the prospect of my own dying.

*Based on Conte, H.R., Weiner, M.B., and Plutchik, R. (1982). *Measuring Death Anxiety*

"The thing to remember is that each time of life has its appropriate rewards, whereas when you're dead it's hard to find the light switch. The chief problem about death, incidentally, is the fear that there may be no afterlife...a depressing thought, particularly for those who have bothered to shave. Also, there is the fear that there is an afterlife but no one will know where it's being held. On the plus side, death is one of the few things that can be done as easily lying down."

Woody Allen

Chapter Two

Week 2:
Picking Up the Pace

Checking In

Richard: Let's begin today with our regular round-robin check-in. This week I'll ask you to focus your attention on last week's homework exercise and what it brought up for you. Who would like to begin?

Raymond: I'd like to begin if I that's all right.

I have a confession to make. Remember last week when I told you in my check-in that I wasn't sick or have a particular disease to speak of? I said I was here only for professional reasons. Well, that's not completely true. I feel terrible for not being more honest, especially since each of you were so candid about your situation.

The truth of the matter is I am at serious risk for heart disease because of my weight and stress level. I've known this for some time, but its seriousness only began to register with me when I was doing the homework for last week. I've been deceiving myself for so long that I didn't even think twice about deceiving you too.

I stopped looking after myself three years ago when I didn't think there was any reason to keep on living. I went through hell with my divorce and saw my family disintegrate before my eyes. I don't even get to see my three kids much anymore. I mean, I see them on holidays sometimes and for a month during summer vacation, but it's not the same thing as daily contact.

The homework assignment made me revisit all of this. I began thinking, if life isn't worth living then why am I so afraid to die? It's not like I think I'll live forever, but I sure as hell could take better care of myself while I'm here. It's funny because I'm very militant about other things like smoking. Why can't I apply the same standards to overeating as I do to smoking? I mean, who do I think I'm kidding? So I apologize to each of you and hope you won't hold it against me.

Kevin: That's funny, I had the same response to the homework as you did, Ray. Lately, I've been playing pretty fast and loose in my life too. I don't want to die, so I had to begin to ask myself, why am I doing the things I'm doing? This past week has really been a revelation. I'm thinking that maybe my fears about dying are really just an expression of how precious life is. I guess I need to be reminded of this from time to time, otherwise I lose my way.

Janice: I'd like to thank you for being so honest with us now, Ray. I'll bet that wasn't easy to admit to strangers.

My week's been okay, nothing really interesting to report. The homework did help keep me focused, however. I decided to take your advice, Richard, and begin keeping a journal. My arthritis makes writing difficult so I'm recording my journal on tape. I'm hoping this little project will help me overcome my feelings of isolation that have been with me since Albert died.

In my journal this week I tried to think of three things I could do to remedy the loneliness I feel all the time. In no time I came up with some really good ideas.

I could join the church down the block from where I live. They have lots of activities after services and they have a bingo game once a month. I love bingo.

Then I thought I could start going to some of the social events at the senior center. It's just a short bus ride from my home and a number of the people who live in my building go there regularly, so I could always go with them.

I was stumped for a third idea until it came to me in a flash. I could start volunteering again for the Red Cross. I've been a volunteer off and on since the Vietnam War. Isn't that great? I'm real proud of myself. Now if only I have the gumption to follow through on these goals, I'll be fine.

Robin: I'm absolutely wrecked. It's been the week from hell. Bobby was cremated on Friday and there was a memorial service for him on Sunday. His parents flew in from Oklahoma, but only after he was dead. Get this...they didn't want to spend the extra money to come when he was still living. What's up with that? They're filthy rich.

Once they got here, they muscled everybody out of the way and took total control over everything. They had this big secret agenda and the whole thing really sucks, man.

The real pathetic part was that Bobby and his parents had this mutual hate thing going on. I mean they never really got off on each other. Bobby thought his parents were super-uptight prudes and they thought he was a totally whacked-out flake. It's like the whole HIV thing was the limit. Get this, they told their friends that Bobby was dying of some weird kind of cancer. What, the truth would've excluded them from the country club or something?

So he dies and they rush in and start recreating history. Bobby can't protest because he's dead, and my suggestions, of course, were completely discounted. His parents hate me. They think I was the tramp who gave him AIDS. So get this, they have this sham memorial service where they only invite certain people, and it's all a great big lie. Why didn't they just stay home and let his friends, all the people who really loved him, give him a proper send-off?

And that's not even the worst of it. Like, you know, Bobby and I lived together for three years. We didn't have much, but what we did have belonged to both of us. Now his parents are saying that all the stuff in our apartment was his and they want to take it back to Oklahoma with them. They don't need any of the shit. Like I said, they're filthy

rich. They just want to bust my hump. And there's nothing I can do about it. I don't have any goddamn receipts for any of it. I can't fuckin' stand it. What am I going to do?

I didn't have time to do the homework, sorry. One thing I know for sure is I don't want to go out like Bobby did. There's gotta be something I can do to prevent my family from busting their way into my life at the end and screwing everything up. That's it for me.

Holly: God, Robin! That's awful. I'm so sorry. And you guys are straight, too. I thought things like that only happened to lesbians and gay men. Gets me to thinking about how everything in life is so precarious and all.

When I did the homework, the thing that stuck out in my mind is that my anxiety about possibly getting sick again is spoiling the quality of my life now. I didn't used to be so panicky about every little thing, but now I'm on edge most all the time. And of course this bubbles right on over into my family life. My lover Jean and I talked about this very thing during the week. By the way, she's real curious about what goes on here.

Richard, Jean thinks that you should run these groups for partners and family members so that they can get in touch with their own death stuff. Maybe then they could begin to understand what us dying people have to go through.

Wait a minute, did you hear that? I just said 'us dying people.' Well, that's a first. And look, the sky didn't fall when I said it either. This is so absolutely amazing. What a breakthrough. I'm stunned.

Mia: Wow, Holly, that is kind of amazing.

I remember the first time I said those words aloud, 'I'm dying.' It was like nothing changed and everything changed all at the same time. Congratulations, Holly, and welcome to the club.

Let's see, my week's been okay I guess. I've just been real tired, that's all. Nothing new came up for me with the homework. All it did was reinforce my fears about dying in pain and not being able to breathe at the end. And I talked enough about that last week. So that's it for me.

Raul: Hi, everybody.

I gotta say, Robin, your story, I mean your check-in or whatever, really freaked me out. I mean, shit man, I never thought parents could be so cold. My parents are totally cool. They'd do anything for me...well, almost. Get this, my mother still comes and holds me and sings to me when I get scared or when the pain's real bitchin'. Just like she used to do when I was a baby. My father works two jobs to help pay for my medicines and doctors and shit. They're always telling me I'm their baby. I know, like that stuff can gag you, but I kinda like it sometimes.

There's a bad side too, though. My mother goes, 'Mi hijo, you must be strong for your madre and get better.' That's when I get all pissed and pull away. Then she gets all hurt and everything is fucked. Shit, man, she keeps messin' with my head. She knows I'm dyin'. So why does she do like that? And why do I mess with it and hurt her even more? But then I think, hey, what about me? Shit, I don't know. Why does this have to be so complicated? I did my homework, but I don't think anything new happened. I'm done.

Max: So what can I say? This week was just like last week, only worse. Sylvia and me aren't doing so good.

I finally had to call a family meeting. My three boys, their wives, and four of the grandkids were there. I tried to put the best face on things, but even that face wasn't so pretty.

Harold, my oldest son, he's a lawyer like you, Mike. Maybe you know him. Anyway, Harold wants Sylvia and me to get some help. He wants to contact an agency and get someone to help out with the housework, cooking and shopping. He says that the family will pitch in too.

Sylvia just sat there and cried. 'God forbid I can't take care of my own home.' 'It's all right, ma. It'll be nice. We'll be able to be together more. Just like the old days.' 'Sure, grandma, we want to help.'

Having this meeting was a big step for me. I don't know if you know that. I'm ashamed to admit, but my pride sometimes gets the better of me. Then I have to back down and eat crow. And I never developed a taste for crow. Oy, it's so bitter.

Thank God I have a good family. They made this much easier than I probably deserved.

Clare: You do have a good family, Max. You should be proud.

Last week's meeting really got me thinking how grateful I am to be here with all of you. I just want to tell you how wonderful it was to be able to sit here with all of you and talk about my dying, without one person telling me not to talk like that. You don't know how important that is to me. I've finally found a place where I can be myself. Even if it is for only a couple of hours a week.

The homework was really interesting. Too bad I'm not able to share this with anyone. Maybe that will come in time. I sure hope so. I'm so tired of carrying all of this on my own.

Mike: I can't believe you guys. We're talking about dying here. Hello. Do you know what that means? It means the goddamn end, that's what it means. And you guys are acting like we're talking about taking a fucking nap. Jesus, what the hell is wrong with you? This is so messed up.

How can you be so calm? Haven't you got any feelings? Doesn't life mean anything to you? And what's this bullshit with this homework? I mean, is it the object of this group to rub my nose in this death stuff? I think that's sick. If it weren't for my wife, I'd leave right now.

I want to live, goddamn it. I don't want to die. Can't anyone get that straight? You remind me of a bunch of sheep being led to the slaughter. It's disgusting. (Mike pauses for a bit to collect himself.)

Listen, you guys, I'm sorry. I didn't mean that. I just don't know what gets hold of me sometimes. I'll be honest. I don't see the point of all of this. Today's the first day since early last week that I've been able to sit up. I've been flat on my back for nearly a week. How do you think that makes me feel? I'm powerless and I'm scared shitless, that's how. The homework pushed all my buttons. Maybe if I didn't have MS, if I had a fighting chance, maybe then I'd be able to face this better.

I always thought I'd go out in a blaze of glory, like some kind of hero. I did, I really did. I had fantasies about being taken out in a hail of gunfire in a courtroom by some crazed shooter, or maybe falling to my death in a valiant effort to save an injured hiker. Anything but slowly wasting away like some rotting carcass. I apologize. After that

outburst, you'll probably all want me to leave, right?

Max: No, no, no. Mike, you stay. We'll all leave. (Everyone laughs.)

Mike: Thank you, guys. I promise to try to keep it together, but it's not gonna be easy. Now you see what my poor wife and son have to put up with. They deserve some kind of freakin' award!

Richard: Before we move on, I'd like to do my check-in.

I've had a rough week. My good friend Karen died on Tuesday. I spent lots of time with her and her family the last couple of weeks and it was worth every minute. What a remarkable woman she was, so full of life and passion and goodness. I will miss her very much.

Karen did this group about six months ago. And although there was a great deal of sadness on the part of her husband and children as she died, there was also this wonderful sense of peace. Thanks to Karen, everyone was prepared. The last two months of her life was spent in pulling her family together, helping them begin their grieving, saying her goodbyes and thank yous.

It was amazing to watch her transform her family's anger and denial into acceptance and celebration. She told me that doing this 10-week group was the best thing she could have done for herself at the end of her life. She likened it to the Lamaze class she and her husband took before the birth of their first child. I was so proud.

Karen died exactly the way she wanted to, in her own home surrounded by those she loved and free of most of the anxiety that plagues other death scenes I've witnessed. Her death had a profound effect on her husband and daughters as well. Each of them told me that this was an event they would never forget. Despite their grief, they were honored to be with her as she died. Her conscious dying liberated them from their fears of death and gave them a shining model for their own dying.

But Karen's death is not the reason I had such a difficult week. My week was difficult because I'm not always able to translate experiences like Karen's into something people who aren't facing their mortality would understand, specifically

people who are in a position to fund this cutting edge work.

While the extraordinary drama of Karen and her family was playing out, I was trying to convince three foundations to support us. I wasn't at all successful. It is so frustrating.

So many potential funders are more comfortable funding programs that fight a disease. That's not surprising, I suppose. A lot of funding decisions are still based on the medical and research model. I try to tell them about our program's successes and the impact it has on people like Karen. I ask, 'How would spending millions of dollars more on cancer research help Karen and her family as she died?'

There is this serious misconception in the popular culture concerning death and dying. We actually think we can eliminate death if only we could cure all the diseases that plague humankind. But I have news for you. No one is getting out of here alive! Disease research and prevention is an admirable thing and there should be plenty of funds available for it, but shouldn't we also recognize that we're mortal, and fund programs like this that help people have a good death?

My Check-In

Richard: Take all the time and space you need to write about your week. Pay special attention to last week's homework exercise. What did the exercise bring up for you? Would you like to respond to anyone in the group?

_____

_____

_____

_____

_____

_____

_____

_____

_____

_____

Group Process

Richard: Moving against the grain of society's conventions is never easy. Consciously facing our mortality in this death-negative culture proves the point. You've probably noticed how little support there is for facing one's death head on.

'Death, death, death — is that all you can talk about? Stop obsessing.' 'Why are you always thinking about dying, shouldn't you be concentrating on living? Do you have some kind of death wish?'

Don't be misled. Contemplating your own mortality and thinking about death is not an obsession. And preparing for the end of life won't hasten death any more than thinking about summer vacation will hasten its arrival.

Dying is hard enough all by itself without adding fatalism and superstition to the mixture. There is no need to buy in to the myth that death is some kind of terrible impending evil or divine punishment. There is nothing life-affirming or empowering in that way of thinking.

A better place to begin is with the undeniable fact that, no matter who we are or how we've lived, each of us will have our turn at dying. Death just is. To read anything more into this simple fact of life is to surrender to the powerful tide of death negativity that can rob us of our dignity.

Last week we discovered that it's easy to fall prey to the crippling emotions of depression, fear, remorse, shame and guilt as we face our mortality. And we were even able to pinpoint where some of these feelings come from. So this week I'd like us to pick up the pace and focus on how we can combat these unsettling feelings.

Let's talk about some of the coping mechanisms that you've developed to resist this tide.

Holly: I've discovered something really interesting. When I'm working in my garden, all my fears about the future seem to disappear. Will I get sick again? Will I die? All that stuff just melts away. There's something about getting down on my hands and knees and messin' around in the dirt that calms me. I feel connected to the earth. And honey, that feels sooo good. I can feel the rhythms of the seasons. Roses are not always in bloom, you know.

No doubt about it, when I'm all hunkered down, watching things real close, I'm able to see the death and decay even at the height of the blooming season. So why all the worry? I ask myself. It's just nature happening, right?

Life has a completely different lesson for me when I'm in the garden. So how is it that I can accept the natural ebb and flow of life when I'm in the garden, but have such a hard time with it later? If only there was a way to bottle my garden feelings and have them available for the other times, like when I get so scared about what might happen in the future that I just freeze.

All this crazy worry is robbing me of precious life. It's like I'm missing the joy of the rose bloom because I'm worryin' about how long it will last.

Robin: I used to use drugs and alcohol to escape from my feelings of dread. But you know what? That shit only made things more dreadful. I was real pretty, all right, full of self-loathing, shame, and guilt. Where did it all come from, I wonder? It wasn't until I got clean and sober that I realized that there's only one way to deal with life and that's to do it head on. So I suppose you gotta deal with death head on, too.

I never really knew how to be honest about my feelings. I was always pretending, trying to please everyone. Somehow I lost any connection with my real self when I was just a kid.

Trying to recover the real Robin has been a mess of hard work. She's been gone for such a long time.

Bobby was my mentor as well as my partner. Somehow he came to this realization about being real long before I did. He wasn't that much older; he was just wiser. He was the best thing that ever happened to me. He never let me get away with anything. He was always saying, "Be real, Robin, don't bullshit me." I used to hate it when he said that, but he was right. Bobby could see right through me. He knew me much better than I knew myself. I'm afraid that now that he's gone, I won't be able to do this on my own.

No, I'm not going to think like that. That's stupid. Of course I'll be able to. And you guys will help, right?

Janice: As I mentioned in my check-in, I've decided to start setting goals for myself. This used to work for me when I was much younger.

For example, I once made up my mind that I wanted to improve my vocabulary. You see I had to leave school in my sophomore year of high school. So I missed out on a lot of things and for a long time I was ashamed that I never finished school. So I decided to learn five new words each week. Charley, who was much better educated than I, would laugh and make fun, but it worked. Even he was surprised. I was so proud of myself. I felt as through there wasn't anything I couldn't do. But that was so long ago. I wonder if it will still work today?

By golly, I'm going to try. I'll set a goal for myself to say hello to five new people this next week. Who knows, I might meet someone real nice. I'm sure there are lots of other lonely older women like myself that would enjoy a new friendship. Maybe if I try to make some friends I won't feel so isolated and frightened all the time.

Mike: What coping mechanisms have I developed? I can't think of anything. I don't even know where to begin. This is so childish.

Richard: Have it your way, Mike. But I doubt there's anything childish about trying to regain lost dignity or making an effort to recover a sense of balance and well-being.

Your anger and frustration are really getting in your way. They're blocking this opportunity for you to make some real progress. I can't believe there is nothing in your life that gives you pleasure, that can pull you out of your self-pity. Is there no passion left in your life? Is it just inertia that makes you draw your next breath? Come on, give it a try.

Mike: Sorry, I did it again. Why am I being such an asshole? If one of my clients did this to me, I'd dump his ass.

I always tell my clients, you either work with me or I'm outta here. Can't let the bad guys get the best of you, and I've had the dubious honor of representing some real scumbags in my day. If I didn't stand up to them right from the beginning, they would have eaten me alive.

I mean, that's it, isn't it? I once was strong and powerful. No petty gangster was going to get the best of me, and they knew it. But look at me now. I'm so goddamn pathetic.

I vacillate between feelings of helplessness and shame. That's why I'm so goddamn angry. Why do I feel ashamed? I didn't do anything that would account for me winding up in this friggin' chair. I was raised to think that men must to be strong. I feel like a failure and I feel guilty for feeling this way.

You asked about what gives my life meaning. It's my wife and kid, of course. I live for them. But I'm destroying my family. I know I am. I know I'm just pushing them away by being such an asshole. It's like I figure that if I make them hate me now, then they won't care if I die. Just like I didn't give a shit when my old man died. And if I push them away now, then they won't see me die all broken and helpless.

Raul: Hey, don't do that, man. They love you, man. There's nothing better than that. Don't be such a dork.

Hey, Mike, it's just bein' sick, you know. It ain't your fault. No one is punishing you for nothin'. Man, give yourself a break.

This is the only good thing about being sick since the day I was born. I never knew what it would feel like to be, ya know, normal. I never had this big macho thing happening. It's workin' for me now though, I don't have nothin' to lose except the pain.

Hey, I got it. Maybe the more you have to lose the more it hurts to die, right?

Dying's no problem for me. Making my family see how I feel is the problem. Man, I wish they would listen to me once in a while. Shit. My parents have this thing goin' on. They act like my dying means that they didn't do something right, that they screwed up somehow. They think that if only they could find the right doctors, they could work some kind of miracle or somethin'. 'Just try this new medicine, Raulito. It will make you better.' Or 'We're going to take you to this new doctor. He is a specialist. Maybe another transplant?' Hell no, man. That's enough already. Why don't you just leave me alone?

They just don't get it. What the hell's wrong with them? Can't they see I'm never gonna get better? I'd be happy if I never had to go to another doctor ever again. Dying's not as bad as living like this. Hey, don't get me wrong, man. I don't want to die. I just don't want to live like this. If I could turn in this crummy body for a new one, I would. But hey, that shit ain't gonna happen.

Mia: Don't you have anyone that can help you work through all of this, Raul? I feel so bad when I hear you talk like this.

Raul: Oh yeah, thanks for reminding me. That's what I wanted to tell you.

There's this new priest at my church. He's cool. Kinda young and ya know, hip. Well, as hip as a priest can get. He hangs with us dudes and plays some mean b-ball. Anyhow, my mother really likes him. So I thought maybe I could level with him on all of this shit. Maybe he'll be different from the old priest who does all the 'burn in hell' shit. Maybe he'd help me talk to my family. That would be way cool, huh? We'll see.

Mia: I'm feeling all turned around these days. And I don't know why. I have

everything I could ask for. Except for my health, that is. My parents are loving and attentive. So are my grandparents. It's all so strange. Shouldn't it be the other way around? It's bizarre having my 83-year old grandmother nursing me, her only grandchild. I wonder what goes through her mind. Does she wonder who will care for her when she's dying? Bad luck for her that she has such a defective for a granddaughter.

The more I think about it, I'm convinced that life is nothing more than a balancing act between good luck and bad luck. It's almost like we have nothing to do with any of it. Listen to me. This is so amazing. I sound just like my parents.

When I was in high school, I used to make fun of my relatives and their crazy superstitions. When I would hear them talk together, I'd be so embarrassed. 'Don't do that. It's bad luck.' Or 'Eat some of this. It's good luck.' These sophisticated, worldly, educated people sounded like a bunch of comic characters in a bad Charlie Chan movie. I swore that I would never become like them. So who do I become? You guessed it. I'm more like them every day. Scary, huh?

The curious thing, and I really hate to admit this, is there is something to this ancient Chinese philosophy. I'm beginning to see that it is rooted in a real fundamental appreciation of the meaning of life. It's not superstition or fatalism like I once thought, it's about fate. And fate is the master of all.

What determines fate? Your guess is as good as mine. What I can tell you is I'm beginning to rethink the whole thing. It's all about balance. If it's a fated thing, then questions like 'Why me?' no longer make any sense. It just is. That's all. I'm beginning to find comfort in all of this for some unknown reason. Go figure.

Clare: I like that, Mia. I like what you said a great deal. We come from such different cultures and backgrounds, and yet we have very similar philosophies. How is that possible? Oh well. Richard, you asked us to talk about how we combat the emotions that unsettle us. My strategy is to avoid thinking that I have been singled out for punishment in some fashion or another. I absolutely refuse to be a victim.

You see, I'm an avid student of nature, always have been. I often hear talk about how humans are at the top of the food chain. It's a way of expressing our superiority, I guess, an excuse for

us to dominate and ravage the natural world. But don't get me started on that. I don't want to get on a soapbox here, but I do want to say that nature doesn't have a top or a bottom. For me the answer is real simple. We humans are enormous creatures compared to most everything else on this tiny planet. And there are so very many of us. I just think nature has provided a balancing agent to keep our species in check. Cancers and viruses do just that. I take comfort in finding my place in the great round of nature. I hasten to add that this way of thinking doesn't diminish the physical pain I have, but it goes a long way in diminishing the emotional pain.

Kevin: Gosh, Clare, do you think that if I sit close to you some of that will rub off on me? I'd give anything to have such a warm and comforting perspective. I confess I'm still floundering around with questions like, 'Why me?' Death and dying still has a distinctly hard edge to it for me.

To tell the truth, I don't think I have a coping strategy. What I do have is a remarkably well-developed ability to avoid things that are unpleasant. And it's clear to me that avoiding things and coping *with* things are not the same thing. Since I don't know how to blunt the hard edge, I've learned to avoid it. I've filled my life with lots of things that distract my attention. Music, the gym, parties, friends, sex...oh, and being a teacher, that's the best.

I guess what I'm trying to say is that I'm too busy living to give much thought to dying.

Clare: But honey, aren't they one and the same thing? Living and dying, I mean.

Kevin: You're right, of course, and that's the problem.

I think if I could somehow integrate these two things in my mind, I bet life would be more enjoyable. I mean I'm doing all this fun stuff, but I'm not really enjoying most of it. I suppose that if I had a better grip on this, I'd probably continue to do all the same things, I just wouldn't feel like I have to do it all at such a breakneck speed. It reminds me of an old movie I saw years ago, *I'm Dancing as Fast as I Can*. Is any of this making sense?

Raymond: I think I understand. Are you saying that even enjoying the good things in life can be a way of avoiding life itself?

Kevin: Yeah, that's exactly what I'm trying to say. A manic pursuit of pleasure is no pleasure, know what I mean?

Raymond: I thought so, good. Then I would have to agree.

I'm having some of the same difficulties. For example, there was a time when I enjoyed food like other people. Then somehow I began to use food as a weapon against myself. This is what I've been thinking about all week. How can I have such a fear and dread of death on the one hand and be actively involved in killing myself on the other? Pretty weird, huh?

I'm beginning to see what you were talking about, Clare. If there is this big disconnect between living and dying, then it opens the door to abuse. Weren't you saying the same thing, Robin, when you were talking about the drugs and alcohol in your life?

Robin: Absolutely. I was out of control, that's for sure. I wasn't caring for myself. Life meant nothing to me. The only thing I cared about was where my next fix was gonna come from.

Raymond: I wonder how someone goes about turning that kind of thing around.

Max: Here's the way I look at it. The closer I get to the end of my days, the more time I want. Mister Death, he's a bastard. You can tell 'em I said so. You can tell him that Max Kapitanoff says he's a bastard. What the hell is he gonna do? Kill me? (Laughs.)

I think a lot about how much time I pissed away when I was a young man. Oy, what a waste. Shame on me.

I see my boys doing the same thing now. I tell them. 'Stop all that running around, already. Sit, talk, maybe have a little nosh.' But no! And what is this with all these little tiny telephones everywhere? Even the grandkids have them in their pockets. I've had enough already. I had to lay down the law. 'No talking on the phone when we're eating.' What the hell is wrong with them?

They're good people, but they just don't know. When they get to be old like me, then they'll know. But then it'll be too late. Crazy! Why is everything so crazy?

Richard: Max, can you tell us how a guy like you gets through the hard times?

Max: I'm glad you asked that. It's simple. I have myself a stiff drink, maybe two if things are real bad. (Everyone laughs.)

Okay, okay, so maybe that doesn't work so good. Seriously, you really want to know? I'll tell you my secret. I have a talk with myself. I say, 'Max, you know this won't last forever. Even this will pass.' That's it, no great mystery. None of the hard times I've seen, and I've seen plenty, lasted forever. Even this dying business will be over one day. I'll just wake up dead one morning and that will that. What can I tell you?

I've made it to eighty-six. That's a miracle in itself. By rights, I should have died with my family in the Holocaust. So I'd say I've been living on borrowed time ever since. My life hasn't always been so wonderful, but nothing in my life has been so terrible as to make me wish I had died in the death camp.

You want to know a little secret? I'm a lot more grateful than I let on. I wouldn't have been able to say this last week. What a difference a few days makes. Since I called that family meeting and got my sons to help out, Sylvia and I are not so nervous. It wasn't so easy doing that, telling them we couldn't make it on our own. But now it's done and I can rest. I did the right thing.

Janice: Oh, Max, I'm so happy for you. It's such a blessing to have family who can help out. You must be very proud.

But I know how you feel about asking for help. Why do you suppose it's so difficult asking for help? I'm embarrassed to admit it, but there have been times that I have gone to bed hungry because I couldn't open a can of soup because my arthritis was so bad. But would I call a neighbor and ask for help? No! Well, there's no fool like an old fool. That's for sure. I don't want this to happen again. Oh, how I wish I had family to count on.

Kevin: Jan, it's not too late to make family. I gave up thinking that a family

is only defined in terms of blood ties a long time ago. Family is who I say it is, the ones who are with me through thick and thin.

When Doug was dying, none of his family could come out and be with him. I sure as hell couldn't do it by myself, although I remember trying. What a mistake! I couldn't handle it all, the endless changing of the bed, the medications and the doctor visits. And when he couldn't walk any longer I had to lift and carry him a lot. I nearly fell apart. I turned into this bitch on wheels. Even Doug, who had the patience of a saint, couldn't take it anymore. 'I'd rather die in some crummy hospital than continue like this. You're killing yourself and you'll hate me before I'm dead. Can't we accept some of the help our friends have offered?'

I was so ashamed of myself for making Doug angry, but his outburst made me think. What was I trying to prove? Whatever it was, it was at Doug's expense. He was getting the short end of the stick, that's for sure. That's when we started "Doug's Family." We actually called it that. We had seven or eight friends who helped out on a rotating basis. It was such a relief to know that there was someone available to do the shopping or to get a meal together when it was needed. And in the last weeks, there was someone with Doug around the clock. I was able to get some needed sleep, go to the gym and do my meditation. It was amazing. What a difference it made.

So take it from me, don't be foolish and try to do this dying thing on your own. It's not worth the heartache. I already have "Kevin's Family" waiting in the wings. And while I'm still in good health, I continue to help my sick friends the same way. I figure what goes around comes around.

Richard: You are so right, Kevin. Thanks.

I would just add that sometimes what you suggest is easier said than done. It's not always simply an issue of pride. Often there aren't any trustworthy people available...a pretty sad comment about the quality of life in this country, huh? Many people die alone or are institutionalized in a hospital or other care facility at the end of their life just because there is no one else to care for them.

Wouldn't it be grand if caring for dying people were, once again, the work of the

whole community? And I don't mean just providing a "place" to die. I mean, people actually getting right in there with sick, elder and dying people and pitching in. Maybe it would be nothing more than holding a person's hand, but it would provide an opportunity for us to learn from and be present to those who go before us. Maybe then our own dying wouldn't be so difficult. Imagine how that would change things.

The greatest wisdom in the world is often squandered. The meaning of life, life's essence, its most profound secrets are frequently lost, because the wisdom that people come to at the end of their life often dies with them. What a waste!

Max: This reminds me of a joke.

A woman accompanied her husband to the doctor's office. After his checkup, the doctor called the wife into his office alone. "Your husband is suffering from a very rare disease and is under enormous stress. If you don't do the following things exactly as I tell you, your husband will die. Each morning, you must fix him a complete and healthy breakfast. You must be cheerful at all times, and you must make sure he is always in a good mood. Each day you must make him a delicious and nutritious meal for lunch and each evening you must prepare an especially nice dinner for him. You mustn't burden him with any chores, or bother him with any of your problems; it will only make his stress worse. And most importantly, you must make love to your husband several times a week and satisfy his every whim. If you can do this for the next year, I think your husband will regain his health and live." On the way home, her husband asked, "What did the doctor say?" "It looks like you're going to die," she replied. (Everyone laughs.)

I'm sorry, I just couldn't help myself.

Mike: Max, you old devil. You're such a card. I'll have to remember that joke so I can tell Maryanne. She'll get a kick out of it.

My Turn

Richard: What gives rise to your feelings of depression, fear, remorse, shame and guilt as you face your mortality? How do you combat these unsettling feelings? What coping strategies have you developed? Take all the time and space you need.

_____

_____

_____

_____

_____

_____

_____

_____

_____

Richard: Okay, you guys. That's it for today. But before we close, I want to walk you through this week's homework. It's a bit more challenging than last week. Hopefully, each of you will rise to the occasion.

I want you to write your own obituary. Just like you would want it to appear after your death. You can be as creative as you like.

Mike: Get outta here, you can't be serious. This is crazy. You can't, I mean how in the hell am I going to do this? Jesus, this is such weird shit. I think I'd rather run naked through the streets.

Richard: Don't worry, Mike, there will be plenty of time for that. Running through the streets naked will be the homework in two weeks. (Everyone laughs.)

Try to remember that this is just an exercise, okay? A wise man once said that we are unable to manage what we cannot measure. And this is an opportunity for you to take measure of who and what you are. Give it some thought. As the saying goes: Things that are difficult for us will tell us more about ourselves than the things we do easily.

AT-HOME WORK

Week 2 — Write Your Own Obituary.

Take some time over the next week to review examples of obituaries and death notices… they're in all the newspapers and online. Now write your own obituary. You died today. What would you like to say about yourself and your death? Model it upon the ones you researched or be creative and design your own. Remember, this is just a snapshot of who you are at this moment. It would be interesting to compare this obituary with the one that you might write at the end of these ten weeks or when it is truly needed.

*"Life doesn't cease to be funny when people die any more
than it ceases to be serious when people laugh."*

— George Bernard Shaw

Excerpts From World Class Obituaries:

"Ronnie loved spur-of-the-moment trips in luxury cars to Vegas with his friends. We would also like to thank the people who issued his credit cards."

"Allison studied cooking to prevent recurrences of memorable culinary disasters and fend off resulting "blond" jokes."

"When you remember Brett, remember he was more than a great set of biceps; he was also an incredible set of pecs."

"She is remembered for her endless capacity to love, her romantic ideals, her wit, her sense of humor, her homemaking and her ability to accessorize."

"Jenette is probably shrieking from the other side now that her true age has been published."

"Handsome and tailored to a fault, he somehow still managed to wear too much jewelry."

"William, the proud owner of an outrageous giant poodle named Orbit, could often be found in his red pumps on Bernal Hill or high in the Sierras."

"Here's to short skirts, tall hairdos, seamed stockings, and bad attitudes!"

"He lived in San Francisco according to the Gospel of Mame and believed implicitly in the virtues of room service and frequent flyer miles."

"Ron loved collecting '50's memorabilia as well as dining out and drinking Merlot and driving his treasured 1961 Cadillac — sometimes unfortunately in that order!"

"She lived by the words of Alice Roosevelt: "If you haven't anything nice to say about someone, come sit next to me.""

"Weary of reading obituaries noting someone's courageous battle with death, Mike wanted it known that he died as a result of being stubborn, refusing to follow doctors' orders and raising hell for more than six decades. He enjoyed booze, guns, cars and younger women until the day he died. So many of his childhood friends that weren't killed in Vietnam went on to become criminals, prostitutes and/or Democrats. He asks that you stop by and re-tell the stories he can no longer tell. As the Celebration will contain Adult material we respectfully ask that no children under 18 attend."

> *"There's an old joke. Uh, two elderly women are at a Catskills mountain resort, and one of them says: 'Boy, the food at this place is really terrible.' The other one says, 'Yeah, I know, and such small portions.' Well, that's essentially how I feel about life. Full of loneliness and misery and suffering and unhappiness and it's over much too quickly."*
>
> Woody Allen

Chapter Three

Week 3:
Unfinished Business

Checking In

Richard: Welcome back. We've got lots to do today, so let's get started.

We'll begin today with our round-robin check-in as usual, but this week we'll do things a bit differently. I want you to read your obituary as part of your check-in. But before you read it, I'd like you to take a few minutes and talk about how it felt to do the exercise. Once we complete our check-in, we'll spend what time remains discussing what we wrote.

You're all smiles today, Mike. That's pretty unusual. I'm afraid to ask. Did you do the homework?

Mike: Yes, teacher, I did my homework. You didn't think I was going to, right? Well, I did and I'm pretty damn proud of myself. But there's a story I need to tell you first.

I left here last week saying to myself, 'Bye bye suckers. I'm outta here.' I had had my fill. I made up my mind that I would call you during the week and excuse myself from the group. I was going to say that I wasn't feeling well enough to continue. I had it all worked out. No one had to know the truth, the truth that I thought you were all a bunch of losers. I was feeling pretty smug and self-righteous till Maryanne got wind of the whole thing. She knew something was up right from the start. She started to grill me about it. 'What happened in your group yesterday? Do you have homework?'

I was pretty evasive at first, but finally she just wore me down. 'Hey, I decided to quit the group, okay, plain and simple.' She looked at me like I had slapped her. She asked me why. I told her about the homework, thinking she would take my side. I expected her to say, 'you're right, honey, that is macabre.' Well, that was a serious miscalculation on my part.

She exploded. 'You pathetic coward! I'm ashamed of you.' She actually called me a coward. That hurt like hell. She went on like that for a good twenty minutes. 'You're right; you're not half the man you used to be. And the part that's missing has nothing with your MS. Somewhere along the line you lost your spine.'

All I could manage to insert into her tirade was a few limp, 'but you don't understand.' She was pissed.

I got the silent treatment for a couple of days until I couldn't stand it anymore. By the end of the week, I told her I had reconsidered. I told her that I'd continue the group just for her. 'Don't do me any favors. Either do the group for yourself or don't do it at all. I'm tired of this charade. This is not about me. You either own up to this or forget it. You got that?'

'Okay, okay, I'll do it, but I don't have to like it.'

So I spent the entire weekend wrestling with what I would write in my obituary. First, I thought, screw them. I can just blow them off with some bullshit. Then, miraculously I started to get into it. I spent hours at the computer going over and over what I wanted to say. I only finished it last night. I asked Maryanne if she wanted me to read it to her. She did, so I read it aloud for the first time. By the time I was finished I had tears streaming down my face. Maryanne was crying, too.

She came over and hugged me. 'I'm so proud of you. Do you realize you're crying?' I hadn't noticed, but it was true. Christ, I was crying for the first time since

I was five at my grandmother's funeral. (Group cheers.)

Thanks, guys. I know, I know. This is so friggin' amazing. So, do you want me to read my obit now?

Okay, but don't be surprised if I fall apart midway through.

Michael Joseph Minetti died yesterday of the massive injuries he sustained earlier this week in a freak accident at the intersection of Lenox and Grand Avenues in Oakland, just one block from his home. Despite his multiple sclerosis, which had confined him to a wheelchair for the last two years, Mr. Minetti is credited with saving the life of a local youngster.

Mr. Minetti was a lifetime resident of Oakland. He attended the University of California, Berkeley during the late 1960's, an experience that became a defining moment in his life. His career in social activism began with the Free Speech Movement, which shaped his enduring commitment to progressive causes. He completed law school at Boalt Hall in 1977, and, after nearly ten years of service to the Alameda County Social Justice Commission, he opened his own law practice in 1986.

Mr. Minetti soon earned a reputation as a flamboyant, in-your-face defense attorney. His courtroom tactics never ceased to amaze and even entertain. A former District Attorney once quipped, "Minetti is not an actor, he just plays one in the courtroom." While there were often raised eyebrows regarding his antics, no one ever questioned his ethics. He was a respected and widely admired member of his profession.

He was the recipient of numerous civic awards and honors. A champion of the underdog, he was as at home defending an alleged drug kingpin, as he was a migrant farmworker. The engraved plaque on his desk said it all. "It's the Bill of Rights, Stupid."

Mr. Minetti's brilliant career was cut short in 2006 when poor health dictated that he retire from his law practice. A particularly virulent case of multiple scleroses crippled his body but not his mind. He continued to serve as a consultant to many nonprofit organizations and authored *It's Your Right*, a popular primer on the First Amendment.

His devoted wife Maryanne and his son Kyle survive Mr. Minetti. He wants them to know that without them he was

nothing. Their love and support helped him reshape his life as he learned to cope with his disability. This was a particularly difficult period in his life. What pain he caused them in the last years of his life was unintentional. You see, he was just trying to find his way.

Services are to be held at St. Joseph the Worker's Church in Berkeley later this week. Donations in his memory may be sent to the charity of your choice.

Janice: My, that was wonderful, Mike.

Now that I've heard your obituary, I don't know if I want to go next. Mine pales in comparison. My life hasn't been special like yours.

I've been reading the obituary page in the paper for years, so I'm familiar with how they look. And I composed one for Albert when he passed. It's funny, but I thought this exercise would be a snap. Well, it wasn't. And I can't really put my finger on why that is, other than the fact that my life is over and it's like it never really began.

I haven't done anything extraordinary, never won an award, never had my picture in the paper, never went to college, never even had a real job. I'm just an old woman who hasn't anything to show for her life. And that makes me sad.

Richard: Excuse me for interrupting, but I feel I need to explain something about this exercise before we continue. This is not a contest. There is no prize for the best obituary, because there can't be a "best" when each is unique. Your obituary is simply a snapshot of how you see yourself at this moment. If there are regrets, and I'm sure we all have them, then they are just part of the picture. Making a judgment call about your life and its worth by comparing your life with someone else's is dangerous and self-defeating. Remember, the essence of life is not in the externals.

My life has meaning because I lived it – a real person in real time living a real life. If I'm going to make a judgment about my worth, let it be by the measure of authenticity.

I'm sorry, Jan. Please continue.

Janice: Thank you, Richard. I'll just go ahead and read my obituary as I wrote it and that will be that.

Janice Rosemary Duba — in San Francisco. Loving wife of 40 years of the late Albert W. Duba.

Born and raised in Alton, Illinois, Janice was the eldest of 10 children. All preceded her in death. She was a loyal Red Cross volunteer most of her life. She died peacefully in her own home of natural causes.

Friends may call after 3:00 PM on Friday. Committal will be at the Evergreen Cemetery.

Raymond: I have to confess, I was having a lot of the same feelings Jan was having. As I reviewed my life for this exercise, I felt really inadequate. Where did all the time go? What happened to all my dreams? It's not like I have a lot of regrets. It just seems like I have very little to show for 50 years. Okay, okay, I'll just read what I wrote and you can decide for yourself.

Raymond Edward Parks, age 50, died of a heart attack while on holiday in Maui. Apparently he was a little late with the relaxing vacation thing.

Raymond was a good friend and a devoted father. His loving children; Amy, 17, Raymond Jr., 15 and Allison, 12, will miss him. He was the world's greatest dad and he had the coffee mug to prove it.

Raymond trained as a social worker at the University of Colorado. He moved to the San Francisco Bay Area in 1991 to accept a position with Visiting Nurses/Hospice. Raymond soon earned a reputation for his conscientious client service. He was a passionate advocate of patients' rights and often found himself at odds with the medical industry that put profits before patients.

Raymond was also a great cook. You could tell by just looking at him. His friends often teased that Raymond never met food he didn't like. While that was a bit of an exaggeration, he knew good food and where to get it. His 4th of July barbecues were legendary. Unfortunately, the secret ingredients of his coveted marinade died with him.

A celebration of his life will be held on Saturday. All are invited to bring their favorite Raymond story and a covered dish.

Robin: That was great, Ray. Too bad I missed those barbecues of yours. I love me some good 'Q.' I really liked that you had a sense of humor in your obituary. That's what I wanted to do in mine too.

I mean, since most of my life has been a joke, I thought my obituary should reflect that.

I'm surprised at how remarkably easy this exercise was for me to do. But I should confess that this isn't the first time I've done this. I once had to write my own obituary for a creative writing class I took a couple of years ago. I was newly in recovery back then, and when I took it out and looked at it last week I was surprised at what I found. Boy, I was really all balled up with myself back then. There wasn't a shred of humor in the whole damn thing.

This would be a great exercise for me to do every couple of years just so I could keep track of my progress.

I liked the analogy of a snapshot that you used, Richard. That's how I was thinking about it too. So without further delay, here it is.

Once upon a time in a place far, far away, a girl child was born to Herbert and Inez Belcher, and they named their daughter Eunice. (What, you actually named your daughter Eunice Belcher?) That's right, they had. They said they liked the sound of Eunice. Well, that was the last time the universe made sense for this girl child.

Eunice simply was never a Eunice and in the 25 short years she lived on this plane she moved through a series of names, each one reflecting her desire to find her real self. She tried Cindy at age five, Moonstone at 15, Sneaker at 19, and finally Robin at 22. And so Eunice Belcher of Medina, Minnesota died as Robin Bell in San Francisco, a bit happier and a lot more self-confident.

All are sorry that Robin is gone, her death coming as it did only one week after her partner and mentor, Bobby Evans, died. (The fourth dimension hasn't been the same since the two of them arrived.)

She was just starting to get things right. She was proud of the fact that she was off the street, clean and sober and enrolled as a journalism student at State.

Robin will be remembered for her wild hairdos, punky outfits, and her inability to carry a tune. She leaves behind her beloved cat, Tuber, her matchbook collection, and her devoted friends, Denise, Julie, and Kelli, who were with her at the end.

Her last words were: 'Don't call me Eunice.'

Max: It's true you don't look like a Eunice. I had a secretary once who was a Eunice. Oy, don't get me started on Eunice.

So what can I say? This week was just like last week, only worse. I'm not doing so good. I was in the hospital for three days last week. I had some terrible pain and was dehydrated. The only good thing was I had lots of time to think while I was in there. What the hell else is there to do?

I know I'm getting close to the end, so I didn't need some fancy-shmancy doctor telling me it was just a little episode. An episode of what? Made it sound like some television rerun. All right, so do you want to hear my obituary or not?

Max Kapitanoff died Wednesday of stomach cancer at the age of 86. Born in Poland, he was the only member of his family to survive the Holocaust.

His parents sent him and his younger sister Rachel to England in 1935 to escape the Nazis. Rachel died in London three months later.

Max arrived in New York in 1941 with just $5 in his pocket. A week later he had a job in the garment district as a pattern cutter. The rag trade would be his home for the rest of his life. He knew the whole business from every angle – production, wholesale, retail, purchasing, managing, you name it, he could do it. And he was good too. Maybe even terrific.

He was forced to retire at 73 when failing health made him sell "Max and Things," a smart ready-to-wear and accessory shop he had on Union Street for 25 years. He hoped in vain that one of his sons would take over the business when he retired, but that didn't happen. It broke his heart to have to sell to strangers.

He was active in many civic affairs and was a member of the Kiwanis, Rotary, Oddfellows, and Toastmasters. He lived by the philosophy that everyone had a responsibility to give something back to the community they lived in. He was an inspiration to many.

Max leaves behind his beautiful wife of 66 years, Sylvia. This is the first time they have been apart in all that time. He entrusts the care of his wife to their three sons, Harold, Sam and Abe, and to their families. They are good boys and he was proud of them even though none of them wanted to follow in his footsteps.

Donations in his memory should be made to your favorite charity.

Holly: Ah, Max, you're so sweet, I could just hug you. That was really nice. I'll bet it was hard to write, though, especially the part about Sylvia. She'll be just fine though, I know it. You have a good family, you don't have to worry, they will look after her.

Let's see, I found this exercise troubling for two reasons. First, it's difficult for me, as you know, to identify as a dying person, so projecting myself to a place after death was, how should I put this, challenging.

Second, this exercise severely tested my faith. I mean, either I believe in the power of the resurrection or I don't. It's easy to say I believe when I'm sitting in church, but if it doesn't extend any farther than that, then it's not real faith, is it?

Anyway, I was finally able to do the assignment, but I don't feel as though I was able to capture what I wanted to say. It was so frustrating. Well, let me just read what I have and maybe you could help me with it later.

Holly W. Wade — Born September 11, 1969. Holly lost her courageous battle with breast cancer, and is finally at peace with the Lord.

At the time of her passing, her devoted life partner of ten years, Jean Hagan, and their daughter Annie, age 14, were at her bedside.

Holly was above all a woman of faith. Those who knew her well believed she had the kind of faith that moved mountains, which was a good thing because there was always a mountain to move. The rugged terrain of poverty, racism, sexism and homophobia all stood as formidable obstacles in her life. But her firm belief in the power of the spirit shook these mountains to their foundations.

She rose up from the crushing poverty of rural Georgia to toil early in the field of the civil rights movement. Her momma, Etta Mae Winslow, a leader in the voter registration drive in their county, was martyred in a bomb blast that destroyed their church when Holly was only nine. Her mother's blood galvanized her for the struggle that lay ahead.

But some of the doors that were pried open by the civil rights movement remained closed to her, not because she was black, but because she was a woman. So her struggle continued. She joined her sisters of every race and color and creed to demand equal access to education and decent paying jobs. Marches and protests and civil disobedience, all the things she learned at her momma's knee, would now be used to shake the system that was responsible for this inequality.

There would be some successes over the years, but there was never any time to rest. One more mountain had to be climbed, and this one would be the most difficult of all. It would be a lonely battle, sometimes just Holly and her God. Former allies disappeared. Even the church shut its doors, all because she loved another woman.

Holly would remember these as her darkest days. She felt cut off and abandoned. Even God seemed to mock her. Could something so beautiful be so wrong? Hell no! Even if she had to climb the mountain alone, she would climb.

Sunday, September 17, 1989 was to be the day of reckoning. Holly's prayers were answered. She was filled with the fire of righteousness, and from the front of her church she confronted the congregation with their bigotry and prejudice.

'Did God deliver us from bonds of slavery and discrimination so that we could enslave and discriminate against others? The only way I'm leaving this church is if you physically throw me out.'

Glory be, the tender, saving love of the Lord softened their hearts and they repented. She gained the friendship of some and the admiration of all that day. She would never have to face another mountain alone.

When the cancer came and went and returned again, her faith community gave her comfort and support. And now that she has gone home, the Mt. Zion Church of God in Christ will mourn and celebrate, wail and sing, weep and smile. The memory of their strong and proud sister fills their hearts.

Holly conquered her last mountain. Only verdant pastures lie ahead.

Raul: Wow, Holly, you did some neat stuff. You really made some heavy waves, huh?

Man, I wish I could say that about my life. I mean, I never got to be more than a kid. That sucks. I always had dreams about what it would be like to do something special, have my picture in the paper, help someone out, be a hero and shit like that. But I ran outta time.

Doin' the homework wasn't hard because there ain't nothin' to say. Oh well, I guess everybody can't be special. Okay, here goes.

Raul Ramon Becerra died yesterday at the age of 18. He suffered his whole life and is finally out of pain. He never had a chance to do anything special in his life, never even got to kiss a girl, but at least he didn't hurt anymore. His parents, Dolores and Emilio, will miss him. They were always real good to him. His five sisters and brothers, Amelia, Maria, Carmen, Tito, and Manuel, will miss him too. The best thing was that by the time he died, his whole family got how hard it was for him and they didn't fight him anymore when he wanted to die.

Raul's funeral will be at St. Peter's Church and he will be buried in Holy Cross Cemetery.

Clare: I thought you said that you didn't do anything special, Raul. You've had to deal with things your whole life that most other people only read about. And you did it with dignity and grace, and in the end, your whole family came to see things as you do. How do you suppose they did that?

It had to be you, my dear. You were the only one that could have freed them from their denial. Both you and I know how difficult that is. So I think you underestimate what a profound effect you've had on your family and friends. I've known you only a short time, but I would be honored to be counted among your friends. You are a very dear, special young man in my tired old eyes, Raul. So it looks like you didn't need to have your picture in the paper after all.

I found the homework more challenging than I thought it would be. I never paid much attention to the obituaries and death notices in the papers. So when I began to take note and examine them more closely, I was somewhat dismayed.

I couldn't exactly put my finger on what it was about them that left me so cold until I started to write my own. For some reason, I thought it was silly to talk about myself in the third person, "she did this, and she did that." If I was going to be talking about myself than I would do so in the first person, like I'm doing now.

This changed everything. In some strange way, it felt as though this would afford me a voice even after I died. I would have one more opportunity to give a gift to those I love so much. I've never seen an obituary quite like this one, so I hope it's okay.

Clare Ann Bencal. I'm dead, not gone, not lost, not passed on, just dead. The leukemia finally killed me, but other than that, I'm no worse for the wear. Things are pretty much the way I imagined they would be. I'm in a much better place now, no pain, no suffering, and I'm still able to be with those I loved so much while I was alive. Death didn't break the connection, just changed the rules of engagement.

Charley, I'm fine and you will be too, I promise. I'm not nearly as far away as you think. You need only listen to your heart. I'll always be able to speak with you there. And don't worry so much about how you'll get by. If you lose one of your dang socks in the laundry, go get yourself a new pair. It's no big thing.

To my dear, dear children who could not bear to see me leave, take some comfort in knowing things worked out just as they were meant to. Samantha, Nancy, Beau, Sandra and Stan, you have made your mother very proud. I hope you know how much I love you. I want you all to get on with the rest of your lives. Live your lives fully. I sure did. Remember, this is not a dress rehearsal. One day it will be your turn to join me here, and I don't want you showing up with a lot of regrets because you were too timid to choose life.

To all my wonderful friends and neighbors, who helped me as I was dying, thank you. I couldn't have done it without you. I invite you to join my family next Sunday for a celebration of my life. Eat and drink until you are full. And when you remember me, do so fondly, for that is how I remember you.

Mia: Clare, that was fantastic. Thank you.

Wow, I only wish I had thought to do the same thing. I also found it awkward talking about myself as if I was someone else. I think the traditional style of obituary, the kind you can find in all the papers, is much too confining. I'm disappointed that I didn't come up with as clever an alternative as you. I'm gonna rewrite mine this coming week using yours as a template and really let loose. For now this one will have to do.

All are invited to a memorial service to remember the life of Mia Mai Wang on Saturday at her home in Palo Alto. Mia died suddenly on Wednesday from complications stemming from a rare lung disorder at the age of 31.

Mia was born in Hong Kong, the only daughter of Loo Wang and Ling Hong. Her family immigrated to California when Mia was just 7. She attended St. Thomas Grammar School and then Galileo High School where she was valedictorian. She completed her undergraduate work at Stanford University with honors.

After graduation, Mia traveled extensively throughout Europe and Asia. She was fluent in seven languages. After serving for a brief period as a consultant in international affairs for her father's investment firm, she returned to Stanford to complete her masters in Medieval Languages. She was just months from completing her goal when she was taken from us.

Mia was an avid sports enthusiast. Outdoor activities of all kinds filled her life. She was most proud of her rock climbing skills and was preparing to climb Half Dome in Yosemite in the summer.

If Mia had been able to say anything before she died, it would have been an expression of her love for her family and friends. She would have wanted you to remember the shared good times, and though she is no longer with us physically, she remains with each of us in our hearts.

_K_*evin:* It's hard to capture your life in a paragraph or two, isn't it? Doesn't it seem all so one-dimensional to you? It sure does to me.

I waver between being really cynical about this. Like I ask myself, who really cares? Friends and family already know all of this stuff, and strangers couldn't be bothered. But then I remember what it was like to write Doug's obituary five years ago. It was a very big thing for me. It marked the end of something very important – a life, a love, and a partnership. I wanted the world to stop and take note of the passing of this special man. Before writing Doug's obituary, I don't think I ever really stopped to consider that there were whole lives behind those little patches of words on the newsprint.

The gay papers do something different than all the other papers I looked at. They run pictures of the deceased to accompany the words in the obituary. I like that because it helps humanize the words. I also remember some years back, during the height of the AIDS crisis, one of the papers ran an end of the year retrospective that included the pictures of all the people who had died that year. There were pages and page of these little pictures, each representing a whole life. It just blew me away. It must have blown others away too, because the paper never did that again.

Man, how did I get off on that? Oh, I know. The reason I was talking about pictures is because I brought along the photo I want submitted with my obituary. It's a relatively recent one, taken just this past summer. I'm looking pretty damn good, if I have to say so myself. It's the picture of a man but I think you can still see the boy in there too. I'm super tanned, my hair's a bit too long, I have this all-knowing half smile on my face, and I'm showing just enough skin to let people know that I had a good bod.

Boy, you must be thinking, what a vain old thing he is. Hey, it's my party, right? Okay, here it goes.

One of the all-time great sun worshipers has finally found the eternal summer. Kevin Matthew Kelly, 1972-. Our boy was known by many names. Kevie, Kevin, Mr. Kelly, Dr. Blue and once, on a dark Halloween night, he was Angie O'Plastie.

Kevie was both son and brother. He was the loving but often misunderstood son of Paul and Polly Kelly of Boston and Coral Gables. Hey, folks, he did the best he could, and he loved you very much.

Kevie was the much-loved brother of three fantastic sisters, Brigid, Mary, and Colleen. They were real tight all through his relatively short life. They would have done anything for one another. In fact, his sisters, each in turn, interrupted their lives to take turns nursing him during his final weeks. Thanks for being with him at the end. Each of you was a big help.

Kevin, on the other hand, was lover and friend. Douglas Webb, who died in 2006, was Kevin's first and only true love. Doug spoiled Kevin for every other man, and even though he tried to find a second Mr. Right, he never did. Well, it looks like they're together again, and all is right with the world once more.

Kevin was also the best friend a person could ever have. Just ask Reggie and Rich and Derik, his fellow pool sharks. Together they terrorized pool tables all over town.

Mr. Kelly was a teacher and mentor. He was the much respected and highly honored music teacher at Bishop O'Dea High School in Oakland. It took fifteen years of tireless effort, but he created the entire music department from virtually nothing. The marching band was the envy of the East Bay Conference, and the school's prize-winning orchestra was a testament to his hard work. He single-handedly raised over $100,000 to refurbish the school auditorium, the site of the annual musical. It will now carry his name: The Kevin Kelly Memorial Auditorium.

Dr. Blue was the jazz and blues man. He was the heart and soul of the Blue Notes, a jivin' jazz quartet. He and his buddies, Nelson, Katz and Jamal, made music for the sheer joy of it. Good thing, too, because most of their gigs were done for free. The Blue Notes were famous for donating their time for every kind of charity fundraiser. Music was Dr. Blue's life and he shared his many gifts freely.

Finally, there was Angie O'Plastie, our boy's way scary drag persona. Mercifully, she appeared only once, a Halloween night we'll never forget.

Kevin was many things to many people. His open heart, his sense of adventure, and his boundless energy marked him as an extraordinary being. He will be deeply missed.

As he requested, his ashes will join those of many of his friends in Bass Lake, the black jewel of Pt. Reyes California.

Goodbye, son and brother, lover and friend, teacher, mentor and fellow musician. Sleep with the angels.

Memorial donations can be made in his name to PARADIGM/Enhancing Life Near Death.

Max: A woman goes into the local newspaper office to write the obituary for her recently deceased husband. The obituary editor informs her that the fee for the obituary is 50 cents a word. She pauses, reflects, and then says, "Well then, let it read: Fred Brown died."

Amused at the woman's thrift, the editor tells her that there is a 7-word minimum for all obituaries. Only a little flustered, she thinks things over and in a few seconds says, "In that case, let it read: Fred Brown died. 1983 Pick-up for sale." (Everyone laughs.)

My Check-In

Richard: Take all the time you need to look over your obituary. When you've finished, jot down your thoughts on how you felt doing this exercise. Would you like to respond to any of the other group members about their obituary?

_____

_____

_____

_____

_____

_____

_____

_____

_____

_____

_____

Group Process

Richard: Good work, you guys. I'm so impressed. Thanks for going the distance with this assignment. I'd be interested in knowing if this exercise was helpful in uncovering any unfinished business. Have you any regrets? Are there unexpressed feelings or unexplored ambitions holding you back from facing your mortality head on? What concrete steps could you take to resolve this unfinished business?

Robin: I have a bunch of regrets. As you could see from my obit, I have some unresolved stuff with my parents that I would really like to take care of now that I'm clean and sober.

They're good people. I don't know why I tortured them for so long. They always tried to do right by me. It's just like we were from different planets, that's all. How this apple came to fall so friggin' far from that tree, I'll never know. I'm gonna put this on my "to do" list.

Writing my obituary made me also realize how important journalism school is to me. Like I said, I am just starting

to get things right. I have something to prove to myself. I'm going to apply myself as if there is no tomorrow. Because you know what? There ain't no tomorrow to count on.

All that really counts is that I make a start, and if I make it to graduation, that'll be gravy. It's the doing and not the hoping and planning that counts, right?

Janice: Oh, I'm so proud of you, Robin. You'll make it, I know you will. You watch and see.

Like I said earlier, I also have many regrets. I don't feel as though my life has had any significance whatsoever. I've always been so passive. I don't want that to be my legacy, but I'm afraid I haven't any time left.

Robin: Come on, Jan. You can do it. Screw it! Let's do it together. Come and take some classes with me at State. I just read in the paper about this woman who got her bachelor's degree at 75. This could be the very best time of your life.

But no more being passive, ya hear. It's never going to just fall into your lap, ya know. I think that you'd be totally rad if you ever started to kick some butt.

Janice: Oh, Robin, how you talk. You make me feel young again. I'm going to take your advice and look into doing some afternoon classes somewhere. You just watch and see. You're right, I could have many more productive years left.

Mike: I'm beginning to see that most of my regrets have to do with my family. This wasn't clear to me before I did this exercise.

Sure I wish that I was still back in the saddle practicing law, but hey, I'm still able to keep my hand in the game working a few hours a week.

It was the part about Mr. Minetti being survived by his devoted wife and son that was the hardest thing for me to write. For years now, I've been harboring feelings of inadequacy as a husband and a father. I suppose that most of my "disruptive behaviors," as Maryanne calls them, are associated with these feelings in one way or another. I guess what I'm trying to say is, I don't want to leave, you

know, die, having to apologize for being an asshole. My family has gone through enough already. They don't need me adding to their problems.

Raul: Hey, I just gotta ask, man, the part about you dying in some kind of accident, what was that all about?

Mike: Crazy as this sounds now, when I was writing my obituary, I couldn't imagine dying a prolonged death from MS. Each time I started to write something like that I wasn't able get past the first sentence. So I created this little fiction where I died in a flash. Beats the alternative if you ask me. Besides, like I was saying last week, I always imagined I'd go out a hero.

Clare: But what does heroism really mean, Mike?

To my mind, maintaining a sense of personal dignity in the face of adversity is the real definition of heroism. And I think I can safely say that I'm sitting in a room full of heroes. I'm even going to be so bold as to include myself in that.

I'm struggling to make this whole end-of-life business work for me. And

I'm trying to do it in the face of great resistance. I want my death to be dignified, but I can't do it alone.

I have all these pressing questions. Will my family, particularly Charley, come around? Will he do so in time? Will we have an opportunity to enjoy one another without all the pretense before it's time to say goodbye? These are the questions that consume me. As far as regrets go, I can't say I have many of those.

Raul: Right on!

I got some regrets too, but they don't come from not doing the best I could. Like I wanted to be a basketball star. I wanted to get laid. Shit, I just wanted to make it to 21 so I could buy some brew with my friends. None of this is gonna happen. So, okay, I can deal with it. Now let me have what I can have, my own death the way I want it. Is that too much to ask?

Mia: I'm dying to know, did you ever get to talk to your priest, Raul? You said you were going to make an appointment to see him.

Raul: Oh yeah, thanks for remindin' me. I did talk to him for a couple of minutes after church on Sunday. We set up an appointment for this coming Friday. Keep your fingers crossed.

Mia: Well, I'm just full of regrets, and they're beginning to turn into resentments. Waves of bitterness have been crashing over me lately, so much so that I hardly know what to do about it. It really scares me too, because it's not like me.

For example, one of my friends from the climbing club came by last week to tell me about her plans to do a triathlon event in Hawaii in a couple of months. I kept thinking, why her and not me? This really sucks!

In the past I would have been overjoyed for her, but all I could muster the other day was a half-hearted 'good luck.' It was so insincere, I knew she was hurt. I mean, she didn't have to come see me at all, and she was only trying to make conversation, trying to cheer me up. Why did I have to hurt her like that? It wasn't like I was just having a particularly bad day or anything. I was just being a bitch.

This kind of stuff is happening more and more often. I'm angry and frustrated and resentful and it shows. All I can say is that this is not me. I don't behave like this. I hate it, and I haven't a clue how to let go of all this junk. It's eating me up inside. Is this happening to anyone else?

Mike: Are you kidding? I'm the king of resentful. If there was a club for resentful people, I'd be the friggin' president, know what I mean?

There's no getting around it, I've had a real good life. So why do I have so much resentment now that it's coming to a close? Is it because I expected it to go on and on without a wrinkle? Hell, I don't know.

You know what? I'm just now finding out that, even more than angry, I am sad. I'm real, real sad. And now that I'm taking the time to notice, my grief feels different than anger and resentment. I guess that in the past all my emotions were jumbled together and everything felt like rage to me. Maybe if I can get in touch with my sense of sadness and grief, my newfound tears will be able to wash away some of my bitterness.

Mia: On one level, I feel robbed too. But I actually know better than that. Maybe if I tap into my grief as you suggest, Mike, I'll be able to move through my regrets and resentment. It's worth a try, because I sure don't want to continue like this.

Kevin: I'm trying to deal with my regrets by fulfilling some of my secret desires. For example, I've always wanted to take a summer off and just kick around Europe for a couple of months. I've wanted to do it since I was in college, but I never made it happen. My rationale for putting it off was simple – there'd always be plenty of time later on. With this homework and all, I've been doing a lot of soul searching. What in God's name am I waiting for?

So I finally decided to make this summer my Europe summer. Just as soon as classes end in June, I'm gonna hop the next flight to London. I have friends all over Europe who want to show me a good time. I figure, what the hell, I'm gonna just go and let things take care of themselves. I'm not even going to have an itinerary. I'm going to let my heart lead instead of my head. Now that will be a novel approach for me. And when I return in the fall I'll decide on the next secret desire to fulfill.

I'm going to keep doing this until I either satisfy all my desires or I croak. This is such a radical departure from business as usual for me that I think it may very well turn my life around. I was getting pretty stale just sitting around waiting for the other shoe to drop.

Clare: That's the ticket, dear.

That's what I was trying to say to my children in my obituary. If there is one piece of advice this old lady would like to impart before she dies, it would be this: This is not a dress rehearsal. Live life fully. You'll have fewer regrets in the end.

I have a question for you, Holly. You said in your obituary that you lost your battle with breast cancer. Do you really feel like a loser?

Maybe that's being too pointed and I apologize if it is. But it really irks me when I hear someone talk like that. As if it isn't hard enough dying, why does it also have to sound like a defeat? If somebody says that about me when I die, I swear I'll come back to haunt them.

Holly: You're absolutely right, Clare. Amen to that.

I guess I wasn't even thinking. It's so amazing how things like that can just slip in to how we talk about ourselves.

I've lived a remarkable life so far. I've overcome some mighty big obstacles in my time, so there's absolutely no way that I'm going to start thinking of myself as a loser now. I'm going to go right back and change that. Thanks for pointing that out to me.

And I'd like to respond to something that you said, Kevin. Since I ain't dead yet, maybe there's more for me to do, more mountains to climb.

I've been getting pretty stale too, just sitting around worrying about what's going to come next. There's still a whole lot of injustice and inequality out there, so I don't know where I get off thinking that just because I'm comfortable, the job's done.

In fact, I think that's my biggest problem. I've been just cowering in the corner, afraid that the big bad cancer is going to come back and rob me of all my treasures. Well, that's not what I learned from my momma, nor is it what I hear preached in church. So I'd better get with it, because if I want to feel alive, I've got to live. Simple as all that.

Raymond: Sounds like there's a consensus forming here.

I oughtn't to be singing the blues either. I've got a good life. Things could always be better, but what the hell, that won't happen if I don't make it happen. The end will come soon enough. I don't have to hurry it along with a bunch of worries.

I still have a few passions in my life – my kids, my friends, and of course food. If I live my life worrying that someday these things will be taken from me, I'm wasting precious time worrying instead of enjoying what I have.

I wanted to say one more thing about my obituary. You know that part where I said, 'The secret ingredients of his coveted marinade died with him.' Well, I've decided to start doing some things differently. For example, I'm gonna to write down that recipe, make copies, put them in envelopes, address them to my friends, and put them with my final papers for distribution after I'm dead. That way my recipe will outlive me and I won't have to listen to my friends bitch and moan about it later.

Richard: Max, you're real quiet today. What's up?

Max: I'm feeling run down today, no pep, no energy. If you don't mind, I'd like to just sit here and be quiet. If I think of something to say, I'll let you know.

Richard: That's fine, Max. Take it easy. We appreciate that you made the effort to be with us, especially if you're not feeling well.

Raymond: OK, I have a joke for you, Max. This 95-year-old guy with a very bad heart buys a lottery ticket and wins five million dollars. His family is afraid to tell him the news for fear the shock will be too much for him. So they ask the guy's doctor to notify him gently. So, the doctor comes to visit the old guy and asks, 'What would you do if you won five million dollars?' 'I'd give half of it to you,' the old man replies. And the doctor drops dead. (Everyone laughs.)

My Turn

Richard: What unfinished business did the obituary exercise uncover for you? What are your regrets? Are there unexpressed feelings or unexplored ambitions holding you back from facing your mortality head on? What concrete steps could you take to resolve this unfinished business? Take all the time and space you need.

_____

_____

_____

_____

_____

_____

_____

_____

_____

_____

Richard: Before we close, I want to call your attention to our schedule. Next week we will be having the first of our presentations. We will be looking at legal issues with Steve Susoyev, Esq. and Emmett Giurlani, Esq.

Since there is so much information to consider, I have divided our time together into two sections. The first half will be devoted to addressing the issue of final paperwork – durable powers, advance directives, and living wills. The second half will be dedicated to looking at estate planning – wills, and trusts and the like.

I've put together two things for you that will help prepare you for next week. Let me walk you through them. First is a brief handbook covering Estate Planning and the Durable Power of Attorney for Health Care. Read this carefully. It will acquaint you with the topics and provide you with a basic vocabulary so that you will be able to understand next week's discussion.

Second is an exercise called "What If?" This exercise will help you create your own checklist for ordering your final affairs. It will help you organize your important papers and other essential items so those things will be in order for those who survive you, especially your executor.

Are there any final questions or comments before we conclude?

Mike: I want to thank all of you for indulging me the past few weeks. I know I've been a real jerk. It's taken me a while, but I think I'm getting the hang of this, finally.

And one more thing, don't anyone even think of showing up here next week with lawyer jokes. Get it? (Everyone laughs.)

AT-HOME WORK

Week 3 — Planning Your Estate and The Advance Health Care Directive

ESTATE PLANNING: PROBATE & TRUSTS

— James B. Creighton, Esq.

Your Estate Plan

What is an estate? Most people think they must be wealthy to have an "estate." But anyone who owns any property has an estate. All of your property, which includes real estate, cash, investments, tangible personal property, insurance policies, retirement plans, and more constitute your "estate."

What is an Estate Plan & Why do I need One? Your estate plan is the expression of the manner in which you wish to manage and protect your property during your lifetime. Your estate plan also directs others regarding the manner in which your property is to be managed and distributed upon your death; including to whom and under what circumstances such property should be distributed. An estate plan usually includes a list of the items of your property and their values. Careful estate planning involves using strategies that will accomplish the sometimes conflicting goals of providing for your loved ones while also reducing or eliminating estate taxes and the costs associated with the administration of your estate.

How to Begin Planning Your Estate

To develop an effective estate plan, you need to define your current and future financial objectives. Of course, most people want to keep estate taxes and administrative costs to a minimum. Another primary concern is to provide for loved ones. So, start the process by taking the following steps:

- **Make a list of all your assets, including any property in which you own a full or partial interest**. Indicate how title to that property is held (i.e., joint tenancy, tenancy in common, etc.). Include all real and personal property. Don't forget to include the amounts that would be paid to your beneficiaries under any insurance policies that you own on your life. Also, remember to include the amounts held in your IRAs, retirement plans, annuity policies, pension plans and the like.

- **List all your debts**. These include real estate mortgages, equipment mortgages and liens, income and property tax liens, promissory notes, deeds of trust, and unsecured (consumer/credit card) debts.

- **Subtract the sum of your debts from the sum of your assets**. This figure represents your net estate.

- **Consider your future distribution objectives**. These may include who should be your beneficiaries, what property should each beneficiary receive and when. Consider contingent events, like future marriages, divorces, and newborn children. Don't forget that one or more of your beneficiaries may predecease you... if that occurs, what should happen to his or her share of your estate?

- **Have your Last Will & Testament prepared**. Your Last Will & Testament is simply a set of written or dictated instructions stating how and to whom your assets are to be distributed. If you die without a valid Will, you will have died "intestate," and the laws of the state in which you live will govern how your property is divided and distributed and to whom. If you wish to avoid the costs associated with the probate of your estate or with establishing a conservatorship in the event of your incapacity, consider establishing a revocable trust.

- **Periodically review and revise legal instruments to reflect changes in your personal circumstances**, such as the death of a spouse or the birth of a child or grandchild. Changes in tax and probate laws can also affect your estate plan. It is very important to periodically consult with your attorney and financial advisor to learn of any changes in the law.

The Probate Process

Every field of the law has its own specialized vocabulary. Estate planning is no different. Before reviewing your Last Will & Testament and any trusts you may have, be sure you understand the basic concepts and consider the advantages and disadvantages of the probate process.

What Is Probate? Probate is an administrative process to provide that a will is valid and that the person who created and signed it was mentally competent and not acting under undue influence when s/he created and executed it.

Your Last Will & Testament is simple a set of written or dictated instructions stating how and to whom your assets are to be distributed. If you have children who are minors your Last Will & Testament should also indicate who should assume responsibility for caring for them. All the assets controlled by your Last Will & Testament must be placed under the jurisdiction of the Probate Court. However, the laws governing probate differ in each state. There are both advantages and disadvantages to the probate process. Often people decide to develop an estate plan that avoids the probate process because of the disadvantages. However, you should study both sides of the equation to determine how probate may affect your estate planning goals and objectives.

Advantages of Probate

1. Creditors Must Present Their Claims During the Probate Process. After an estate has been "probated" and all of the estate assets have been distributed to the beneficiaries, any creditors who did not have their claims paid during the probate process are out of luck; they cannot make a claim against the beneficiaries for the deceased person's debts.

2. Court Supervision. Another advantage of probate is that there is court supervision over the entire process. If the estate's debts have not been paid or assets distributed within 18 months of death, the executor must answer to the court and explain the delay. The executor must also prepare an accounting for the court, detailing the executor's actions with regard to receipts and disbursements for the estate.

Disadvantages of Probate

1. Probate can be costly. Law sets your estate's attorney's fees, but they only cover ordinary services. If the attorney has to do "extraordinary" work, the fees may be greater. Also, your executor is entitled to charge fees to administer your estate. Law also sets the executor's fees and the rate schedule is the same as that for your estate attorney. These fees are based on the gross value of your estate. These fees do not include other fees fixed by law or assessed by courts or other agencies, such as appraisal fees, title search costs, or any publication costs set by the publisher.

2. Probating an estate can be time consuming. The settlement of an estate often takes between one and two years. Moreover, assets in probate often suffer from lack of management during the settlement process. It can often take a month or more to obtain the probate court's permission to see an asset. Because of these delays, the executor must be conservative during the probate process because they can be held personally and financially liable if their actions with regard to assets in the estate are deemed less than prudent.

3. Probate is a public process. The public nature of probate gives unknown creditors an opportunity to make claims against the estate. Therefore the will must be a matter of public record.

More often than not the avoidance of probate will be an important consideration in the development of any estate plan. However, consider your goals before deciding whether to develop an estate plan that will avoid probate.

The Revocable Living Trust

A revocable Living Trust is a device whereby owners of property transfer to themselves as Trustees the legal title to their property. Take the example of Beth Taylor who established a revocable trust after her divorce. She transferred the legal title of her house from *"Beth Taylor, an unmarried woman"* to *"Beth Taylor, Trustee of The Beth Taylor 2012 Trust."* Beth is free to direct who will receive her house upon her death. Beth also transferred all her other assets (e.g., stocks, bank accounts, other real property) to the trust. During her lifetime, Beth can freely move assets in and out of the trust by merely changing title to the asset.

Other important advantages of a trust include:

1. Avoidance of Probate. Avoiding the costs and delays associated with probate is probably the best reason to establish a revocable living trust. Assets in the trust are not subject to probate administration because the assets were transferred from the individual to the Trustee;

therefore there is nothing in the decedent's name to probate. Avoiding probate saves court costs and fees, and greatly reduces the time needed to distribute the assets.

2. Avoiding Probate in Other States. Assets in a revocable living trust also avoid probate in other states. For example, Beth's primary residence is located in California, but she also owns real property in Utah. Upon her death, if the property in Utah were in her name alone, the property would be subject to probate in Utah. To avoid this Beth transferred the title to the Utah property to her California revocable living trust and thus avoids probate in both states (assuming the California property had been transferred to the trust).

3. Avoiding Conservatorship in case of Incapacity. Beth's trust is written to provide for her well-being and the management of her assets if mental or physical incapacity occurs. Should the occasion ever arise when Beth becomes unable to manage her affairs, a successor Trustee whom she named in the trust document takes over the management of the trust for Beth's benefit. This procedure enables Beth to avoid the costs and burdens involved in the necessary court proceedings to establish a conservatorship for her. Moreover, the annual costs associated with her conservatorship are eliminated.

4. Control Even After Death. Beth has her trust written so that, upon her death, assets can be distributed outright to her children or can be held in trust to be distributed to them over a period of time. Beth doesn't have to worry about her children receiving control of assets before they are capable of managing them.

5. A Revocable Living Trust Ensures Privacy. A special advantage of the living trust over a will is privacy. If Beth were to die without having established and funded a revocable living trust, her will and all of her probate assets would be probated and become a matter of public record. But a living trust rarely, if ever, becomes public. Beth's fully funded revocable living trust will remain private even after her death. There are no public records or court files to reveal ownership of the trust assets, debts or liabilities, or to whom the assets will go. In addition by avoiding probate, the successor trustee will not lose control of the assets or of any income flow from those assets to Beth's children. Of course, since there is little if any court supervision in the administration of a revocable living trust, the Settlor must be careful to choose a trustee who will act in the settlor's best interest. In short, the trustee must be trustworthy!

6. Difficult to Challenge a Trust. Another advantage of trusts over wills is that it is more difficult to contest the provisions of a trust than it is to contest the provisions of a will.

THE ADVANCE HEALTH CARE DIRECTIVE

— James B. Creighton, Esq.*

Kate just went through the tormenting experience of watching her husband, Jack, die a slow and painful death. He had a massive stroke and was in a coma. Even though he was not expected to survive, his condition was stabilized because the doctors had placed him on life support before they located Kate.

Kate knew that Jack did not want to be placed on life support, but he had never recorded his wishes. Now, the burden fell on her to make this difficult decision: should she ask to have Jack be taken off life support?

Jack could have spared Kate a lot of anguish had he signed an **Advance Health Care Directive** ("**AHCD**"). An **AHCD**—which has also been referred to as a **Durable Power of Attorney for Health Care**—is a written document in which Jack could have authorized someone—Kate, or one of his children, or someone else—to be his Health Care Agent to make health care decisions for him if he were unable to speak for himself.

How and When is an AHCD Used? If you become unable to communicate with others because of an illness or injury (whether permanent or temporary), your Health Care Agent under an **AHCD** can make health care decisions for you, carrying out your wishes. If you don't have an **AHCD**, your health care providers and institutions will make important decisions for you, even if you would have disagreed with these decisions.

The "Living Will" Compared to the AHCD. A "living will" is sometimes confused with an **AHCD**. The two are not the same. The living will is a written statement to your physician of your wishes regarding the use of life-prolonging medical procedures. The living will becomes effective only if you are unable to provide directions to your medical providers regarding your medical treatment. The scope of a Living Will usually is limited to the administration and/or withdrawal of life-sustaining or life-prolonging procedures in the event of a terminal illness or injury. By contrast, the **AHCD** is more encompassing and flexible than the Living Will in several important ways:

First, with an **AHCD**, you appoint a Health Care Agent to act on your behalf. Therefore your Health Care Agent can represent your interests during any consultations with all relevant medical personnel *before* any decisions regarding treatment are made.

Second, with an **AHCD**, you have granted to your Health Care Agent broad decision-making power over a spectrum of issues that normally arise with any kind of hospitalization or medical treatment including but not limited to the administration and/or removal of artificial life support. The Living Will simply states your wishes regarding the administration and/or removal of artificial life support.

Third, with an **AHCD**, you can include specific instructions to, and place limitations on, your Health Care Agent's authority regarding: (a) medical treatments you approve of or those you want to avoid; (b) the disposition of your remains upon death; (c) the performance of an autopsy; and (d) the donation of organs or tissue.

The AHCD is Still Relatively Uncommon. Studies have found that while 3 out of 4 people agree that an **AHCD** is important, only 1 out of 3 people actually has an **AHCD** in place. *Why?* The researchers found that because people don't like thinking about death and dying they often wait until it's too late to sign an **AHCD**.

The researchers also found that patients often wait for their physicians to initiate the discussion about the administration or withdrawal of artificial life support. On the other hand, physicians interviewed for these studies said that while they would be delighted to discuss this issue with their patients, they don't want to upset them or their families by initiating the discussion.

What Does the AHCD "Say"? The single most important part of an **AHCD** is the appointment of a Health Care Agent to make health care decisions for you if you are unable to speak for yourself. The document includes other sections such as: (a) provisions regarding the scope of and limitation on your Health Care Agent's powers; (b) specific directions to your Health Care Agent and health care providers regarding the administration and/ or withdrawal of artificial life support and other life prolonging treatments related to a terminal illness or injury; (c) a provision in which alternate or successor Health Care Agents are named to serve should your primary Health Care Agent be unable; and (d) provisions designed to ensure the legal validity and effectiveness of the **AHCD**.

The AHCD is Easy to Terminate. You may revoke or terminate an **AHCD** at any time. There are a number of ways to do this. The most effective way is to (a) notify your Health Care Agent in writing of your decision to terminate the **AHCD**, (b) physically destroy the **AHCD** document itself and (c) notify your physician and any other health care providers verbally and in writing of the termination.

Issues to Consider Before Executing an AHCD. Before executing an **AHCD**, you should consider the following issues:

First, determine your attitudes and personal feelings with regard to physical or mental disability and the final stages of life. Communicate your values and feelings on this subject to your loved ones and medical advisors. Consider your religious beliefs and how they affect your feelings on this subject. How might your personal relationships affect your feelings? Under what circumstances, if any, would you feel that the administration of artificial life support would be appropriate?

Second, consider whom you would appoint as your Health Care Agent and successors. The choice of an agent is the single most important decision you can make when instating an **AHCD**. It is vital that your Health Care Agent be someone whom you would trust completely to act on your behalf. Speak to the person or persons whom you wish to appoint and explain your intentions. You may be surprised to learn that some family members wouldn't be able to act on your behalf without letting their own feelings "get in the way," while others could act objectively and willingly on your behalf.

Third, to the extent you have specific wishes or preferences regarding your medical care, particularly if your death would occur without the use of artificial life support procedures, you should clearly state those wishes or preferences in the document itself as well as to your Health Care Agent and health care providers. This will help ensure that your wishes will be honored. However, be aware that regardless of the completeness of the directions you provide to your Health Care Agent, s/he will still need considerable discretion and flexibility because it is impossible to foresee all circumstances.

Fourth, realize that some physicians, hospitals, or other health care providers may still be unfamiliar with or resistant to the **AHCD**. Some physicians may have personal views or values contrary to your stated desires. As a result they may not want to recognize your **AHCD**. The best way to avoid this problem is to speak with your physician and other medical providers beforehand to ensure that they understand the **AHCD** and have no objections to honoring it. If you discover that objections arise, attempt to work them out, or choose another physician or medical provider.

You Should Review Your AHCD Periodically. Once the **AHCD** is signed, it should not be tucked away in your files. Rather, you should check periodically that you have not changed your mind about any of the provisions in the document, particularly as they relate to the withdrawal or administration of artificial life support.

Usefulness of the AHCD Is Limited to its Visibility. When you are in the hospital, you should have a copy of your **AHCD** added to your medical charts. Keep copies of the **AHCD** accessible. Give a copy to each of your Health Care Agent(s) and your physician(s).

Communication is the key to unlock this difficult area of life. We encourage you to initiate discussions regarding artificial life support and life-prolonging treatment with your loved ones and medical advisors. Decide which of the persons in your life could best carry out your wishes and desires as your Health Care Agent and ensure that s/he is willing to serve. Then, sign an **AHCD** that includes your wishes and desires. Peace of mind will be your reward.

* James ("Jay") B. Creighton, a specialist in ESTATE PLANNING, TRUST and PROBATE LAW.

He maintains offices in San Francisco and San Mateo, CA.

AT-HOME EXERCISE

Week 3 — What if? Creating a Final Affairs Checklist

What if you died yesterday, what would your survivors be dealing with today?

This exercise is designed to help you get organized. It provides you with an opportunity to consider the many loose ends that your friends and family will have to deal with today if you died yesterday.

The object of this exercise is to create a checklist of things you can do in advance, to spare your survivors much of the chaos that can follow a death. Remember, having things up-to-date, implemented and organized is one of the greatest gifts you can give those who survive you.

Here are ten general categories of concerns. The first part of this exercise is to fill in the blanks. See if you can list at least three things in each category that needs to be put on your personal final affairs checklist.

Once you've completed your checklist, review it with an eye to what still needs to be accomplished. You might want to highlight the things that are still outstanding and need your attention.

1. Advance Directives

_____

_____

_____

_____

2. After Death Care

_____

_____

_____

_____

3. **Estate**

4. **Legal and Financial Instruments**

5. **List of Assets and Liabilities**

6. **Distribution of Keys**

7. **Death Notification**

8. **Personal Papers Assembled for Distribution or Destruction**

9. **Names, Addresses, and Phone Numbers of Your Professional Advisors**

10. **Household**

Chapter Four

Week 4:
Details, Details, Details

Checking In

Richard: Today, we begin a new phase of our program, the seminar or presentation phase.

With us today are two of my very favorite people. They are my good friends and trusted advisors, Emmett Giurlani, Esquire and Steve Susoyev, Esquire. Both are lawyers. They're here to help us work through one of life's most daunting tasks, making sense of what is commonly referred to as end-of-life legal issues. But I have a problem with that designation. And I'd be willing to bet that both of our guests feel the same way. There is no need to wait until the end of your life to deal with these things.

Estate planning and advance directives, such as the Durable Power of Attorney for Health Care, are not only for people at the end of life to consider. No adult should be without them. In fact, if more people took care of these things before there was a pressing need for them, there'd be less panic and superstition associated with them when they are actually needed.

Getting one's affairs in order and keeping them updated is really very simple. A little bit of advance planning now will bring great peace of mind in the long run. And those who survive you will be grateful that you took the time to take care of these things. But enough sermonizing.

Let's do our check-in. This week I'll ask you to briefly comment on the homework. For example, was it helpful in framing the issues? I'd also like you to mention where you stand in the process. Have you completed an estate plan and executed your advance directives? Or are you avoiding these things completely? Max, you mentioned when you arrived that you have something on your mind. Would you like to begin?

Max: Yes, I was at the hospital again this week, this time for just overnight. I saw a new young doctor who I liked because he talked straight with me.

'Mr. Kapitanoff, you're dying. But I think you already know this.' 'Of course I know. I'm an old man, I know everything.' I asked him, 'How much longer?' 'Do you really want to know?'

'No, I'm just playing a game with you. Oy!' 'Then I'd say you have six weeks or less.'

You know what I think? I think he's right. Plain and simple.

So, you want to know how I feel? I feel like, okay, so it's over. It's a relief, if you really want to know the truth. I had a long talk with Sylvia. She knew too. How could she not? She's been my better half for nearly 66 years. She surprised me, very few tears. She was all business. She gets like that sometimes.

'Max Kapitanoff, don't you dare leave me with a big mess. You know I won't be able to handle it on my own. Do the right thing! Call Jacob!'

Jacob is our lawyer and good friend. He's been after me for years to make a will. 'Think of Sylvia and the boys.'

Why did I wait so long? Who knows? I'm crazy like that sometimes. I wish I'd listened to Jacob years ago. With so little time left, I can think of a million things I'd rather be doing.

My sons think I'm a stubborn old fool, holding out so long. I think they're right. The homework helped, though, especially that checklist. Who woulda thought there was so much to do? And

to think I came this close to dumping this all in Sylvia's lap. Shame on me.

Clare: Oh Max, don't be so hard on yourself, not now anyway. Maybe this is what was supposed to happen. If these are your last weeks, and I believe you'd know if they were, I urge you to spend them with Sylvia as free of as much stress as possible. The paperwork is important, of course, but it's nothing compared to being close with your wife. That's what I'm trying to do, put Charley first. And I think he's beginning to get the message.

This past week I asked him to help me with the checklist we got for homework. He was uncomfortable at first with my frankness, but I didn't cave in this time like I usually do. I was very businesslike. I told him there isn't any time for silly nonsense, and that I wanted to do this right. And when Charley started to get all moody, I just stood my ground. 'Help me, Charley,' I said. 'I can't do this by myself. Can't you see how much this means to me?'

Luckily, I did an estate plan years ago, and, thanks to my son Stan, I executed my Durable Power of Attorney for Heath Care over a year ago. Stan's my only ally in the family, the only one who really supports me in taking care of my unfinished business while staying out of denial about dying, so he accepted the responsibility of making sure my wishes will be honored. Gosh, I hope the rest of my kids don't give him a hard time. He's doing this not because he wants to, but because I asked him to.

Raymond: God, my life is so full of contradictions. In my professional life I take great care in making sure my clients have all these things in order, especially the Durable Power of Attorney for Health Care. I'm aware of how patient rights groups fought their long battle to secure this fundamental right. So you'd probably assume that I have mine completed, right? Wrong! I am so embarrassed.

I've never taken the time to execute my own durable power, and here I am sitting on a potential heart attack or stroke or even worse. It's a funny thing about us professionals. We think we're exempt from the things that plague normal people.

And while I'm on the hot seat, I might as well tell you that I never bothered to

update my will after my divorce either. I mean, hello! Earth to Raymond!

I'd say I'm way behind the curve on this one. Maybe I could make an appointment with either one or the other of you, Steve and Emmett, to help me pull this stuff together.

Janice: I'm happy to report that I have my durable power document completed. I found out about it only after it was too late for Albert, I'm sorry to say. Had Albert signed such a document before his final hospitalization, none of the terrible things that we had to go through at the end would have happened.

I also found out that there is another directive that is equally important. I think it's called a Do Not Resuscitate Order. Am I correct? Will we be talking about that today too?

Richard: Good point, Jan. I'm sure Steve will walk us through that one as well.

Janice: Good. I want to make sure all my bases are covered. I don't want any mishaps like when Albert was dying. As far as my will is concerned, I'm afraid that I don't have one and so I'll need help with that too.

Raul: Man, this is so wild. A week ago I never heard of this, what do you call it, durable power of something. Attorney, yeah, that's it. Anyway, this is so freaky, because in one week, I hear about it twice. First I read about it in the homework and, get this, Father Diego tells me about it when I went to see him last Friday. Nobody ever said anything about any of this when I was in the hospital all those times. What gives? I guess you gotta be 18 or somethin'.

I had a really good talk with Father Diego. He's way cool. He says that it's not a sin to stop doing my treatments, even if I should die. It's not suicide. It wouldn't be like I'm killing myself or anything like that. He said it's just like letting nature take its course, that's all. He said that he would help me talk to my family about this. I told him about this class and he thought that this was a real good thing. This is so cool, man. Finally, I'm so relieved I found someone who can help me with this.

Guess what? I invited him to our house for dinner. I want to get this goin' right away. My mother, she don't get it.

She's all worried about the house being a mess and what she'll cook. But she's real proud that a priest is comin' to dinner. I hope she still thinks so after she finds out what this is all about.

Oh yeah, I don't have a will or anything like that. I mean I don't need one, right? I don't have any stuff or money or anything.

Robin: Good news, Raul. Funny how things come together like that.

I'm sure glad that we're talking about all this legal stuff. Like I said right after Bobby died, I want to make sure that when it's my turn to kick, no one is going to come around with a truck and start hauling stuff away that doesn't belong to them.

Right now I haven't got any kind of will or estate plan or anything. But one of my friends said that she has this software program that creates a will and all that stuff right on your own computer. That sounds so easy, I'd be interested to know what Emmett and Steve have to say about this. If it's cool, then I could pound out a will in no time.

Mike: I have all my legal affairs in order, but you'd probably expect that since I'm a lawyer myself. It's funny, being as phobic about dying as I am, I never thought that having a living trust as part of an estate plan and executing a durable power was tempting the fates. But I sure know lots of people who do feel like that.

Like you said, Richard, there is a great deal of superstition out there about making a will. If I had a quarter for every time I've heard someone say, 'why should I make out a will, I'm not dying?' I'd be a wealthy man.

I suppose we all have our blind spots when it comes to end of life concerns. God knows I do. So I'm not about to be ridiculing anyone else for his or her fears and superstitions. In fact, if anything, I'm more sensitive now to the difficulties others may have in organizing the end of their lives. I think I'm going to do some writing about this and see what I come up with.

Holly: Jean and I and our lawyer, Ruth, put together an ironclad living trust for the two of us. We're particularly vulnerable because even though we've

been domestic partners for 8 years and own our home, our partnership is not recognized or honored in the same way a heterosexual marriage is. So we've had to go to extraordinary lengths to protect ourselves from the whims of anyone who has misgivings about lesbian relationships.

Like the time I was in the hospital right after my breast surgery, there was this nurse who insisted that Jean couldn't be with me, because she wasn't kin or my spouse. Can you imagine? Luckily for her I was too out of it on pain meds to know what was going on, because if I had known I would have really pitched a fit. As it was, Jean was just beside herself with worry. It was a very cruel thing to do. That nurse should have known better.

I'd be interested in knowing if our visitors know of anything else Jean and I can do to protect ourselves and our daughter Annie from such craziness.

Mia: Oh God, this is freaking me out. I'm completely unprepared. It's just that this stupid lung thing surprised me by coming out of nowhere. It's like I went from being well one day to dying the next.

I'm absolutely wrecked. I mean, not just emotionally, it's everything.

I'm having this recurring nightmare where I'm in this big classroom. A final exam is about to be given. Everyone around me is all hunkered down ready for the ordeal. There is even an air of confidence radiating from everyone but me. I rush in late, can't find my seat, and I don't even know what the examination topic is. And so I break out into a cold sweat. I've never failed a class in my whole life. The lowest grade I ever got was a B+.

I've never really failed anything in my life, so I can't even begin to express to you how terrifying this nightmare is to me. Just recounting it makes my hair stand on end. This is precisely how I'm feeling as I confront my own death. If anything, this workshop has only highlighted just how far behind I am.

Last week's homework left me completely numb. I've never given any of this end-of-life stuff an ounce of thought. I'm screwed for sure.

*K*evin: Whoa, Mia, darlin'! Hold on there. You're painting yourself into a corner. At this rate, your anxiety will get ya long before your lungs fail. I was gonna say take a deep breath, but considering who I'm talking to, I think I'll rephrase that.

Come on, it's not so bad. It's true, being presented with this stuff all at once and for the first time is definitely overwhelming. I got my initiation into all of this the hard way too. Doug was dying, my whole world was collapsing around me, and I was feeling none too good myself. I didn't know shit about any of this legal stuff. And to tell you the truth, I didn't much care about it either. I figured, Doug was dying, I was dying, so why not just go limp?

Like in everything else, Doug had to lead the way. He was always a much stronger and insightful kind of guy than me, even when he was dying. I kept telling him that I didn't know where to begin.

I was confused, depressed, and angry that my life was being interrupted like this. Doug insisted that I contact what was once called AIDS Legal Services. There were a bunch of lawyers volunteering their time to make house calls to AIDS patients. So I make the call, and in days this absolutely to-die-for lawyer (no pun intended) named Jay came to the house and helped us through the whole thing.

He was extremely patient and in no time we had everything done. I'm so glad that we did that. It restored my sense of being in control. So take it easy, Mia. It'll all fall into place, you'll see.

One thing I need to do is pull all that stuff out again and go over it. I haven't taken a look at it in over five years. Like my friend Roger, who I asked to be my executor, died a year ago so I gotta update that for sure. I've postponed this redo for way too long. I better get on the stick.

Richard: My week's been okay. I've been busy arranging another PARADIGM group. I have ten people lined up to start in a couple of weeks. This next group will be an evening group.

I always tease the participants who are only able to attend evening sessions because of their work schedule. I tell them that evening groups are specifically designed for those busy dying executive types who can't make time during the day. (Everyone laughs.)

Poor people, they don't know what to make of me yet. Do you remember how nervous you all were just three weeks ago? I'll bet each of you thought I was some kind of freak.

Robin: What do you mean, THOUGHT? You're the wackiest guy I know. And that's sayin' something coming from me. (Everyone laughs.)

My Check-In

Richard: Take all the time and space you need for your check-in. Please include your evaluation of the homework. Have you completed an estate plan and executed your advance directives?

_____

_____

_____

_____

_____

_____

_____

_____

_____

Group Process

Richard: Now I'd like to turn everything over to Steve and Emmett. They'll introduce themselves and then they will field your questions. Don't be shy, they're masters of their craft.

Steve: Well, hello, my name is Steve Susoyev. It's an honor to be here with you. Thank you for the invitation.

Let me begin with a little background on me. I went to UCLA Law School in the early '80's. And by the time I finished school, a couple of friends had died from a mysterious new disease. These were young men, much too young to die. At least that's what I thought back then. In time, the reality of the situation set in and I was struck with the realization that we are all mortal. I had never really considered that before. HIV was the consciousness-raising event of my life. It started me thinking in real terms about death and dying. And I'll admit I'm grateful for that, because without HIV I would have remained in denial about death and dying for a much longer time.

As a result of my early work with the HIV/AIDS community, I began to get more involved with other support services for people with life-threatening conditions. A whole new world was opening up for me.

Many people ask how I can do this work, because they assume it must be terribly depressing. I tell them the opposite is true. This is the most uplifting, life-affirming thing I do. People like all of you who are courageously facing your mortality, getting the most out of life and trying not to leave a mess behind for those you love, are a great inspiration to me.

Before we get to last week's homework exercise, I have some general comments to make.

There are many reasons people don't do estate planning or complete advance directives. From my point of view, the biggest reason people avoid this topic is denial. Some people believe it would be tempting fate to execute a will or a Durable Power of Attorney. Curious, isn't it, we aren't as superstitious about other things, like carrying insurance on our car, for example. Carrying insurance does not invite accidents to happen. So wouldn't the same thing be true when contemplating our mortality? Take it from me. Planning for the end of life will not hasten its arrival.

Unresolved anger can also get in the way of taking care of business. I've noticed that we often have more power in death than we do in life. For example, a person could be ignored his whole life, but once he dies the entire judicial system bends over backwards to try to fulfill his wishes.

Leaving a mess behind or purposely sabotaging efforts to tidy up your affairs can be a way to punish your survivors. But wouldn't it be a shame to go out all angry and spiteful? I'm sure that it's much easier to help a person resolve his or her anger before they die than it is to undo the damage done by neglect and sabotage after his or her death.

But let's face it, people usually die the way they live, and there are lots of very angry people around. So if there is just one thing I can accomplish in my work with you today, I'd like to help you break down your walls of resistance, anger, and denial.

Okay, let's turn to last week's homework. You were asked to complete the *What If — Creating A Final Affairs Checklist* exercise. Did everyone get that done?

Good. I'd be interested in finding out what things you placed on your own personal checklist. We can start with #1 and work our way to the end. Would someone like to begin?

1. Advance Directives

Janice: In this category I put down the Durable Power of Attorney for Health Care and the Do Not Resuscitate Order. And I also just included one I just read about a bit ago, The Durable Power of Attorney for Property Management.

Steve: These are all excellent. There is also the Durable Power of Attorney for Legal Affairs. Are there others?

Clare: I put down a living will on mine. I don't know what that is, exactly, but a friend mentioned she had one. Could you clear that up for me?

Steve: In practical terms, there's very little difference between a "Living Will" and a "Durable Power of Attorney for Health Care," but I always recommend the Durable Power because it is more flexible.

A Living Will simply directs the physician to withhold or withdraw life-support in the event of an incurable or irreversible condition that will cause death within a short time. There's nothing to guarantee the physician will follow your wishes.

With the Durable Power of Attorney, you actually appoint an agent, a person you know and trust, to make the decisions for you after you're no longer able to do so on your own. Your agent is your advocate and has the power to argue on your behalf even if it means going to court to have your wishes enforced.

2. After Death Care

Robin: My list includes advance payment for cremation and an outline of my memorial service. I want things done my way. I want the memorial to be for my friends. I don't want to put on a show for outsiders like what happened at Bobby's memorial. That doesn't sound too anal, does it?

Richard: Not at all, Robin! If you have a prepaid funeral and burial plan, be sure to have this paperwork as well as any deeds to cemetery plots in an easily accessible place. I believe that some health insurance policies have death benefit clauses. If yours does, it should also be on your checklist.

Max: The lawyer cabled his client overseas: "Your mother-in-law passed away in her sleep. Shall we order burial, embalming or cremation?" Back came the reply, "Take no chances - order all three." (Everyone laughs.)

3. Estate

Raymond: See how you are, Max?

I'm not sure I understood what this category means, so I used it as a kind of "catch-all." I put down Executor and alternate. And since I didn't know where else to put it, I added birth, marriage, and military discharge papers to this category.

Oh, I almost forgot, I also included prior state and federal tax returns. I just found out about this from Joann. As her executor, I will have to file a final tax return for her with both the state and federal government. Good thing she kept all her old returns, because I wouldn't have known where to begin.

Steve: Good for you, Ray. That's one that is often overlooked. Without previous returns, your survivors can be stuck trying to figure out how to complete this final return. Or worse, they would have to pay an accountant thousands of dollars to dig around for your old records.

Remember, you can always ask your accountant this question. If I died yesterday, what would my survivors be dealing with today? When he comes up with the answer, the two of you can take care of all the outstanding things right then and there.

4. Legal and Financial Instruments

Mike: This was an easy one for me. I have a big list. My will and/or trust; organ donor cards; personal and business balance sheets; list of charitable donations; list of personal stuff to be distributed prior to my death.

Thanks to my secretary, I have all my important papers assembled in one place. Insurance policies including life, health, accident, and liability, you name it. It's all there.

Steve: I'm real glad that you brought up the issue of charitable donations, Mike. Consider all the organizations that helped you during your life, or all the great causes that hunger for support. This is a perfect time for you to show that you have a social conscience. You can even direct your survivors on how to make charitable donations as memorials after you are dead.

5. List of Assets and Liabilities

Holly: I could only come up with a few, but I'm sure there are a whole lot more. My list includes insurance policies and employee benefits with a note to make sure I have the correct beneficiaries for each. Then there is bank stuff, checking, savings, and loans, that kind of thing. Oh, and real estate too.

Clare: My list included credit cards, credit union, safe deposit box, and savings bonds.

Raul: My list has my comic book collection and my leather jacket. Hey, no one mentioned a car. Wouldn't that go here? Boy, I wish I had one.

Steve: You guys are right on top of things.

You can make your beneficiary the co-signor on your bank accounts, or designate the account 'pay on death.' If you have real estate or a motor vehicle, you can put the beneficiary's name on the title right along with your name now, before you die. This can work for real estate, too, but only between next-of-kin family members. All the deeds can be made out in joint tenancy. These have what is called the "right of survivorship," so after your death the asset will pass directly to your beneficiary without becoming part of your estate. Of course, if you owe money on that house or car, your survivor will still have to make the payments, unless you have mortgage life insurance. If you do own a house, check

with your lawyer. A living trust may be needed to avoid taxes.

Holly, your point about having the "correct beneficiaries" is a very important one. You'd be amazed to find out how many people's life insurance policies, pension funds, or even savings accounts name beneficiaries who are already dead.

We'd better not forget to detail liabilities as well – outstanding loans, mortgages, and credit card debt.

6. Distribution of Keys

Max: I put house keys, car keys, and safe deposit keys on my list. Wait, I just remembered our cabin in the country. Where are those keys, I wonder?

Richard: Don't forget to pass along the combination to any safe or strong box you might have in your home. This is often overlooked until it's too late.

I once had a friend who had a safe hidden in his home. He would often refer to it, but no one knew where it was. He said it contained jewelry and gold and perhaps other stuff I didn't want to know anything about. Months before he died, he demented. He not only was unable to give us the combination to the safe, we never found its hiding place. The people who own the house now probably have no idea that they are sitting on a fortune.

7. Death Notification

Mia: I assumed that this category meant who should be notified of my death and when. Is that correct?

I made two lists. The first list names the people who should be notified immediately, family and close friends. The second list is composed of people who should be notified when time permits. I also included my obituary under this heading. I couldn't think of anything else.

Steve: There is also the issue of the death certificate. You won't have to worry about this yourself, but your executor will. Securing a death certificate can be an arduous, time-consuming task, especially if there is an autopsy or inquest after you die. Hopefully you will have chosen a strong, capable person to be your executor, someone who is good with paperwork and handling bureaucracies.

Being an executor is not fun. It's a lot of work and is often a thankless task.

8. Personal Papers Assembled for Distribution or Destruction.

Kevin: This one was easy. I keep a journal. I have off and on for twenty years. My journals are very private and I don't want them being passed around after I croak. There's nothing bad in them really. They are just my private thoughts and that's the way I want to keep it. I plan to destroy them before I die, but just in case I miss the opportunity, my friend Reggie said he would do the honors.

On the other hand, I could see there might be a reason for keeping and even publishing someone's collected writings or letters. That happened to a friend of mine. He was a writer. When he was dying, he called a bunch of his friends together for a little ritual. He knew everyone wanted to read the novel he had been working on, especially since he told us that we were all in it, but no one thought it proper to ask. We didn't want to look like vultures, after all. He must have known this, because in his ritual of farewell, he handed us a stack of computer disks that held the treasure. With a smile on his face he said, 'Make me live.'

He died a few hours later. His partner, with our help, published the novel. It was fantastic. What a tribute!

Steve: You make a good point, Kevin. Many people appoint what is called a literary executor, someone who will follow your directions on what to do with your private papers.

Raymond: That's really got me thinking about what to do with my stuff.

Oh, and I wanted to chime in here with another concern. I know that some people collect sexually explicit material. One would probably want that stuff handled in a delicate fashion, right? This isn't about shame; it's about prudence. I think that falls under this category too.

Clare: I'm not sure if this is the correct place for this or not, but I have on my list some final letters to family and friends. I'm in the process of jotting down short notes to my children and grandchildren and a couple of dear friends. I though a personal message of thanks and love

would help bring them peace after I'm gone.

9. Names, Addresses, and Phone Numbers of Your Professional Advisors.

Raul: My list has my doctor and Father Diego on it. I couldn't think of anyone else.

Steve: Let's see, we could add lawyer, accountant, stockbroker, and insurance agent, just to name a few. Are there others?

Holly: I didn't think of adding my pastor's name till Raul mentioned Father Diego. Thanks, Raul.

10. Household

Clare: This may sound funny but I've made a catalogue of important household items and where they are located. I've even catalogued some of my closets and cabinets. My daughters will be helping Charley after I'm dead and they're no longer familiar with where I keep things. I'm just trying to make things a bit easier on them, that's all.

I've also made of list of some of my more precious personal possessions, jewelry and antiques and the like, and to whom I would like them to go. I'd just as soon give these things away before I die, in a nice ritual like Kevin's friend, but my family won't hear of it.

Kevin: You are so amazing, Clare. You've thought of everything.

I put a petty cash fund on my list in this category. It sure came in handy when Doug was dying. If I wasn't around, and someone needed to run to the store for some bread or milk or something, they just dipped into the petty cash box. No one ever had to use his or her own money. It really helped make things run more smoothly, that's for sure.

Steve: I noticed no one mentioned pets. Don't overlook Binky and Fluffy. If you have pets, you'll want to consider what will happen to them when you die.

My Turn

Richard: What items did you include in your personal Final Affairs Checklist? Did you find the suggestions made by the other group members to be helpful? Are there items that the group overlooked? What concrete steps could you take to get all your final affairs in order? Take all the time and space you need.

_____

_____

_____

_____

_____

_____

_____

_____

_____

_____

Steve: You guys, you did a fine job. Congratulations! This is a much easier exercise when done in a group, isn't it?

Let's turn our attention to the issue of advance directives.

As I said before, each state has something similar to this. I want to walk you through the document step-by-step, so that by the time we're finished you will have completed and executed this very important directive.

I'll give you a few minutes to take a look at the document itself. You will notice that there are six sections and a signature page. The format is relatively simple and straightforward.

Section 1: <u>Creation of Durable Power of Attorney For Health Care</u>. This paragraph explains what the document is, how it is used, and who can use it.

Section 2: <u>Appointment of Health Care Agent</u>. You begin by filling in your full name in the line that begins: I, _____ , hereby appoint. Next there are spaces for the name, address, email address, and phone numbers of the person you are choosing to be your agent.

Robin: I haven't actually talked to the person I want to be my agent yet. Should I wait until after I have an opportunity to speak with her about this?

Steve: By all means, talk to the person you wish to select as agent before you complete this form. I suggest that you even go so far as to have a conference with your agent and your doctor at some point. It's always good to introduce the main players to one another. It'll help build a working relationship. After all, your doctor and agent may be called upon to have to work closely together to make difficult decisions one day at a time when you're not able to help.

For now, Robin, you can just pencil in the name. Remember this is just an exercise. My objective is to acquaint you with the form. If you can walk away from here today with a completed, signed and witnessed directive, all the better.

Raul: I don't know who I want. Do I have to pick my parents or another relative?

Steve: It doesn't have to be a parent or relative or a lover or a spouse. In fact, you may actually wish to spare such a person this task.

The rule of thumb here is to choose a person who will have the strength of character to honor your wishes even under difficult circumstances if other people disagree. Clare was telling us earlier that her son Stan is her only ally, and she knows that other family members may oppose the decisions he makes when he's following her express wishes.

You're going to want to choose someone who will fight for you if necessary. Sometimes it would be best to choose someone other than your dearest and closest.

Raul: I think I'm gonna get Father Diego to be my guy.

Steve: It sounds like he'd be a perfect choice for you, Raul.

Be sure you check it out with him first. You'll probably also want to clue in your parents about your decision. This shouldn't come to them as a bombshell.

This document will be effective for an indefinite period of time unless you limit the duration of its effectiveness in the optional space at the bottom of page one.

Section 3: <u>Authority of Agent</u>. This is a general statement of what authority your agent will have in the event of your incapacity.

Section 4: <u>Medical Treatment Desires and Limitations</u>. First there is a general statement regarding withholding and removal of life-sustaining treatment. This is what lawyers call boilerplate language. It's the bottom line. Read this statement carefully. If you agree with its provisions, you can initial it in the space provided.

So far, the document is pretty uniform.

Now we are presented with several lines, and even additional pages if necessary, for you to personalize your Durable Power of Attorney. You can make it absolutely clear what it is you do and do not want in terms of end-of-life care. Take a moment to consider what things you would like to add or define. Let's work together on this and see if we can come up with some suggestions. Be creative.

Raymond: I have a real phobia about gagging. I don't want any medical procedures that will cause me to gag. I don't want airways and I don't want any kind of nasal-gastric tubes.

Clare: The document I have at home simply states the thing I do want. I only want pain medication, no heroics. I want sufficient pain medication even if it hastens my death.

Holly: I'm gonna put down that no one can prohibit Jean from being with me for any reason. I suppose one we could also list the people one wouldn't want to have access, right?

Steve: That's right. If you anticipate a problem, spell out the solution here.

I hope you are beginning to see that the more specific you are in this area, the more you will be helping your agent.

Have compassion for your agent. Eliminate as much gray area as you can, so that if and when the time comes for this directive to come into play, your agent won't be faced with a huge moral dilemma. He or she will then be able to say with confidence that you yourself made these specific requests and the agent is here simply to see that your wishes are honored.

Janice: I don't want to be on a ventilator, no artificial means of keeping me alive. Period.

Kevin: Sometimes a ventilator is a good thing. I had a friend that was vented for 24 hours to help him through a very serious bout of pneumonia. He's alive and well today because of that intervention.

Steve: Good point, Kevin.

You can spell out the conditions under which you may want life-sustaining interventions. Suppose you have cancer, but you are not actively dying and you have another emergency like a car accident, then life-support might be in order. You may wish to have a timeline for the use of such treatments, three days, for example. You can write in the space provided at the end of section four — "Remove me from life-support after three days if there isn't significant improvement in my condition."

Mike: I guess what you're saying is everybody should have one of these directives. This is not exclusively for dying people.

Max: Yeah, like a bus could hit me on my way home.

Steve: Exactly, Mike. That can't be emphasized enough.

Because our time is limited, we need to move on. But I hope you understand that this standardized form can and should be personalized in order for it to be effective.

Section 5: <u>Appointment of Alternate Agents</u>. Although this form suggests that this is optional, I would strongly encourage you to consider naming at least one alternate agent. After all, your primary agent could be in that crosswalk with you when the bus runs the red light. This just makes sense from a logistics point of view.

Section 6: <u>Use of Copies</u>. Unlike a will, a photocopy of this document is just as good as the original. Make copies and pass them around. Nothing will come of this directive if, after it is completed, you just file it away somewhere.

Give a copy to your agents, to your doctor, to your lawyer, have a copy put into your medical chart in the hospital, carry a copy in your purse, briefcase or backpack. There is also a little card that comes with this form in most states that refers to the fact that you have this advance directive. Keep that in your wallet.

Now all there's left to do is the signature page. Just fill in the blanks, sign, and date. You'll need two witnesses and since there are plenty of us here we can be witnesses for one another.

Any questions?

Mia: Do I need to have this document notarized?

Steve: No, Mia, you don't.

Janice: Could you comment on the Do Not Resuscitate Order?

Steve: One thing you need to realize about the Durable Power of Attorney for Health Care is that it takes effect only after you are in a medical facility. It has nothing to do with what happens to you before you get the hospital. That's where The Do Not Resuscitate Order comes in to play.

You should know that any time an ambulance or paramedics are called to either an accident scene or a sickbed, they are required by law to do everything in their power to save your life and keep you alive until they get you to the hospital. This is particularly troubling to people who are actively dying.

Suppose someone attending you as you are dying has a panic-filled moment and calls the paramedics. If there isn't a Do Not Resuscitate Order in plain sight, the paramedics will do everything in their power to revive you and keep you alive.

In other words, a Do Not Resuscitate Order is like an insurance policy against the miscommunication or anxiety attacks that may, and often do, occur at the end of life.

This order frees up any medical professional from the responsibility to try to save your life. It also shields them from any liability should you die in their presence.

Some people wear a medical bracelet, like the ones that alert for allergies or diabetes, which states the wearer has

a Durable Power of Attorney for Health Care and/or a Do Not Resuscitate Order.

This may be a tricky issue for someone who is not actively dying. So if you choose to employ this directive, you must realize the consequences. Basically this is a quality of life issue. This document is designed to protect an individual from invasive and perhaps fruitless life-sustaining efforts if the procedures are not going to lead to enhancing the quality of life.

Max: Could you say something about the Durable Power of Attorney for Property Management and Personal Affairs that was mentioned earlier?

Steve: Some states have streamlined the process that has always been handled through a conservatorship. A conservatorship gives the probate court power to supervise both the ongoing medical care and management of financial affairs for anyone who is unable to handle these things for him or herself.

The problem is that a conservatorship can take up to a year to implement, and it is very expensive. So if you think this situation may apply to you one day, you can prepare accordingly.

You can make it easier for your friends and loved ones by signing a "Durable Power of Attorney for Property Management and Personal Affairs" now, while you are still able to manage your own affairs. Then, if the time should comes when you are unable to handle your own affairs, the person you designated as your agent will have the power to manage your property and finances for you.

My Turn

Richard: What advance directives do you need to bring you peace of mind? What is your plan for getting the necessary paperwork you need to execute these directives? Be specific and give yourself a timeline. Don't lose the momentum.

Steve: That's all I have time for today. I realize I didn't have enough time to answer all of your questions, but I hope I covered the basics. You will want to consult your own personal advisors for any further information you might need. Remember that the follow-up on this is your responsibility. I'd now like to turn the floor over to Emmett.

Emmett: Thank you, Steve.

My name is Emmett Giurlani, and I am an estate-planning practitioner. I was educated at the University of Santa Clara for both undergraduate and law school. I've been practicing law for well over thirty-five years, the last twenty-seven specifically in estate planning. I'm delighted to be with you today.

I have had the good fortune to be a frequent presenter here at PARADIGM. I believe this is my fifth or sixth visit since Richard and I met. A mutual friend, Todd, who is now a PARADIGM mentor, introduced us.

Even though I am well versed in the law, every client and every opportunity to speak to a group like this brings a fresh perspective and an interesting new challenge to my work. So I hope you've done your homework and have lots of good questions to ask me today.

If I may, I'd like to begin by responding to your check-in statements. I've taken some notes and would like to begin with you, Max, since your concerns seems to be the most pressing.

I understand that you've been taking care of your wife since her stroke, and now you have you own health issues to cope with. Let me begin by bringing to your attention a couple of fundamental issues. From what you tell us, I assume that you and your wife will need care. So when you get together with Jacob, and hopefully you will do this very soon, please consider executing a Durable Power of Attorney for Health Care for both you and Sylvia. As you know from your homework, this document will disclose to all caregivers, doctors as well as hospital personnel, exactly what kind of end-of-life care each of you want.

Secondly, even if you may not have anything else prepared, it is essential that you and Sylvia execute a Durable Power Of Attorney for Property Management and Personal Affairs. Notwithstanding any other documents of this nature you may have in place, it is becoming increasingly apparent that in California this document is essential. It will secure the management of your affairs until your death even if you have nothing else in place.

My concern is for your estate. I assume from what you tell that your community property estate has a value of approximately $1.5 million dollars.

You should know from the outset that the first death in a marriage is tax free, because there is an unlimited marital deduction. However, since both you and Sylvia are in your 80's and both of you are dealing with life-threatening illnesses, the possibility of close-to-each-other deaths is real. This makes for a special concern in planning your estate.

You need, at the very least, an estate plan that sets aside the "exemption equivalent" amount of $625,000 this year. A well-drafted document would say that whatever the exemption is in the year of your death, that amount can be set aside for the survivor of the marriage. And it would be tax-free.

The survivor's portion of the estate would be taxed at rates between 37% and 50%, once the estate exceeds the exemption amount in the survivor's year of death.

You would be well advised to consider an inter-vivos trust, or "living trust." Not everyone agrees with me on this, but I'm a firm believer in trusts, because I've seen them work efficiently after a death.

The trust would be set up for the benefit of the surviving partner of your marriage. You would name a successor trustee, perhaps one of your sons, who would after your death take care of Sylvia, according to your wishes. If you believe you may die before Sylvia, you can prepare accordingly. You will want to make sure that she is completely cared for and that her side of the estate would be depleted first. The part that is set aside to save taxes would be depleted last, if need be. Only after her death would the remaining estate be divided between your secondary beneficiaries.

Basically, Max, you need three sets of documents – a Durable Power of Attorney for Health Care, a Durable Power Of Attorney for Property Management and Personal Affairs and finally, a Living Trust. These three things will go a long way to giving you the peace of mind that you seek. Of course, there are other documents that are sometimes drawn in a case like yours, but with these three your objectives could be realized.

Max: How do I begin? Do I just call Jacob? Will he know all of these things? And what is the turn-around time for all of this?

Emmett: If Jacob is an Estate Planning Specialist he will most likely know about "Exemption Equivalent Trusts" and other bypass legal vehicles. They are not difficult to master, really, but they can be tricky in the drafting.

Call Jacob today, Max. There shouldn't be more than a week turn-around time for all of this. Each lawyer is different, of course, but in extreme cases, I know that suitable documents have been put into effect in 48 hours.

There is one caution, however. Drawing up the proper paperwork for your Living Trust means nothing unless you implement or fund it. Doing this simply means that all your assets, bank accounts, properties, stocks, retirement plan, whatever you have, are transferred into the trust. You'll need the help of a professional for this. You'll want to be sure all things are properly done and in order. Otherwise the paperwork is useless. And as I said, all of this can be done in a matter of days.

Raymond: My situation is a bit different from Max's. I have three minor children living with my ex-wife in Oregon. I haven't updated my will since my divorce. Do I need to start all over again?

Emmett: One rule of thumb you can work from is this: Whenever there is a birth, a death, a marriage, or a divorce, you should think about your estate plan.

Your divorce did not invalidate your will. If that will leaves everything to your ex-wife, which is the generic kind of will that people with young children make, then upon your death your ex-wife will inherit your estate.

Raymond: That's precisely what I don't want to have happen. Without getting into it all, I don't want her to benefit from my estate. Everything should go to my kids. And I want to set it up in a way that ensures that she can't interfere with my wishes.

Emmett: If that's the case, then you must decide if you want to establish an inter-vivos or "living trust" or stick with a simple will. I noticed that your homework for last week contained a good presentation of the pros and cons of avoiding probate, so I won't go over that now. Either way you proceed, your estate plan should include a trust for the benefit of your children.

Of course, from what you've just said, you'll probably want to choose someone other than your ex-wife to be the trustee after your death. A will or a trust is an "ambulatory" document. This means that either one goes where you go geographically. It also means that your will or trust provides for your children regardless of where they live. Your executor or trustee, however, should live near the assets that comprise your estate.

When it comes to contesting a will or a trust, no testamentary document is airtight. Unfortunately, there are unscrupulous people out there who can cause real problems for your intended heirs in situations like this.

Greed is a powerful motivating factor for many people. There really is no way to completely insulate oneself from the bad will of others. That being said, there are steps you can take to ensure that your will or trust will be upheld if it is contested.

Raymond: What would happen if I died without a will or a trust?

Emmett: The law is clear. Your property would naturally go to your children. They are minors and in such a case the law would create a resulting or "constructive" trust over your estate.

The problem is that in this situation, your ex-wife could be the named trustee by a court. You can avoid this likelihood by creating either a will or a trust. Then nominate a trusted person to manage your estate in the event of your death. It's that simple.

Janice, let's move on to you. I notice that you have your Durable Power of Attorney for Health Care. Good for you. It is a well-considered decision, especially in light of the unfortunate death of your husband Albert. You mentioned that Albert died without a will and you don't have one either. As Albert's intestate surviving spouse, you must have received the community assets, correct?

Janice: There wasn't an estate to speak of. It was a big mess. I had to sell our home to pay outstanding taxes. I was left with virtually nothing. That's why I'm living in subsidized senior housing now. All I have to live on is Social Security.

Emmett: The unfortunate situation that occurred after your husband's death could have been avoided if you and Albert had planned ahead.

Sadly, your story is not uncommon. A surviving partner in a marriage can be left in poverty because of inadequate foresight.

There's nothing we can do about your tragedy now, Jan, but this situation can serve as an example to others.

I am a firm believer that both partners in a marriage are equally responsible for estate planning. I have seen many women whose husbands kept them completely in the dark about the financial affairs of the marriage, who then discovered serious problems after their husbands' deaths. I realize that this sort of marital arrangement was prevalent in the past, but it is not prudent in this day and age.

Janice: You are absolutely right, Emmett. I did blind myself to the financial workings of our marriage. Albert always took care of those things, like I took care of the cooking and shopping. Looking back on it all now, I can see that we were terribly shortsighted. I should have been more involved. The disaster that resulted was as much my fault as Albert's. What were we thinking?

I guess we both imagined that we would live into our golden years and always have adequate resources. How foolish we were. That's why I want to make my own will now.

There is very little that I can call my own. When I lost the house, I had to sell most of the furniture too. But there are still a few precious things that I want to pass on to my sister's grandchildren. These things should stay in the family. I don't want to make the same mistake twice.

Emmett: A simple will would suffice in your case, just a series of specific bequests. Did you know that most communities have inexpensive or even free legal advice available for seniors?

Check it out. You can call your county Bar Association for referrals.

Raul: Hey, what about me? I don't have a will, but I ain't got anything either. I still live at home. It would be way cool to have a will, but you gotta have some stuff to put in it, right? I don't wanna look stupid or anything.

Emmett: You're 18 now, right, Raul? In California you need to be 18 to execute a will.

You should have a will for one very good reason. Your will says to the world that Raul Becerra was here, and that you made a difference.

Each of us will die. You probably know that better than I. And death is the great equalizer. You don't have to be rich and famous to have a will. Your will, like that of anyone else, states your desires regarding the distribution of your assets after your death.

Do you have personal possessions, Raul?

Raul: Yeah, I have this rad comic book collection and a real fine leather jacket.

Could I leave this stuff to, say, my friend Ernesto?

Emmett: Absolutely. Just make a list of the things you want to bequeath, decide who should receive what and put this list in your will. It's quite simple.

Besides, this is an elegant statement to your beneficiaries that you cared enough about them to entrust your possessions to them. Your will is a powerful tool for communicating your love, concern and thanks to those who survive you.

Robin: Emmett, I'm wondering about the software program I've heard about. I think it's called WillMaker.

Emmett: That's the software put out by Nolo Press in Berkeley, I believe.

Nolo Press is a widely respected resource for many legal concerns. They have an abundant library of both printed material and computer software. I'm not personally familiar with this particular program, but I want to believe that if it weren't legal and up-to-date, it wouldn't be out there on the market. This resource may be perfect for your needs.

You brought up another interesting issue in your check-in. You have a concern that after your death unauthorized people might come into your home and pick over your possessions. I imagine you're referring to what happened after your partner Bobby died.

I wish I could tell you there is an absolute way to prevent this kind of thing from happening, but I can't. There are, however, a few things you can do to make this kind of unpleasantness less likely. The first line of defense is your will. Then, of course, there are all the common sense things you can do.

For example, you can make sure that only trusted people have keys to your home. You can carefully choose who will attend you as you die. And most importantly, you may want to disperse some of your possessions before you die. You can even make a ritual or a party of it. There's less of a chance that things will go awry if you plan ahead.

Another issue that can be the source of much disruption in a family is the disposition of remains. There can be a conflict between your wishes and those of, let's say your parents, about what to do with your remains.

If you anticipate such a problem, you can leave explicit written instructions on what is to be done with your remains. You will also need to name a trusted person as your agent who will ensure that your wishes are honored.

Take care that these instructions are not hidden away somewhere. At the time of your death, your survivors will be worrying about just getting through the day. They shouldn't have to go rummaging through your possessions or rifling through your papers to find your directives. Give them a break. Keep all your important papers in one easily accessible place.

You can also arrange for the disposition of your remains before your death. Buying a cemetery plot or arranging your cremation in advance can short-circuit lots of problems. And the services will cost less if you pay for them in advance.

Again, it pays to be prepared. You may wish to call the Neptune Society and speak with one of their representatives.

Mike: My situation is a bit different from that of my friends here. As I said, I've completed an estate plan. I have a Living Trust and my advance directives are all executed. However, this is my second marriage and my son Kyle, who is from my first marriage, lives with Maryanne and me.

Emmett: Mike, you are the exception to the rule. Most lawyers don't have their affairs in order. You've been wise. Congratulations!

I have some thoughts that I'll throw out to you in an effort to help you evaluate your estate plan. First, I hope that your Living Trust takes advantage of all the available marital deductions.

Second, since your son is from a previous marriage and he is still a minor, you probably set up separate trusts for him and Maryanne. Funding these separate trusts can be tricky, so I would advise that your successor trustee work with a professional after your death.

It seems as though "composite families," children from different marriages living with remarried parents as one family, are becoming the norm these days. The intricacies of these arrangements are reflected in the growing legalities and case law governing estate planning in situations like this.

Particularly troublesome is the issue of custody of minor children after the

death of a biological parent. Custody battles can have tragic consequences, so it's wise to stay on top of this by considering various possible outcomes. You should bring your concerns to the attention of your estate-planning expert.

Holly: This "family" thing is a concern to me as well. My partner Jean and I and our daughter Annie are family together. You talk about your "composite families!" And it works. It works just fine. Needless to say, Jean and I are concerned that our family will stay together even if one of us should die...me, for example. We've worked real hard putting together this ironclad trust that will ensure that. But we don't live in a perfect world, do we?

Emmett: No, we don't. This bears repeating. There is no such thing as "ironclad" or "airtight" when it comes to wills and trusts. And as you suggest, Holly, some people are more vulnerable than others. I wish this wasn't the case, but it is.

At the same time, I don't want to suggest that you and Jean are at the mercy of backward-thinking people. There's plenty you can do to protect yourselves. The old adage, forewarned is forearmed, applies in this case. And it sounds like you've done your homework.

Let me ask you a few questions. How old is Annie? Is she your daughter?

Holly: Annie's fourteen. And honey, she's every inch a fourteen year old, God save me. Jean is her biological mother and I'm her co-parent. Annie calls both of us as momma, that is, when she's talking to us, if you know what I mean. We've been together as a family for eight years. We're good together, real good.

Emmett: The first thing that comes to mind is that it's appalling that our legal system does not afford your family the same status as a traditional family. Great strides have been made to remedy this, but many inequities still remain.

The trust you and Jean executed is considered, in the eyes of the law, a contract between two people, pure and simple. Nothing more, nothing less. So when you ask, "Is it immune to attack?" I would have to answer no. However, what you have in place is much better, by far, than if you had done nothing at all. Having all your assets in one trust is

the smartest thing you could have done. It is tangible evidence of the communal nature of your relationship with Jean.

Mia: Like I said in my check-in, I'm completely lost and don't know where to turn. I'm not sure that I could even formulate an intelligent question about all of this. I'm so intimidated.

Emmett: Mia, this isn't that complicated. You're an intelligent woman; you'll be able to figure it out. I understand you being frightened. Perhaps you feel pressured by what you perceive to be a time constraint.

You should be acknowledged for your courage to talk about and be with your emotions. Most people feel just as you do when a crisis dictates that they face these things before they are ready. You're a good example of taking care of business before crisis time.

That being said, let's see if I can't provide a bit of direction. You've heard me talk about the Durable Power of Attorney for Health Care. Begin there. The rest is also simple, especially if you are working with a specialist in estate planning.

You've mentioned that you come from a wealthy family. You are the beneficiary of a trust yourself, is that correct? The beneficial interest in most trusts ceases at death. It is not an asset you can pass along to someone else. So unless you have assets of your own, a simple will is all you'll need.

My only advice is that you not let your fear and anxiety get in the way of some thoughtful planning. Take it slow and seek help when you need it.

Kevin: See, I told you, Mia. There's nothing to it when you take it step by step.

So Emmett, can you provide some advice for me?

Emmett: From your check-in I gather that you've experienced this once before with Doug. Your comments to Mia are well considered and correct. The only thing I would add is that all this paperwork is useless unless it's kept up-to-date.

Kevin's predicament holds a lesson for us all. You say, Kevin, that the person you chose to be the executor of your will died last year. These things do happen.

Here's a good rule of thumb: Make an annual review of all your documents and advance directives as well as your estate plan. This way you are sure to keep all your things up-to-date.

Another suggestion: Name at least one alternate for every important position. You should have an alternate executor or trustee, as well as alternate agents for your advance directives.

Kevin, it appears that you have one of those estates that materializes at death: life insurance, a pension, etc. Right now you say that you haven't anything of consequence. Your estate, however, will garner significant assets.

Kevin: So I'm worth a whole lot more money dead than alive? I'd better not tell my friends this or I'll be sleeping with the fishes by next week. (Everyone laughs.)

You think I'm kidding. You don't know my friends. (Everyone laughs.)

Emmett: It's true, Kevin, your estate will be considerable. I'm glad that you see the humor in that.

This is a very common occurrence nowadays. We set things up in such a fashion as to provide for those who survive us even if we don't benefit ourselves. That's what insurance is all about. You're betting that you're gonna die and the insurance company is betting that you won't.

If you don't do anything, your estate will be administered in court after your death. The court will then hand over your affairs to a professional administrator or trustee, who will receive a good-sized fee for settling your estate. I don't think this is the way you want to go. So at the very least, you need to update your will by codicil. You just name a new executor. Or you could start fresh, by revoking your old will and writing a completely new one.

Clare: I guess that leaves me.

Emmett: We've saved the best for last.

Clare: Thank you. That's sweet.

Emmett: Looks like you've got most everything together, haven't you, Clare? Unfortunately, you also have this distressing family stuff going on. I have to tell you, I was really touched by your

story. Imagine! You were only 20 years old when you married your husband. Now, 53 years later, your time together is coming to a close. This must be incredibly difficult for him...for you both.

Notwithstanding the love and comfort level you must share, your frustrations are real. Consider the impact your dying must be having on him. I'm sitting here wondering how I would react if I were Charley. I wonder how gracious I'd be if I had to watch my life partner prepare to die.

I applaud your fortitude. Your commitment to create a good and wise death for yourself is enviable, but I also empathize with your husband and family. These things are rarely easy. Perhaps there is still time for your family to come together. I wish you luck. You are an amazing woman.

And with that I'll conclude my portion of this presentation. Thank you for inviting me to join you today. It has been a distinct pleasure.

My Turn

Richard: What are your concerns about your estate? Have you completed a will or trust? What is your plan for getting the paperwork you need to complete this task? Be specific and give yourself a timeline. Don't lose the momentum.

_____

_____

_____

_____

_____

_____

_____

_____

_____

_____

Richard: Thanks, Steve and Emmett. You guys have been fantastic.

Next week we'll be taking a look at the issue of spirituality. Joining us will be Reverend David Pettee, MSW. So before we close, I want to set you up with this week's homework. I have prepared a series of questions that I think will be helpful in organizing your thoughts about this very important issue. It is called: *Examining the Spiritual Dimension.*

Are there any final questions or comments before we conclude?

Mike: I have a joke. An attorney, cross-examining the local coroner, queried, "Before you signed the death certificate had you taken the man's pulse?" "No," the coroner replied. "Well, then, did you listen for a heart beat?" The coroner answered, "No." Did you check for respiration? Breathing?", asked the attorney. Again the coroner replied, "No."

"Ah," the attorney said, "So when you signed the death certificate you had not taken any steps to make sure the man was dead, had you?" The coroner rolled his eyes, and shot back "Counselor, at the time I signed the death certificate the man's brain was sitting in a jar on my desk. But I can see your point. For all I know he could be out there practicing law somewhere."

AT-HOME WORK

Week 4 — Examining the Spiritual Dimension

Here are 5 simple questions to help you evaluate your spiritual path.

1) **What does "God" or spirituality mean to you?**

   _____

   _____

   _____

2) **Have you ever had a spiritual (religious) experience?**

   _____

   _____

   _____

3) **What makes an experience a spiritual experience?**

   _____

   _____

   _____

4) **How do you know if you are having a spiritual experience or are "in the presence of God?"**

   _____

   _____

   _____

5) **Is there a relationship between your spiritual path and your mortality? For example, how do they connect or intersect?**

   _____

   _____

   _____

"Why do some men go through life immune to a thousand mortal enemies of the race, while others get a migraine that lasts for weeks? Why are our days numbered and not, say, lettered?"

Woody Allen, *Getting Even*

Chapter Five

Week 5:
Going Home

Checking In

Richard: Welcome back, everybody.

Before we get started, I have some news. Max is unable to join us this week. His son Harold called yesterday to say that he hasn't been out of bed all week. Apparently he's very weak. He has been bleeding internally and has been having a great deal of pain. His doctor put him on a morphine drip earlier in the week and now he seems to be resting more comfortably. But Harold says Max is somewhat dazed by the drugs.

The doctors told the family that there was a modest chance Max could rally again, but that no one should get their hopes up. 'And Sylvia and the rest of the family? How's everyone doing?'

'My mother's a trooper. This is very hard on her, but she's holding up okay. Dad never gave her much credit for her stamina. I think he secretly believed he was indispensable. Mom and dad are spending all his waking moments together. It's both sweet and sad. They're like school kids – touching and holding and whispering and joking. It's breaking my heart. I love my father. We all love him. We're all taking turns being with

him. I guess it's time for saying goodbye, but I just don't know if I'm ready. By the way, my mother said to tell you that dad finally completed his will and not a moment too soon. Isn't that amazing? After all these years. We're all very grateful to you for helping get dad off the dime.'

I asked if Max was up for visitors. He said, 'I think so, but you should probably call beforehand to check on his condition.' I told him that that I'd stop by over the weekend, because I'd like to meet the family. Let's send some good energy Max's way.

Okay, time to begin. Today, we have with us my good friend and colleague, Reverend David Pettee, MSW. He's here to help us focus our attention on spiritual matters.

I'd appreciate it if, in your check-in this week, you could speak a bit about your own spiritual journey and your reflections on last week's homework. After check-in, David will lead us in our discussion. Robin, would you like to begin?

Robin: I miss Max. He's such a funny old dude. I think I'll give him a call and tell him that I miss him.

I'm still reeling from the barrage of information we got last week. Steve and Emmett really know their stuff. I'm glad we're turning our attention to more ethereal matters after that dose of legal reality. Personally, I think I'm better suited to thinking about lofty things. The mundane, everyday stuff of life confuses me.

Let's see, about my spiritual journey – all I can say is I've spent my whole life searching and I guess I haven't found what I'm looking for, because I still feel kinda empty.

I've dabbled with all kinds of stuff in my life and religion is no exception. I was baptized a Lutheran as an infant. That didn't last very long. It was way boring. I got involved with an Evangelical church when I was 10. Man, what a difference. Those people were wild, at least compared to the Lutherans. Then at 19 I decided I was a Buddhist. That was cool. I mean I wasn't really a Buddhist any more than I was ever a Christian. I just mimicked what I saw and picked up a few buzzwords. Can't hardly call that spirituality.

While I was in recovery I became a 12-stepper. That was more of a religion for me than any of the others. Maybe because it was something I needed to survive. It like totally helped me kick the drugs and get straight. But after a while that got pretty confining, and so I left that behind too.

Now, jeez, I don't know. I'm nothing, I guess. I mean, I don't practice any religion. I try to meditate everyday and I guess I pray too. I believe in God and all.

Boy, I'm really being articulate, aren't I? I have all this stuff swimming around in my head, but I can't seem to find the right words to express myself. I'm looking forward to our discussion though. I'm dying to hear what you guys think about all of this stuff.

Kevin: I'm a cradle Catholic, Boston Irish, it's actually one and the same thing really. No, let me rephrase that. I was a cradle Catholic. Oh, screw it. The truth is once a Catholic always a Catholic.

What I'm trying to say is that at one time I was deeply religious. In fact, I was on the fast track to the priesthood when I was in high school. Then, while in college, I realized I was queer and that put an end to that. I bolted from the flock, so to speak. I was unwilling to sacrifice my sexuality on that altar.

Now I feel lost most of the time. I miss the Church a lot, especially at Easter. I love the liturgy and the ritual. I know there are lots of other traditions out there that are less phobic about the sex thing, but they don't appeal to me. It's like I'm unwelcome where I'd be comfortable and uncomfortable where I'm welcome. I guess I'm just a lost soul.

I really got into the homework though. I wrote pages and pages about it in my journal. I'd probably spend more time talking about this stuff if my friends allowed it, but they don't. Bringing up religion at a dinner party is almost as bad as bringing up death.

Hey, maybe that's the answer to question 5, 'Do you sense a relationship between your spiritual path and your mortality?' Yeah, you can't talk about either one in polite company.

Janice: I've been looking forward to this topic, too.

I don't think I'd describe myself as a particularly religious person. I was born and raised Methodist, but it didn't leave a very distinct impression. I sometimes think about God and heaven, or hell as the case may be, but I can't seem to make any sense of it. Unlike you, Robin, I'm better suited to the practical, everyday things. I don't think I've ever had a religious experience, at least not that I know of. To be perfectly frank, I couldn't even tell you what a religious experience is. Who knows, maybe I've had one, and I didn't even know it. Is that even possible?

I still think I'm a good person though. I always thought that being a moral person was much more important than attending church. I've seen too much hatred and fussing about by church-going folks to ever believe that a person has to belong to a church to be good person.

Raymond: Gosh, I'm sitting here really missing Max. Do you think he'll be all right?

That's a dumb question, isn't it? Why do we say things like that? Here we are doing a class on death and dying and still the old cultural conditioning comes shining through.

Why can't we just accept the fact that he's dying? I'm sorry, I should rephrase that. Why do I say things like that?

Why can't I just accept the fact that he's dying?

I'm like that with Joann, too. She's pretty close to the end now. Her doctors say it's only a matter of weeks, but I continue to relate to her as if she has a bad cold. I don't get it. Why can't I get it through my thick skull? This makes me so damned depressed.

Richard: It appears to me that your depression is connected, for the most part, with being unable to adjust to the fact that Joann and Max are actually dying. Often our own disorientation is the source of most of our sadness, grief, and depression. After all, our world is being irrevocably changed.

How many times have you heard someone say, "I lost my husband, wife, daughter, whomever," when speaking about the death of a loved one? When I hear someone say something like this, I always respond in the same way. "Where did you lose him or her? At the mall?" This, of course, is a real conversation stopper.

I believe it's important for us to hear how we talk about death. We sometimes talk about the death of someone we love as if it were our fault.

If I say, 'I lost my keys,' or 'I lost my jacket,' I'm telling you that I've been careless in some way. I haven't been able to keep track of my things. In other words, it's my fault. But if my wife, lover, grandmother, son, whomever dies, it is not my fault. I may experience a sense of loss with the death, but I didn't lose the person. They're dead, not lost.

Remember the work we did our first two weeks together? Many of you said that dying is hard because your death would be the source of anguish for someone you love. Aren't we talking about the same thing here? I'll bet if we checked in with Max or Joann they would talk in terms of dying, not in terms of abandonment.

Death doesn't end a relationship. Sure, the relationship is altered by death but it endures, at least in memory. And memory is a very powerful thing.

Many people believe that death is not the end of things. I believe that myself. But if my vocabulary does not reflect this, then what kind of double message am I giving myself and others? That's one of the reasons why we're talking about spirituality, to see if we can flesh out what we really believe about life and death. I'm sorry I interrupted you, Ray. Please continue.

Raymond: You're right, Richard, I just don't have confidence that my world will be the same without Joann. She keeps telling me that she's not abandoning me and that I shouldn't feel the way that I do, but I can't seem to shake it. Maybe if I had some kind of belief system that would reinforce this for me I'd have a better time of it. But right now I have nothing in place and so I'm floundering.

Holly: Wow, I don't know what I'd do without my faith. It means everything to me. My belief in Jesus has got me through many hard times. I just don't see how folks get by without faith. Believing is how I was raised, honey, it's bred in my bones. But it's more than that. It's a cultural thing too.

In the rural south, where I'm from, our churches are the center of the black community, its very heart and soul. The civil rights movement began there. Everything that I'm most proud of has its roots there.

Don't get me wrong, just because I have faith doesn't mean I don't have my doubts. Like I was saying last week, my faith is being tested now as I face my own death. It's a troubling time for me. I keep asking myself, what if my faith isn't strong enough to bring me comfort when I die? What if I die in agony because I feel like God has abandoned me?

Excuse me, I'm sorry, I can't help crying. It's just I'm so afraid. I just get to feeling real lost at times.

Mike: I'm pretty much adrift with this stuff too. If you ask me, religion is for kids and old ladies. I stopped going to church when I was sophomore in high school. It all seemed like a bunch of pious mumbo jumbo. Even now the whole thing still gives me the creeps. In fact, the last couple of times I was in a church, like for a wedding or a funeral, I was real uncomfortable. I felt like the proverbial criminal returning to the scene of the crime.

At the same time, I am proud to count among my good friends a number of priests and nuns. They've taught me just about everything I know about social justice. I've always been amazed at the level of their commitment and I know that their commitment comes directly from their faith. It's real powerful stuff.

So as you can see, I'm in a bit of a conflict and my ambivalence about all of this really came into focus when I was doing the homework.

I was thinking that if I were dying I would want my friend, Father Joe, to give me the last rites. I know this is a contradiction, and I'm hard-pressed to explain it myself, but that's what I want. And like it said in my obituary, I want a full Catholic funeral. I want the whole enchilada, all the bells and whistles. I want them to pull out all the stops.

Has this got anything to do with religion or God? Your guess is as good as mine. One thing I know for sure, and I can almost hear Max saying, 'it couldn't hurt.' A guy like me wants to have all his bases covered, you know what I mean?

Mia: There was never any formal religion in my home when I was growing up, but I did get a taste of it when I went to Catholic grammar school right after we moved to America. It was a lot like the private British school I attended in Hong Kong, with the uniforms and all. But the Catholic school here in San Francisco had one thing the British school didn't have. It had a bewildering array of religious statues and pictures.

They were everywhere. And they really frightened me at first.

I remember some of the pictures and statues were all bloody and others had exposed body parts, like hearts and whatnot. I remember asking myself, 'What does all this mean?' I was afraid that if I didn't behave these terrible things would happen to me. Even today, as an adult, I don't like seeing that sort of thing.

I've never given spirituality much more thought. I don't feel as though I'm deficient in any way. Actually, I feel a lot like you, Jan. The world is full of religious-generated violence and hatred. I find that offensive, I really do.

Quite frankly, I'm a non-believer. I don't believe in God or an afterlife. I mean, how could there be a God when there is so much misery in the world? Bad people prosper while good people suffer. And the concept of an afterlife always seemed to me like so much pie in the sky. A carrot on a stick that keeps the poor and unfortunate gazing upward instead of focusing on finding a solution to their plight here and now.

As far as I can see, religion is just a way of subjugating people. I'd just as soon have none of it.

Was that too harsh? I hope I didn't offend anyone.

Raul: Man, I can't even imagine growing up without religion. My family is way religious. Sometimes I think it's way too much. Our house is full of the same kind of pictures and statues like you were talkin' about, Mia. And I guess I never really thought about how scary all that stuff could be for kids.

Why does everybody have to hurt so bad? That's what I'd like to know. Didn't any of them saints have, you know, a nice life or anything? My mother is always sayin', 'Raulito, Jesus suffered a lot, you'll never suffer more than him.' I hope I don't go to hell for sayin' this, but shit, man, Jesus had only one really bad day, right? All the other times he was hanging with his friends drinking wine, goin' to parties and helpin' sick and dyin' guys. Sounds okay to me.

Besides, I don't like goin' to church. It's boring. I do like bein' in church, though. I like it when I'm there all by myself. All them little candles burnin', it smells real nice and like it's real quiet. Sometimes when I'm in church all by myself like that I think I hear God talkin' to me. Sometimes when that happens I just start cryin' like a baby. Shit, man, I never told anyone that before. Do you think I'm crazy? You just have to tell me to shut up, okay?

Ya know what I want to know? I wanna know what heaven's gonna be like. I asked Father Diego about it, but he just started talkin' about all this weird stuff I never heard of before. Just between you and me, I don't think he knows. Maybe no one does. Maybe there ain't a heaven. Shit, man, that would really suck.

Clare: I believe there's a heaven, Raul. I haven't any idea what it's going to be like, but I know there is one and it's going to be simply wonderful. Life is too charged with energy to have it all end in death. Besides, I feel the presence of many of those who have gone before me, just like if I were there with them. I sometimes hear them calling to me. My parents, sisters and brother, everyone who has died before me is just waiting for me to arrive. How could that happen if there isn't an afterlife?

I sometime have little conversations with them. As I get closer to the end, these conversations have become all the more intense. To tell you the truth, it's often hard to come back to the land of the living after one of these lovely encounters. They are very comforting to me. My anxiety just seems to melt away.

When this first started, about six weeks ago, I tried to talk to my family about it, but I didn't get anywhere. My daughter, Sandra, said that I was probably hallucinating because of the pain medications I'm taking. Sandra is a good daughter, but believe you me, she can be a real pill sometimes. I wanted to tell her how beautiful it is so that she wouldn't worry. But all she did was reduce the whole thing down to a chemical reaction. My, my, my, how can she be so stiff? And what if it is the medications? It's no less real to me.

Why are people like that? I'm sure glad that I can talk about this here. What I'm telling you *is* real, really it is. I'm not just a crazy old woman. You have to believe me.

Richard: I believe you, Clare. I've heard many people say similar things at the end of their lives. In fact, that's what my check-in is about. I'm currently working with my friend, Robert, who is actively dying. Robert and I have known each other for years. He's been in and

out of hospitals for as long as I've known him. In fact, that's how we met.

A few weeks ago Robert began confiding his dreams to me. He recently told me of a particularly vivid dream where his hospital room suddenly filled with dozens of other women and men, some old, some young. 'It was like some big party and I was the guest of honor. I thought it was odd that it was happening here in this little hospital room, but what the hell? A party is a party, right? Everyone was being so friendly and when I awoke I was alone, but not at all frightened.'

Robert is dying in a room at a local hospice. I've visited that room many times over the years and I've known some of the people who died there and I told Robert this. He was silent for a few minutes. 'Imagine how many people have died in this room, in this very bed. No wonder the room was filled to overflowing in my dream.

This is a sacred place, isn't it? It's like a shrine.'

'It's kind of like you're being born, Robert. You're straddling two worlds now. You appear to have one foot in the next world before you've completely left this one and you now have the ability to communicate in both. How does that make you feel?'

'Well, I'm not afraid anymore. To tell the truth, I'm finally ready for the adventure to begin.'

My Check-In

Richard: Take all the time and space you need for your check-in. This week, I'd like you to address the issue of your own spiritual journey and your reflections on last week's homework.

_____

_____

_____

_____

_____

_____

_____

_____

_____

Group Process

Richard: David, it's all yours. Please take a few minutes to introduce yourself and then you could help direct us in our discussion, okay?

David: Thank you, Richard. And thank you, everyone, for the invitation to join you today.

My name is David Pettee. I am a Unitarian/Universalist minister affiliated with the Unitarian/Universalist Church here in San Francisco. My ministry is hospice social work.

This often surprises people. 'If you're a minister, why aren't you a chaplain instead of a social worker?'

Actually, there is a good reason. When I was a hospital chaplain at a hospital in San Francisco, I felt that my access to patients was limited by my job title. Only a small fraction of the patient population invited a visit from the chaplain, and even then few would engage me about anything of consequence in their life. On the other hand, the hospital social workers I knew were always very busy, even to the point of being overwhelmed.

So I decided, what the heck, I'll just change my job title. And it worked. Now, as a hospice social worker, I have access to all the hospice clients and my connection with them is considerably deeper.

Hospice care, by its very nature, addresses all manner of end-of-life concerns. And many of these concerns are about who we are, in relation to all that there is. In other words, end-of-life issues are often spiritual issues. So I figure, it really doesn't matter to me how I get to the issues, either by being a social worker or by being a chaplain, just as long as I get to the meat of things.

A word about my connection with PARADIGM. I read about Richard some years ago in an article in one of the local papers. Then, some months later, I saw a flyer advertising this group so I decided to call and finally made the connection.

At the time, I remember feeling pretty dry in my work at hospice. Things were becoming routine and I knew I needed to make some kind of adjustment. Besides, I had my own mortality issues to address, but because of professional boundaries

I couldn't bring these concerns to work with me. I needed an outlet for dealing with what was on my mind. So I thought, what the heck, I'll join PARADIGM.

I started with a group, but had to drop out after only one week. You see, my wife was diagnosed with cancer at that very same time. I needed to focus all of my attention on my wife and family, so I wasn't able to complete the course. Interestingly enough, my wife later joined a PARADIGM group of her own and went on to complete the ten weeks I only started.

Well, enough about me, let's turn our attention to the topic at hand. I would like to break open this discussion by tackling at least some of the five questions given as last week's homework. They're pretty broad in their scope so we should be able to include everyone. How about question 1? What does "God" or spirituality mean to you? Would someone like to begin?

Raymond: It's so good to finally meet you, David. You and I are in the same line of work, well, the social work part anyhow. You have such an interesting take on your work; I'd really like to learn more. Maybe we could have coffee sometime. I'd love to pick your brain.

I'll be honest with you, I haven't a clue about what God or spirituality means to me. I just can't seem to get behind the whole religion thing. However, I do have a craving for something deeper in my life. Why in the world am I going first? I'm not making any sense. Sorry.

David: Let me begin by cautioning you not to confuse the notion of spirituality with religion. Sometimes they go hand in hand, but not always. Religion is a place to exercise one's spirituality, but I don't think it's the only place one can find spirituality.

For me, spirituality is a constant but gentle tugging that takes place in me. My spirituality is always calling me back into relationship – relationship with myself, with others and ultimately with what I consider to be universal. That presence is always there. And at the risk of being too linear, I would suggest that there are choices that I can make to either enhance this connection or create division. I think we have those kinds of choices all the time.

For me, God is the energy prompting this call to relationship. It is a call to love and compassion.

Raymond: That's spirituality? I never thought it could be so simple. I thought spirituality was all about dogma and rules and regulations.

Mike: That was my understanding too. Maybe I know more about spirituality than I thought.

David: I believe that we are continually given opportunities to make contact with others. It's all about relationship, even as are lives are coming to a close. And these relationships can be nurtured without using words. A touch or a look can heal wounds that have been festering for years. A simple gesture like extending a hand in forgiveness or a smile by way of blessing can radically change the whole scene.

Of course the opposite is true as well. Godlessness, to my mind, is the rejection of relationship – the state of being grossly out of communion with one's self, with others or ultimately with one's God. Relationship makes us accountable. And this accountability takes place in the form of communication, honesty, and love. When we are out of relationship, all of the "glue" that binds us together dissolves.

I am often asked what hospice is all about. And I always respond the same way. Hospice care is about helping dying people discover if they are in "right relationship" with themselves. If they discover that they're not in right relationship with themselves and they want to be, then hospice can help them bring about reconciliation. Hospice invites them to expand the circle to discover if they are in right relationship with family and friends. If they're not and they would like to be, hospice can help bring about reconciliation there as well.

And finally, hospice invites its clients to expand the circle of discovery to include their relationship with God or whatever they perceive to be universal. And if they discover that they're not in right relationship with their God and they would like to be, hospice can help them with that reconciliation too.

Mike: I'm trying to follow you here, but you lost me at the end. I think I understand right relationship with myself and with others, but I don't know about God. I'm a non-believer.

David: This is where my work gets a little tricky, Mike. This is precisely where the dialogue often breaks down. You said something interesting in your check-in that I thought I'd mention here. You said you felt like a criminal returning to the scene of the crime when, on occasion, you find yourself in a church. Interesting analogy, wouldn't you say?

Seems to me there's a relationship problem there, otherwise why would you feel guilty?

Here's a simple little test that I use to evaluate my relationships. If I can find even a shred of guilt, shame or anger in any relationship I have, be it with myself or with another person or with the universe, I know I have a problem.

Mike: Well, I guess I've really got my work cut out for me. As my friends here can tell you, I'm pretty much consumed with all three – guilt, shame, and anger. And there's no doubt that my relationships, especially with the people I love the most, are in jeopardy.

God, I feel like a 10-year-old going to confession. I'd better quit while I'm ahead.

It's just now beginning to dawn on me that things can't continue the way they've been going. I've really messed up big time.

Clare: They say confession is good for the soul.

Mike, I really admire you. You are so transparent. I'll bet you don't think of yourself as being transparent, but you are, and I find that very appealing.

David, as you heard in my check-in, I'm facing a great deal of resistance from my family when I attempt to bring closure to my relationships with them. And since we appear to be making confessions, I have one myself. The more resistance I meet, the more frustrated and, yes, angry I become. I know I'm dying and I don't want to die angry and frustrated.

David: It is frustrating and even maddening to be unable to bring reconciliation or closure to a relationship. But sometimes circumstances prevent us from making amends for the mistakes and hurts that we have caused each other and ourselves. Sometimes we don't even get the opportunity to say goodbye.

So you have to ask yourself, what can you do in a situation like that? Some religious traditions have rituals for reconciliation, like confession in the Catholic tradition. People in these traditions are lucky. They have a whole belief system that can help them get them through some really rough stuff.

But what if you don't belong to tradition like that? What do you do then? Well, I guess, you could always create your own ritual. Do you see the power in that? You could put together your own ritual of reconciliation, Clare. You could ritually let go of all these heavy burdens that you are carrying. You could forgive your family their inability to join you in your good death, and you could forgive yourself for your anger and frustration. Forgiveness is all about getting back into right relationship and sometimes that begins by forgiving ourselves first.

Kevin: As you heard from my check-in, I'm alienated from my religious tradition. It's too bad that things are the way they are, but I'm not gonna get all balled up in feeling sorry for myself. Maybe God is calling me to forge my own path. It's a hell of a lot more work, but maybe it will be just as rewarding.

Holly: It breaks my heart every time I hear you say that, Kevin. It would sure enough kill me to be cut off from my church. It almost happened once and I don't ever want that to happen again. But then I keep wondering, is God calling me out of this comfortable place to a place that is more challenging? Is this why I'm having this crisis of faith? I know my faith is more alive when it is being challenged, but dear Lord, I'm scared.

At the moment I have this big disconnect between what I believe in my heart and what I feel in my guts. I want to believe that God loves me, but I sometimes feel like I've been abandoned. Is this making any sense?

David: I assume people go through this kind of thing on a regular basis. The Christian mystic, John of the Cross, called this kind of experience the dark night of the soul. Some instances can be more pronounced and longer lasting than others. But inevitably, even these come to an end. The question then is, how will I respond when I'm having such a crisis? Will it be with bitterness and anger, or will it be with humility and acceptance?

Mia: I fall squarely into the first category, no doubt about it. I am full of rage. What kind of God would do something like this to me? I was just hitting my stride. I'm not about to roll over in humility and acceptance and say, 'fine, no problem, who cares if I can breathe or not?' I could just scream I'm so pissed.

Look at me, even talking about this makes me short of breath. Damnit, I can't even express myself without my lungs failing me! You tell me where the goodness is in all of this.

Richard: I generally get to feeling sorry for myself when I have a sense that I have been singled out for unfair treatment from the universe. It's only after the crisis abates that I'm able to have a perspective on what I've just been through.

I've learned that when I'm having a crisis of faith, it is nothing more than one of my many illusions being destroyed. And I have plenty of illusions about everything – about me, about the world, about God and how I think the world should run. The more ingrained the illusion, the more that I'm wedded to the idea, and thus the greater the crisis will be when the illusion is destroyed.

Sometimes it's a minor crisis, 'Why am I aging so quickly? Why am I losing my hair? Hey, this wasn't supposed to happen to me.'

And sometimes it's a major crisis, one that shakes me to my very foundation. 'How could my Church have destroyed my priesthood, this beautiful thing that I worked so hard to achieve? How could they rob me of this for their own selfish reasons?' The death of that illusion nearly killed me. It took me fifteen years to make my peace with the end of that dream.

But I think you're right, David, when you said that a difficult path can change one for the better. The anguish I experienced for so many years over the destruction of my priesthood and ministry brought forth something beautiful. The death of my priesthood is what gave birth to PARADIGM.

There is no doubt in my mind that my church-related crisis of faith was as real a death as any I've ever seen. That's why I believe that life presents us lots of opportunities to rehearse our physical death.

Robin: Hey, I'm with you on that.

Like I always say, my HIV diagnosis was the best thing that ever happened to me. I know that's not the politically correct thing to say, but screw political correctness. It's time for the truth.

My diagnosis turned my whole life around and gave me one last chance to live before I die. I came dangerously close to dying physically and, as you know, I was already spiritually and emotionally dead. So why didn't I just die? I guess I had stuff I had to do yet.

For one thing, I needed to learn how to let go. Bobby was helping me learn how to surrender to fate when he died.

By the way, when I say surrender I'm not talking about giving up, I am talking about relinquishing control. When I was in charge of my life, I really fucked things up. Since I started to practice the art of surrender, I've been able to clean up my act a little bit.

This is what I mean when I say I'm in recovery. I'm recovering from Robin being in charge.

David: Now that's what I call spirituality. And you didn't think you had one.

I'll go back to what I said at the beginning. There is always something calling us back to right relationship with ourselves.

My mother suicided when I was 19. Some people say that this is the worst possible experience a child can have. I understand why they say that, but over time it's become clear to me that I had a choice. I didn't have to let this event be only a tragedy. My mother's untimely death was the source of all the personal growth I've been able to make since. It even inspired my career in social work and ministry. I wouldn't be who I am today had my mother not died the way she did.

That is not to say that I'm grateful for her death, but my agony became fertile ground for my own growth. I'm grateful for the grace that helped me respond to her suicide in the way I did. And I insist it was a graced event because I could have easily responded to her death in a completely different way. I could've shut down back then and effectively ended my life before it even had a chance to begin.

So you see, it's not like any of us will make it through life without knowing pain, hardship, sorrow and death. The point is, what are we going to do with this stuff when it arrives on our doorstep? As my grandmother always used to say, 'it ain't a sin to have roaches, it's just a sin to keep 'em.' (Everyone laughs.)

Mike: What about social justice and doing the right thing? Isn't that a big part of being in right relationship?

David: Good point, Mike.

Doing the right thing is at the very heart of a right relationship. And it is compassion, the other divine attribute, which calls us to practice what theologians have called "ultimate concern."

See, in no time at all, we've been able to identify the two faces of God, love and compassion, right relationship and doing the right thing. You guys are amazing. I thought you said you were amateurs in the spirituality department. Good for you!

Let's move on and take a look at Question 2 from last week's homework. 'Have you ever had a spiritual (religious) experience?'

Janice: Before we began this discussion today, I was convinced I hadn't. I didn't

even know what such a thing was. But now I'm not so sure.

I've been a Red Cross volunteer all of my adult life, and over the years there have been many occasions when I've been moved to tears by the love and concern of strangers for one another. I always say that disasters bring out the best in us. Each of these experiences has been very powerful. Maybe they could count as a religious experience.

David: I think you've got it, Jan. Being a witness to the compassion of one person for another is exactly what I would call a spiritual experience. These are the real God-filled moments. Too bad most people are always looking for the kind of miracles that Cecil B. DeMille might produce – big, brash, and showy, while the truly miraculous events in their lives go unacknowledged.

I remember an occasion some years ago when I was in the desert. It was night and I was lying on my back looking up at the stars. There was a moment when I suspended thinking about what I was doing and for a brief instant I just WAS. I was connected to and a part of that vastness. I saw God that night.

Clare: Oh, David, that's how I feel too. I've had similar experiences and they have filled me with a tremendous sense of awe and wonder and joy.

David: Being present at the birth of my eldest daughter was another profound spiritual experience for me. And I know the same thing can happen at the end of life as well.

On more than one occasion I have had a God-filled experience as I've attended the death of a client. Something miraculous and inexplicable happens, at the end of life, when all the pretense and illusions are finally stripped way. I can't really describe it to you other than to say that there is a serenity that fills the air and I am transformed. Everything stops. There is a timelessness and other-worldliness that changes everything.

Mia: I'm so glad that we're talking about this instead of what generally passes for spirituality in this culture.

I've had timeless and otherworldly kinds of experiences too, but mine occur during meditation. It's like being lifted out of my pain-racked, anxiety-ridden, day-to-day existence and being transported to a higher level of awareness.

I wish there was some way I could capture that feeling of transcendence and have it available to me all the time, especially when I get frightened, because when the panic sets in, I just lose it.

David: What you seek, Mia, comes only with practice. If you're not doing so already, maybe you could try a daily meditation. You'd probably have a better chance of mastering your fears. You might also consider meditating with a partner. I think it's easier if you have someone to work with. Groups are also an option. Do you have someone you can work with?

Mia: I don't, but your suggestion is a good one. I'll have to look into that. Thank you.

David: There are many ways up the mountain, but in the final analysis spirituality is simply about unification and connection.

I often hear people at the end of life speak of encounters they are having with deceased relatives and friends.

Just like you mentioned, Clare. They are peak experiences for them, religious experiences, if you will. And if you ask me, it's all about reunification and completing the circle.

Clare: Thank you, David. That's just what I needed to hear. I didn't think I was just a crazy old lady. My dreams DO have meaning. Thank you.

But how do I know if I'm having a spiritual experience or am in the presence of God? Like question 4 of our homework.

David: I know this is beginning to sound repetitious, but the things I look for are simply unity and relationship.

Right relationship, being connected, being in the moment, surrender, all the things we've been talking about are, to my mind, proofs of God's presence. And the gifts of God's presence are always the same – peace, serenity, well-being and healing.

It makes me sad to think that most people would find this is a completely foreign concept. It's no wonder we don't heed the signs of God's presence. We are unable to perceive them.

We are indeed products of our age – broken, fractured and disconnected from the earth, the unifying spirit and ourselves.

Richard: So I suppose from what you are saying, there is a relationship between one's spiritual path and one's mortality, which is our final question.

David: Yes, I do, but it is difficult to appreciate the connection when there are so many conflicting messages.

All indicators point to the fact that we are mortals. Like you say, Richard, "None of us is getting out of here alive." But all the messages that are coming from our culture contradict that. "Don't worry about it, you'll live forever." It's the ultimate disconnect. No wonder our world is in such a state.

If you can accept the fact that you are going die someday, then I think you would be well advised to practice your dying everyday.

That means practicing detachment, dealing with your sense of loss, encountering your fears and resistances and accepting your limitations. So when the time comes for you to actually die, there won't be chaos. You will have been living your life that way already.

Experience the liberation that comes with knowing one of life's timeless truths – everything is transitory. Each fleeting moment of our allotted time is unique. It will never appear again. When it is over, it's over. Live now as if there were no tomorrow, because none is guaranteed.

Dying is not just about dying, it's about living. And living is not just about living, it's about dying.

Raul: Yeah, yeah, yeah. Now you're beginning to sound just like Father Diego. Can we cut to the chase? Is there a heaven or not? It's a simple question. How come I can't get a simple answer?

David: It's not as simple a question as you might think, Raul. I don't think struggling with the concept of living authentically is avoiding the issue of an afterlife. In fact, it might very well be the only way to know if there is a heaven.

With all the intense interest in the afterlife, it's curious that we rarely talk about the "before-life." I have a question for you, Raul. Where did you come from?

Raul: Hey man, I don't know all this stuff.

I guess I think like they told me to think in religion class – God made me.

David: Then I believe that you will return to God. I hope that gives you some comfort.

Kevin: This reminds me of a joke. This one's for you, Max.

This guy dies and finds himself in Hell. He's really depressed as he stands in the processing line waiting to talk to the admittance devil. He says to himself, "I know I led a wild life, but I wasn't that bad. I never thought it would come to this." Looking up he sees that it is his turn to be processed into Hell. With fear and a heavy heart he walks up to the devil.

Devil: You look depressed, what's the problem?

Sinner: I'm in hell, what do you expect?

Devil: Hell's not so bad. We actually have a lot of fun.

Do you like to drink?

Sinner: Sure, I love to drink.

Devil: Well, then you're gonna love Mondays. On Monday we drink up a storm. You can have all the whiskey, rum, tequila or beer that you want. We party all night long. And you'll never have to worry about a hangover or ruining your liver, because you're already dead. You'll love Mondays.

Do you smoke?

Sinner: Yes, I do.

Devil: You're gonna love Tuesdays. Tuesday is smoke day. You get to smoke the finest cigars and the best cigarettes available anywhere. You can smoke to your heart's content without worrying about cancer, because you're already dead. You're gonna love Tuesdays. How about drugs?

Do you do drugs?

Sinner: Well, in my younger days I experimented a little, but I never inhaled.

Devil: Well, you can experiment with anything you like on Wednesdays. That's drug day. You can toke, snort, drop or shoot any kind of drug you'd like and you don't have to worry about overdoses or getting hooked, because

you're already dead. You're gonna love Wednesdays.

Do you like to gamble?

Sinner: Sure, I love to gamble.

Devil: Well, Thursdays is gambling day. We gamble all day and all night – blackjack, craps, slots, horseraces, everything. You're gonna love Thursdays.

Are you gay?

Sinner: No I'm not.

Devil: (Winces.) Oh, I'm afraid you're gonna hate Fridays. (Everyone laughs.)

David: I want to leave you with one final question before I call it quits. It's the question I ask each of my clients and it generally gets to the heart of the matter.

What is your life prayer? What is it that you ask for in the privacy of your own heart? The answer to this question should give you an idea of the quality of your relationship with the great mystery that is life. And with that I'll say amen.

Thank you so much for this opportunity to join you in your search. It's been an honor.

My Turn

Richard: Are you in "right relationship" with yourself? Are you in right relationship with family and friends? Are you in right relationship with God or what is universal? If not, what concrete steps could you take to make it so? What is your life prayer? Take all the time and space you need.

_____

_____

_____

_____

_____

_____

_____

_____

_____

_____

Richard: Thanks, David. You are wonderful.

Next week we'll be taking a look at the issue of sexuality and intimacy. The renowned sex educator and therapist, Dr. Cheryl Cohen Greene, will be joining us. So before we close, I want to set you up with this week's homework. I have prepared a series of questions that will be helpful in organizing your thoughts about this very important topic. It is called: *Some Questions About Sexuality and Intimacy.*

Are there any final questions or comments before we conclude?

Raymond: Thanks for taking the time to be with us, David. This has been a real mind-opening experience.

AT-HOME WORK

Week 5 — Some Questions about Sexuality and Intimacy

Here are 5 simple questions to help you focus your attention on your sexuality and intimacy needs.

1) **How important is sexuality in your life?**

   _____

   _____

2) **Is there's a difference between sexuality and intimacy?**

   _____

   _____

3) **Do you have a range of options in which to experience your sexuality? If yes, what are some of them?**

   _____

   _____

4) **How well are you able to communicate your needs for sex and/or intimacy to your partner(s)? Are there any specific issues that get in the way of asking for what you need?**

   _____

   _____

5) **What are your biggest concerns about your sexuality as it relates to your disease, aging and/or dying process?**

   _____

   _____

"Exactly what do we mean when we say, man is mortal? Obviously it's not a compliment"

Woody Allen, *Side Effects*

Chapter Six

Week 6:

Don't Stop

Checking In

Richard: Welcome back, everyone.

Let me confirm what most of you already know. Max died on Tuesday. I wasn't with him at the time, but Sylvia told me that he had a peaceful, good death. The family is planning a formal memorial gathering in the next couple of weeks so I'll keep you posted on the details as I learn them. In the meantime, I'd like to propose that we do a kind of ritual of our own to mark Max's death.

Before we move on to our check-in, perhaps you'd like an opportunity to respond to this news.

Holly: I'm stunned. I can still see Max sitting in that chair, all smiles, and full of mischief. He sure went fast, didn't he? I suppose that's a blessing in a way. I like the idea of doing a ritual of remembrance; it would help bring closure to my relationship with him.

Robin: Wow, this just blows me away. I just talked to him by phone on Sunday. He said he was okay, but then again, he wasn't one to let on, was he? I like the idea of a ritual too, but I wouldn't know where to start. Bobby's memorial is still pretty fresh in my mind, so I have a much better idea what not to do than what we should do. Is someone gonna take charge of this?

Kevin: This is gonna sound strange, but Max is the first person over 45 that I've known who has died since my grandparents died when I was a kid. No kidding. I'm so used to guys in their twenties and thirties dying that I almost forgot that other people die too. Isn't that amazing?

I liked Max and I'm sorry that he's gone.

Listen, I'll volunteer to coordinate this ritual thing if you'd like me to. But I'll want input from each of you on what you think we should do. So give it some thought and I'll contact you during the week. Together we'll do something real nice. We'll give old Max a good send off. What do you say?

Janice: That's so sweet of you, Kevin. Thanks for taking charge. Even though I'm sure Max had a good long life and I believe that he's at peace now, I can't help feeling sad. All I can think about is Sylvia being all alone now. I remember how I felt right after Albert passed. Poor dear, it must be terrible for her. Maybe we could say a little prayer for her too.

Raymond: Well, this just makes my day. I have an announcement of my own. Joann died on Tuesday. The same day as Max! Jeez, I'm reeling from these two body blows right now. I think I'm in shock.

Mike: Just when I thought I was getting a little more comfortable with the whole death thing, this happens. God, I feel trapped. I suppose I'm okay talking about some of this stuff, like the legal and spiritual stuff from the last couple of weeks, but no one was supposed to die. This really makes me nuts. Get me outta here!

Mia: I thought for sure that I was going to be the first one to die. I guess I was wrong. I'm not sure how I feel about this. I guess I'm wondering who will be next.

Raul: Hey, this ain't some kind of weirdo death contest, Mia. You talk like there was gonna be a prize for bein' first. Shit, man, I could tell Max was dyin' right away, when I first saw him. He was an old dude and sick too. I knew he was gonna die real soon and I think he knew that too.

Clare: Yes. I can't say that I'm particularly surprised by the news either. He was much closer to death than he let on and I think he knew it. I will miss him though. I like the idea of creating a ritual to mark his passing. I'd like to work with you on this, Kevin, if that's okay.

Richard: Thanks for being so honest with your feelings. I appreciate that. So we will have our Ritual of Remembrance as part of our time together next week, okay? Good.

Now we need to turn our attention elsewhere. This beautiful woman sitting to my right is one of my favorite people in the whole wide world. She is the nationally known sex educator and therapist, Dr. Cheryl Cohen Greene. Cheryl is also a PARADIGM mentor. She has gone through this program more than once herself, and she's a frequent presenter. Cheryl is here to help us focus our attention on the issues of sexuality and intimacy.

I'd appreciate it if, in your check-in this week, you could speak about your own sexuality and intimacy concerns. You might want to begin by responding to last week's homework. After our check-in, Cheryl will lead us in our discussion.

Who would like to begin?

Raymond: Last week was hell week. I still can't believe that Joann and Max are dead, and on the same day. What were the odds of that happening?

I was with Joann as much as I possibly could the last three days of her life. But believe it or not, she died when I wasn't there. I'm all broken up about this. I mean, I left her side for no more than a half-hour to run to the store for some milk. When I got back, her attendant said that she sighed one last sigh and died.

What was I thinking? Was the trip to the store all that important? I shouldn't have left her. She died alone because I was so thoughtless.

Richard: Hold on, Ray. Why are you punishing yourself for something you had no control over?

Listen, I've heard this same lament many times over the years. 'I interrupted my death watch for only 10 or 15 minutes to use the bathroom and make a cup of tea, but when I returned, I found that my friend, husband, wife, lover, son, daughter, whomever had died in my absence. Why wasn't I there? How could this have happened? I was being so diligent. I was gone for only a few minutes.'

This is such a common occurrence that there must be a message in it. I haven't any proof of this, of course, but I believe that some people need privacy to die. Why else would they die in the only few minutes out of the day they are left unattended?

That's why I have a rule of thumb when I'm attending a death. I always give the dying person twenty minutes out of each hour to be alone. This way, if they need private time in which to die, they'll have it. I use the twenty minutes I have for myself to regroup and pace myself, which is important for maintaining my sense of balance and well-being during the vigil.

So, Ray, please cut yourself some slack. Joann died just the way she wanted to.

Raymond: I never thought of it like that. It makes sense though, especially in Joann's case. She was going to do it her way if it killed her. (Everyone laughs.)

I feel like I've been through the wringer and yet I also have this great sense of relief. I mean, I'm sorry she's dead, but she's also not suffering anymore. And my world hasn't collapsed, as I feared it might. There is a void, for sure, but I think I'll be able to get through this okay. Boy, I'm sure glad I have this group to come to. You've helped me more than I can tell you. Thank you for being here.

Okay, let me make a quick comment about today's topic. I've never been comfortable talking about sex, particularly my own sexuality. To be honest, I've replaced sex with food in my life. I'm not proud of this, but turning to

food was a lot easier than trying to figure out the whole sex thing.

My divorce devastated me. I never had much confidence that I was a good lover, and when my wife left me, I figured it was because I was lousy in bed.

Intimacy, on the other hand, is a different story altogether. I'm real good at that. In fact, I believe that more intimacy is possible over a dinner table than in the bedroom. I mean, just think about it. Intimacy is about a meeting of souls. Sex is about bumping parts. Maybe what's why I excel in the kitchen. I'm a much better chef than a lover.

Mia: I need a minute to clear up something.

When I said earlier that I thought I was going to be the first to die, I didn't mean to suggest that this was a contest. Perhaps I didn't express myself properly. What I was trying to say is I've been so caught up in my own fears of dying that I wasn't paying attention to what was going on with Max. I feel real bad about this, because the reason I wanted to do this group in the first place was so I could have the opportunity to learn from others who had more experience than I.

I feel as though I've missed something really special.

About the homework...I've been looking forward to your visit, Cheryl. I have so many questions I don't know where to begin. I have two problems actually. First, because of my lungs, I no longer can engage in any kind of vigorous activity, so when it comes to sex, even masturbation wears me out.

And secondly, my illness has destroyed the terrific sex life I was having with my boyfriend Troy. He's so spooked by the whole thing that he's now afraid to touch me, so he doesn't.

To make a long story short, I have the same libido I had a year ago, only now I haven't either the ability or the outlet to satisfy my desires.

Raul: Shit, man, you said masturbation. I never heard a chick say the "M" word before. This is gonna be hot.

Oh, and Mia, sorry about making you upset when I said that thing about the death contest. I'm hurtin' pretty bad today, and when that happens I sometimes don't think about what I'm sayin'. Sorry. You just gotta tell me to shut up, okay?

I'm a little nervous talking about this sex shit, ya know, in front of everybody. I already said a couple of weeks ago; I haven't got any sex yet. I'm 18 and I've never even made out with a chick. All my friends have their old ladies and they get sex all the time. Couple of guys even got girls pregnant, so you know they're gettin' some. Me, I'm gettin' nothin'! This is such a drag.

I never told anyone this, but what the hell, Mia said masturbation, so I can say this, right? My friends, Ernesto and Ramon took me to a prostitute for my birthday. She was nice but not so pretty, but she was gonna, ya know...and like, I wanted to real bad because I wanted to see how it feels, but I had a lot of pain that day and I couldn't even, ya know.

Shit, man, what a loser. I just know I'm gonna die before I get laid. I don't want to sound like a baby, but that's cold, real cold.

Janice: You'll have to excuse me, but this topic makes me very uncomfortable. I guess I'm just old fashioned. I was brought up believing that ladies don't talk about such things in polite company.

Raul: Shit, man, you must think I'm some kind of pervert for sayin' that. Sorry.

Janice: No, Raul, I don't. And I'm glad you're not all tied up in knots like I am.

You see, I've been with only one man my entire life, my husband Albert. Our sex life was very conventional. And if the truth be known, there wasn't even much of that. I always wondered if I disappointed him. I guess I'll never know now.

To tell the truth, I don't miss it at all. The sex, I mean. But I do miss the companionship. I'm so very lonely now. I mean, you get pretty attached to a person after thirty years together. What I wouldn't do for just one more hug from my Albert. It's the predicament of so many women that I know. The senior center is filled with widows who are starving for affection. It's so unfair.

I have this fear of dying alone. And I don't mean alone as in solitary. I would feel just as alone if the only people attending me as I die were people I didn't know. So it's not about care, really, it's about being loved. Is that so much to ask? Maybe I should just stop now.

Robin: Aw, Jan, I know what you mean about being lonely. Bobby and I were together for only three years and I miss him so much. I can't imagine what it would be like if we had been together for as long as you and Albert. I miss the intimacy and companionship too, a whole lot more than the sex.

I've had a real twisted sex life. Until I got clean and sober, I could only have sex when I was loaded. I lost my virginity at a concert when I was 14. It was the first time I did speed. I don't remember it at all. I just know it happened. When I was living on the street, I turned tricks to feed my smack habit. There was plenty of survival sex too. A lot of times I had to fuck some guy just to get something to eat or get a place to crash. Sex was never about pleasure. It was a commodity.

But Bobby changed all that. I remember the first time he approached me for sex. We had known each other for only a few months. I wasn't like gaga for him or anything. He was all lanky and bony, definitely not my type. But he was nice and I said what the hell and started to strip. I turned off emotionally like I always did. I mean, it was the only way I knew how to get through it.

Of course Bobby backed off. He said he didn't want to fuck a corpse. In fact, he didn't want to fuck at all. All he wanted to do was hold me and be held by me. What did I know? This was a totally new concept for me.

'Affection, what the hell is affection? You don't just want to jump my bones?'

Bobby left my room that night without so much as a peck on the cheek. It took him weeks to break down all my negative conditioning, but I'm sure glad he made the effort. I had my first orgasm with Bobby, another new concept. Now that he's gone, I fear that I'll never find anyone like him again.

I'm only 25 and if this HIV cocktail that I'm on continues to work, like it has for so many of us survivors, then I may be here for a long while yet. I'd hate to think that I've already peaked-out on sex.

And what's more important, I want to start a family.

Mike: I'm not used to being part of such a frank discussion about sex. I'm more comfortable with the locker room bravado that passes as sex talk for guys. At least in that situation I don't have to be honest. This is very intimidating.

I want to be straight with you. I wasn't looking forward to this week's topic at all. I really didn't want to come here and have to discuss last week's homework questions about sex and intimacy, because I was afraid that you'd want to know how a gimp like me does "it." I was afraid that I would have to tell you that a gimp like me no longer does "it" because he can't get it up anymore.

I'd probably then have to tell you how frustrating it is for me not to be able to make love to my wife, and how this is a source of constant friction between Maryanne and me, how she accuses me of throwing out the baby with the bathwater, how she doesn't care if I have a hard-on, all she wants is for us to be close.

So you see, if I told you all these things I'd really be embarrassed. So I'm not going to say anything at all. Next!

Clare: I guess this means that you don't want to talk about "it," right? (Everyone laughs.)

You're such a hoot, Mike. You make me laugh. And I always feel better when I laugh.

Speaking of things to laugh about, take my sex life. No, that's not fair.

I've done the best I could under the circumstances. I was well into my thirty's when the woman's movement began. It was a time of great awakenings for me. Charley was threatened, of course, but I was able to win him over in time. It was only then that our sex life started in earnest. I finally realized that sex could be about pleasure and not simply about duty. What a liberating experience that was!

Even now Charley and I are intimate, or were until the last six weeks or so. In the last few years our sex has not been like the old days, all heated and hormonal, but it's just as special. Oh, I'm so glad we're able to talk about this.

My major concern is the medications I'm taking for the pain. I'm woozy when I take them, but irritable without them. I want to be more available to Charley for the closeness that's so important to each of us, but I'm often too out of it. This is a problem for Charley too, because he doesn't know how touch me anymore. And so, I'm afraid, he keeps his distance. This only makes matters worse for the both of us.

How do I change this, I wonder? Or maybe there's no changing it. Maybe it's just over. What a sad thought.

Kevin: Like I was saying a couple of weeks ago when we were talking about the regrets we have. My sexuality has always been a driving force in my life, but sometimes I simply feel driven. A manic pursuit of pleasure is no pleasure, if you know what I mean.

I don't want to suggest that I'm a sex addict or anything, but I sometimes feel out of balance. I know a lot of this has to do with my relentless pursuit of love.

I had real love in my life once with Doug and I would desperately like to have it again. I know this is a big trap...sex and intimacy are not one and the same thing. But I always wind up acting like they are the same. I always have it in my head that maybe my next sexual encounter will bring me love. It's maddening.

Holly: Let's see...I'm dealing with some big-time body issues. I had a radical mastectomy a little over three years ago. It scarred me psychologically as well as physically. I didn't realize the dimensions of all of this until I had finished the chemo and radiation I was doing. For a good six months after the surgery, I was so sick from all that poison that the thought of sex of any kind made me nauseous. I didn't even want to have Jean in the same bed with me. It was awful.

Over time the nausea diminished and I was able to resume some semblance of intimacy with Jean. We were able to be close and do some touching just as long as it wasn't sexual.

Then about eight months ago, Jean and I had this big blowout. We were screaming and yelling about God only knows what when she finally blurts out: 'Can't you see I'm starving? I have needs too, you know. For as much love as I get from you, I could be living on the moon. Are we ever going to resume our sex life? Because if I wanted to live like a nun I woulda joined a convent. Your sex aversion is making *me* sick.'

I had completely forgotten about Jean and her needs. I knew I still loved her, of course, but after the surgery I didn't feel whole. I didn't feel like a woman, know what I mean? But Jean persisted, thank God. 'I'm doing this as much for you as I am for myself. You gotta deal with this, babe.'

I was starving too, but I was too afraid and ashamed to admit it. We've made

some movement since then, but it's still not like the old days.

My God, in the old days Jean and I were like wild women, letting it all hang out. Some of that was female pride, but it was also a kind of "in-your-face" protest. 'These are my breasts, damnit! Get over it!' I don't see how I can ever regain that.

At the same time, I have an incredible respect for the women with mastectomies who are able to display their scarring. Like there are several books out now; photo essays of women who have gone through the same thing I have, but are proud instead of ashamed. This just blows me away. As you can see, I'm all turned around on this one.

Richard: I'm glad last week is over. It seemed as though I didn't have ten minutes to myself, which brings me to my perennial complaint when it comes to the topic we're discussing today. I'm so busy in my role as caregiver, therapist, Father confessor, or whatever that I rarely take the time to love and be loved.

Don't get me wrong. I like what I do. It's just that I'm usually putting out a whole lot more than what I allow to come in. This is not a good thing. I'm not

Superman. I need to take better care of myself, that's for sure.

One thing I can say on my behalf is that I'm much better about my sex and intimacy needs than I was a few years ago. At least now I know when I'm suffering from touch deprivation. So when I'm feeling particularly depleted, I treat myself to a massage or some other form of bodywork. Sometimes I'm even able to scare up a date. What a difference that makes!

I need to be more conscious about nurturing myself. After all, I never let myself get so hungry or thirsty that I'm liable to pass out, so why do I let myself become so needy for affection and touch before I do something about it?

One difference, of course, is that I can feed myself, but when it comes to affection and touch, well, that involves other people and I have to ask for what I need. I guess I'm just like most everyone else in this regard. I still find it difficult to reach out in times of need. I have lots of work to do on this yet.

My Check-In

Richard: Take all the time and space you need for your check-in. This week, I'd like you to focus your attention on your own sexuality and intimacy needs. You can begin by reviewing your responses to last week's homework.

_____

_____

_____

_____

_____

_____

_____

_____

_____

_____

Group Process

Richard: Cheryl, it's all yours. Would you take a few minutes to introduce yourself before you direct us in our discussion?

Cheryl: Thanks, Richard. My name is Cheryl Cohen-Greene. And I am so glad I have this opportunity to be with you today. This is a homecoming for me. I completed this same 10-week program over a year ago, and now I'm a PARADIGM mentor. I probably should begin with a few words about how I came to be involved with PARADIGM.

In the summer or 1993 I was diagnosed with lymphoma. I subsequently went through six rounds of chemotherapy, or as us veterans like to call it, "chop." I met Richard three years later, in June of 1996, at the wedding of our mutual friend Louanne. All three of us had been working in the sex field for years, Louanne and Richard as verbal therapists and I as a surrogate partner. Yet this was the first time Richard and I had an opportunity to meet. Richard officiated at the wedding, and later at the reception dinner he told

me about PARADIGM. It sounded like the perfect thing for me, so I participated in the very next Access Program.

It was a wonderful ten weeks, so wonderful in fact that I repeated the experience a few weeks later. Actually, the reason I repeated the program was to accompany my friend Carla to the group. She had cancer too, but she wasn't well enough to make it to group on her own, so we carpooled to the City each week.

I did my first presentation on sexuality and intimacy that second time around. I thought it went very well. Everyone seemed receptive to the information I presented. But you have to remember that I was a member of that group, so the other participants already knew me. I think they found the presentation less threatening and they were more eager to join in the discussion because I was a member of the group myself.

It's not always like that though. Coming into a group cold, like I'm doing today, makes this particular presentation a little more challenging. So I hope you will bear with me and not hesitate to join in the discussion.

Sexuality and intimacy are important topics for us to consider, because there is so little information out there about these things for elders and those of us who have life-threatening conditions. The assumption, I suppose, is that sick, aging and dying people don't have sexual and intimacy concerns, so why even bring it up?

That ridiculous assumption is so prevalent, even among healing and helping professions, that I'm forever having to confront it with, 'Hey, we're not dead yet.'

Let me tell you a little about what I experienced when I was being treated for cancer. To be blunt, the cancer and subsequent chemotherapy destroyed my sex life. The thought of being touched in an intimate way made me very uncomfortable. I wasn't even able to have an orgasm. My life was shattered and I couldn't find anyone to help me piece it together again. I was on my own.

I had to learn to cope with the dramatic changes in my body, changes that not only interfered with my personal sexual life, but also effectively halted my professional life as a surrogate partner. Finding a way through this mess wasn't gonna be easy because I had my partner's feelings to deal with as well as my own. I couldn't very well put him on hold indefinitely.

In the beginning the hardest part was the communication with my partner. I had to learn an effective way to talk to him under these very trying circumstances. The bottom had fallen out of our sex life and neither one of us knew how to deal with that.

It wasn't just that I was feeling tired and sick all the time; I was having no sexual feelings at all. But I was also painfully aware of his desire to connect with me. He was so afraid that I was going to die and yet he didn't know how to be close to me anymore. It was a stressful time for both of us.

Doing the ten weeks of PARADIGM, even three years after my diagnosis, really made a big difference. Thanks to this group, I was able to confront these very intimate concerns in an honest manner. PARADIGM was a catalyst for enormous change in my life.

So as we begin today, just remember that once, not very long ago, I was right where you are now. And thanks to this program and the openness and support I found here, I'm feeling much less frightened, confused, and alone.

Let's begin. I took some notes during check-in so that I would be able to mirror back to you some of my impressions of what you said. I'd also like to work on last week's homework, because the questions get right to the heart of the matter we're going to discuss.

How about if we start with you, Raymond?

From your check-in, I gather that this is not your favorite topic and yet there is no avoiding it, is there?

Our culture is plagued with mixed messages about sexuality and intimacy. We can easily become obsessed with the image of the perfect body, with youth and beauty. All of this can get in the way of finding a comfortable place for us to express ourselves as intimate and sexual beings.

Raymond: I'll say.

Sex was a taboo subject when I was growing up, just like death and dying, come to think of it. And since I never even came close to conforming to the ideal body image, I always had a hard time of it. I was teased mercilessly as a kid for being fat. Boy, kids can be really cruel.

When I was older, I guess I still let that haunt me, because I never had any confidence about my role as a husband and lover either. I know there wasn't any expertise involved in getting my wife pregnant. In fact, I wonder how many of us would be here today if conceiving a child involved any kind of skill at all.

No, you're right, Cheryl, this is not my favorite subject.

Cheryl: Can I ask you a question? How important is sexuality in your life? Some people haven't any interest in sex, and that's just fine for them. But I sense that you're not like that. Am I correct, or are you content with the status quo?

Raymond: God, I hate talking about this.

Okay, okay, I'll admit it. I'm not satisfied with the way things are. Joann, God rest her, was the only person who had the patience to talk me through this. She actually got me to a point where I could admit that I've built up this wall of fat to keep people out. And now I can see that this crazy defense mechanism of mine will most likely kill me if I don't get a handle on it. Listen, I don't aspire to being the world's greatest lover, but it would be nice to stop running for cover every time the subject comes up.

Cheryl: I believe it's never too late to relearn new and healthy ways to deal with our sexuality. This re-education process begins with dispelling the myths and misconceptions that our culture passes off as sex information.

I suggest that you begin by doing some reading around the topic of male sexuality. I think you will find it both informative and supportive. There are a number of good books available, and I'd be happy to suggest some titles, if you like.

Once you're more comfortable with the basics, you could then move on to being with a partner. In your check-in you said that you feel that more intimacy is possible over a dinner table than in the bedroom. An interesting thought. And that leads me to a suggestion! Why not bring some of the intimacy of the dining room into the bedroom? This way you would be combining something you know how to do really well with something you're just learning. You could invite a partner to join you for dinner in bed. Eating could be part of your sex play. Plan a menu of finger food, and other things you could feed one another. Oh, and don't forget the whipped cream. Make it playful. Sex, like eating, shouldn't be work. And maybe when you get real good at eating in the bedroom, you could try being sexual in the dining room.

When you've finished your sex play, take a long walk together. The exercise will do you good and you'll have a perfect opportunity to do some talking about sex.

I don't think couples talk nearly enough about sex with one another. Learning to communicate is key to having a happy and healthy sex life. Talking about sex is especially important for couples that have been together for a long time. It keeps them from getting stale and prevents them from presuming each knows all there is to know about their partner.

Why not get interested in life again, Ray? Have a little fun. Sexuality isn't a mystery. It's a wonderful miracle.

Mia: Wow, I love the idea of eating in bed. I can see it all now, Ray, especially the whipped cream. Go for it, you wild man.

Cheryl, my concerns have to do with how my disease process is interfering with my sexuality. Like I said in my check-in, this is happening on two fronts. First, my lung condition keeps me from enjoying all the physical activities I once loved. It has virtually put an end to my sex life, including masturbation.

The other problem has to do with my boyfriend Troy. He is afraid to touch me. I think he's afraid he'll hurt me if he tries. So you see, my libido's the same, I just don't have the ability or the outlets I once had. It's so damn frustrating. I hate it!

Cheryl: Let's tackle these issues one at a time.

First, if you are exhausting yourself while masturbating, perhaps you should consider a new technique. I often suggest to women with disabilities that they try using a vibrator when stimulating themselves. There are so many different kinds on the market these days that shopping for one can be half the fun. You may find that your vibrator will also come in handy when you are being sexual with a partner, which gets us to your second point.

I know from my own experience that after the cancer and chemotherapy I had to take the lead in re-sensitizing my partner about how to be close to me. This was a very delicate issue because he only knew how to be sexual with me in the ways he had before the cancer. He wanted us to resume being close but he didn't know how to do that. And I wasn't sure what would work either. What I did know was that if we worked on this together it would be better than struggling with it independently.

We started slowly at first. For example, when I was feeling well enough for some cuddling we did some spoon breathing. Do you know what that is?

It's a great exercise! I highly recommend it. We lay together like two spoons on our sides, his front to my back. Then we would try to match one another's breathing pattern. First he would match mine then we would change positions, my front to his back, and I would try to match his breathing. This exercise can be done with or without clothing.

It's a wonderful place to start rebuilding a sense of confidence about being together. As time went on, our spoon breathing embraces became more adventuresome. When I was feeling up to it, I would take one of his hands in mine and guide it over my body in a way that was comfortable for me. I would show him the kind of stroke and pressure that was pleasurable for me. This was a very effective way of reestablishing a threshold for what was possible between us.

Guided-hand sensual touch like this can be expanded to include genitals if and when you desire. You could help educate Troy on how to pleasure you in a way that would allow you to be more of a passive recipient rather than an active participant in your lovemaking.

If intercourse is no longer an option for one reason or another, there are always other ways to have an orgasm. This is where your vibrator may come in handy. Are you able to go through the sexual response cycle? Can you accommodate the tension and energy required to reach a climax?

Mia: Yes, I can still have an orgasm. It's just hard to do on my own.

Cheryl: Then the key is to discover what is physically possible for you now. You and your partner can experiment with different positions and activities until you find what works for you. My only advice is to keep it playful. If you begin to reach your limit, back off. Don't work at it. Stop when it's no longer fun.

For example, when I'm working with a client in this sort of situation, I always call for a moratorium on having an orgasm. I don't want our time together to be goal directed. When having an orgasm is the goal, a couple can easily lose sight of the joy and pleasure that comes from all the other touching and intimacy involved in sex play.

You might consider putting a similar moratorium in place so you can take some of the pressure off your partner. If your time together is about intimacy and play, there will be less performance anxiety for him.

Raul, are you okay? You look upset. Am I making you uncomfortable?

Raul: No way, man. I mean, okay, yeah, a little bit, maybe. I also don't feel so good. I shoulda stayed home today, but I didn't want to miss this for nothin'. But now that I'm here, I see this ain't for me.

Cheryl: Why do you say that?

Raul: I don't got a girlfriend or anything so I can't even do any of the stuff you're tellin' Mia about. This sucks. I ain't never gonna get laid.

Cheryl: I'll bet there are options you haven't even considered yet. If you have sexual issues you need to work on and you don't have a partner, you might want to consider working with a surrogate partner.

Raul: Hey man, I don't even know what that is. What's a surrogate and where do I get one?

Cheryl: I'm a surrogate, Raul. The word surrogate simply means a substitute. I'm a substitute sexual partner for people who, for one reason or another, are without one. A surrogate is a highly skilled, well-trained sex therapist who does hands-on therapy with her/his clients. A surrogate works in tandem with another therapist, like Richard, who does the verbal part of the therapy. Does that explain it for you?

Raul: You mean someone like you would have sex with someone like me? Hey, that's cool, I guess, but why? I mean, like, shit man, I never done it before and I'm all skinny and shit. Girls don't even like me. Why would a beautiful lady like you wanna have sex with messed up dude like me?

Cheryl: Because that's what a surrogate does. We have experience working with all kinds of people. Some of our clients have disfigurements and disabilities that are worse than yours. We are committed to helping our clients overcome whatever obstacles may interfere with their achieving a happy, healthy and integrated sex life for themselves.

Our interest is in our clients' inner beauty, not the externals. It's this inner beauty that makes them attractive and interesting to us. And while our relationship is not a love relationship, a bond of real affection can develop between the surrogate partner and her client.

As I was telling Mia, a surrogate partner is a sex educator and the object in surrogate work is not intercourse, so having an erection isn't all that important. A surrogate would be able to help you explore your body's unique pleasure zones. She would also be available for you to explore her body. And if you wanted to try intercourse she would help you with that as well.

A surrogate supports and encourages her clients as well as informs them. In fact, I would hasten to add that working with a surrogate would better prepare you for the sexual experiences you will no doubt go on to have on your own.

Richard would be the one to talk to about setting up an appointment with a surrogate partner. So if you are interested, I'm sure he'd be able to help you.

Raul: Yeah? I mean I didn't know anything about any of this stuff. Hey, Richard, I gotta talk to you pronto. Thanks for being so nice, Cheryl.

Man, this is hellacool.

Janice: I must confess, I didn't know what a surrogate partner was either. Thank you for the explanation.

I've never had much of an interest in sex and I don't see that changing at this late stage in the game, but I do continue to be interested in intimacy. Since the death of my husband I've been very much alone. I so miss the companionship we used to share. Do you think it's too late for a person like me to find that kind of thing again?

Cheryl: Of course it's not too late, Jan.

May I ask you if you are taking hormone replacement therapy? I'm assuming that you are post-menopausal. Am I correct?

Janice: I went through menopause years ago, but I've never taken hormone replacements. Why do you ask?

Cheryl: The reason that I ask is many women find that their libido, their interest in sex, disappears after menopause. It's simply a chemical thing that happens as our bodies age.

Many post-menopausal women don't know about this option and so they go through some of the best years of their life without knowing the joys of sexual intimacy unfettered by concerns of becoming pregnant.

I've had both of my ovaries removed, so I can speak about this unpleasant shift in libido first hand. I used to be a strong advocate of natural hormone replacement for all post-menopausal women. However, nowadays I encourage women to engage their doctors in a frank conversation about the pros and cons of this therapy. There is a known connection between hormone replacement therapy (HRT) and breast cancer. Breast cancer survivors who took HRT to relieve menopausal symptoms had more than three times as many breast cancer recurrences as survivors who did not take HRT.

The benefit of discussing this issue with your physician is two-fold. First, you'll get information you need to make an educated decision about the therapy itself. And second, you will have established a working relationship with your OB/GYN on the topic of your sex life.

If you find that your doc isn't comfortable talking to you about sex in general or your sexual practices in particular, then you need to start looking around for someone who is up for the task. We are all best served when we are conscientious consumers of our health care.

Besides, Jan, I bet there are plenty of options open to you if it's simply companionship you seek. You're living in a senior complex, right? Have you met your neighbors? Why not strike up a conversation? Join in the planned activities. What are your interests? How about taking a class? Do you like to dance? Maybe you could do some volunteer work.

There is so much going on, and I'll bet you have loads of leisure time. It is often said that an acquaintance is a friend just waiting to be discovered. And if that's true, then a friend could become a companion, and a companion could even become a lover or partner. But like everything else that's worthwhile in life, it will take some time and energy on your part.

You mentioned something very touching in your check-in. You spoke with such eloquence about the plight of all the lonely senior women you know. Have you considered having another woman as a companion? With all the lonely people in the world it's a crime to be lonely alone.

Intimacy is not a gender issue; it's a human issue.

Robin: What a great idea, Cheryl. I can see me doing that in thirty years, me and a girlfriend getting an old Airstream and cruising the highways. We'd be just like Thelma and Louise. Yeah, right, I should live so long.

Actually, I'll be happy to make it through my twenties. I know the HIV drugs I'm taking are keeping me alive, but there are days when my body simply can't tolerate the stuff. The side effects are deadly. I sometimes get so sick I can't see how I'll make it through the day. That's when I really feel alone. I start to wonder if I honestly think anyone would be interested in planning a life with damaged goods like me.

But on my good days, when I'm feeling strong and healthy, I see the whole thing in a different light. I see me, the kids, a white picket fence, and hubby schleppin' home from the office.

When I hear myself say this out loud, I don't know which is more deluded, thinking of myself as damaged goods or seeing myself as June Cleaver.

Cheryl: I can see you making a family. You certainly have the strength of will for it. I would only encourage you to broaden your concept of family to include the possibility of less traditional definitions.

Family is all about intimacy and connection and community. I believe that we can pretty much design family to be whatever we want it to be. I know that's what I did. I was a young wife and mother with two small children in tow when we uprooted from the East Coast and moved to Berkeley. We left all semblance of a traditional family behind when we left Massachusetts. But now, all these years later with my kids grown to adulthood, I can look back with pride on the family that we created together.

So a hubby and a white picket fence is nice, but it's only one model.

Mike: I suppose it's the gimp's turn now, huh?

Cheryl: Do you really see yourself as a gimp? Or is that just a term of endearment you use for yourself?

Mike: What do you think? Just look at me. I'm one fine specimen of virile manhood, wouldn't you say?

Raul: Don't listen to him. He's always like this.

Cheryl: Is that right? Well, maybe you are a gimp then. I wouldn't have guessed by just looking, but after that introduction, maybe I should take a closer look.

Mike, it doesn't have to be this way. I'm currently working with a client who has a more advanced case of MS than you have. We began working together some weeks ago, because he was interested in knowing what he was capable of sexually. As it turns out, despite being a very large man and being bedridden he is a remarkably good lover. He has a vivid imagination and an exceptionally talented mouth. He is affectionate and gentle and there is absolutely no hint of a chip on his shoulder.

His pleasure comes from giving pleasure to others. I like him very much. Maybe you would like to meet him some day.

Mike: I owe you an apology. I'm not myself today. Or maybe this is what I've become. I know my wife and son think so.

Cheryl: Is all of this rage about being unable to have an erection?

Men are so amazing!

Mike, many women don't care at all if their partner has an erection or not. In fact, most report that when their partner's penis is hard it generally means only one thing and it's rarely about them. It's the old "get it up, get it in, get it on, get it off and roll over" routine, which is not particularly fulfilling for a woman.

Losing the ability to have an erection may be a humbling experience for a man but his partner may have an altogether different experience. For her it may signal the possibility of some really good sex.

How do you feel about your oral sex technique, Mike? If Maryanne wanted you to pleasure her orally would you be comfortable doing that?

Maybe she would prefer hand stimulation. My MS client can't use his hands very well so I use them for him. I take his hand and stimulate myself with it. He loves it. Would you feel comfortable if Maryanne used your hand like that?

How well are you able to communicate your needs for sex and intimacy to Maryanne? Are there any specific issues that get in the way of asking for what you need?

Mike: We stopped talking about sex about the same time I got sick. Actually, we never really discuss it at all. What generally happens is Maryanne will bring it up, I'll get angry and she gets hurt. That's how "discussions" about sex go in our house.

I wish I could tell her how I really feel, how ashamed I am, not just for being such a bully, but for being such a coward. I wouldn't even know how to begin such a conversation. I can't seem to get past saying 'I'm sorry.' I'm sorry, all right, real fuckin' sorry. I'm afraid of what would happen if I opened this can of worms. Would I ever be able to look her in the eye again? Sometimes I wish I were dead.

Cheryl: So you're not talking to your wife. Are you talking to your doctor about your erection concerns?

Mike: Nope, I just figured there wasn't anything to talk about. Besides, it's too goddamn embarrassing to admit.

Cheryl: You may want to reconsider that. I have two pieces of advice.

First, begin a dialogue with Maryanne. Let her know that you are serious about working through your problems as a couple. Engage a professional if necessary. Richard can refer you to a number of good sex therapists in the area.

Second, contact your doctor as soon as possible and initiate a frank discussion about your erection concerns. A great deal of progress has been made recently in understanding and treating male erectile dysfunction.

Most men occasionally experience the inability to have an erection, but repeated problems, whether they are organic or situational, constitute what was once referred to as impotence. Men with chronic erection problems are often too embarrassed to ask for help, and they may not have the impetus to do so if they don't have a partner. So statistics on how widespread this concern is among men are hard to come by, no pun intended.

It used to be that erection problems were dismissed as mostly psychological in nature, which of course didn't help get men to seek the help they needed, or they were written off as inevitable side effects of medications. But finally things are beginning to change for the better.

Getting an erection for a man is like lubricating for a woman. Both processes combine complex emotional and biological functions. So it's clear that either a physiological or psychological problem can interfere in the arousal stage of the sexual response cycle in either women or men.

For example, a relationship problem, depression, anxiety, prescription medications, excessive alcohol consumption, a hormone imbalance, cardiovascular disease, a neurological problem, being overweight, even some over the counter cold and allergy medications or even something as simple as a poor diet can contribute to arousal dysfunction.

Sadly, there was very little research done in this area until about twenty years ago. Before that, the treatments for this common dysfunction were unattractive and painful options. If the erection problem was diagnosed as

organic in nature a man had the option of hormone replacement therapy, or injecting a muscle relaxant directly into his penis, or inserting a hormone pellet into his urethra. Other options included penile implant surgery or using a vacuum suction device.

If the erection problem was diagnosed as psychological, the only real option was sex therapy.

As you undoubtedly know, a major breakthrough in treating erection problems was made by a chance discovery in the mid 1990's. A researcher who was studying the effects of a new heart medication noticed a remarkable side effect in some of his male subjects... erections. When Viagra hit the market it revolutionized the industry. And because this medication is in a pill form, it's more convenient and less painful than the old injection or insertion therapies.

It's important to note that this medication as well as all the other erectile dysfunction meds out there are "erection enhancers" not "erection inducers." I say that because without proper stimulation, these medications will not cause an erection on their own.

There are some reported side effects to these medications and one can only get them by prescription, so you better talk to your doctor as soon as possible.

So you see, Mike, there are options. Stop thinking about what used to be and start working at finding out what is currently possible.

Richard: Cheryl, in previous presentations you've mentioned the work you've done with disabled couples. Can you speak a bit about that now?

Cheryl: Sure. Seriously disabled couples, like the couple with cerebral palsy I am currently working with, are unable to enjoy their sexuality because of mobility problems.

When I first met this couple they were very shy, even embarrassed. No one had ever talked to them about their sex lives. They had been married for seven years, but never had intercourse. We spent some time getting to know one another and when they felt comfortable enough with me they asked if I would help them have intercourse for the first time. My role was to facilitate their union.

I helped them out of their wheelchairs and out of their clothes. I put them in bed and positioned them as they directed me.

It was sometimes awkward, but we all did a lot of giggling to relieve the tension. And when the time is right, I help guide the man's penis into the woman's vagina. It's a remarkably tender moment. It's times like this that make my work so enriching.

Richard: This reminds me of something really important. People who live in an institutional setting like an extended care facility, hospital or hospice, may have a problem securing enough privacy for their intimate and sexual moments. Even though you have a right to your privacy, you may find that you must be very proactive in securing this right for yourself. Many of the attending staff in these settings are sensitized to a patient's privacy needs, but the patient may still have to ask for what he/she needs.

I always carry a "Do Not Disturb" sign with me when I visit people in these settings. And I make it my practice to consult with the attending personnel to make sure that my visit won't conflict with other previously scheduled activities. I try to be very accommodating, because I know that having the support and understanding of the staff makes securing private time a lot easier.

Holly: Cheryl, could we go back to something you said earlier about vaginal dryness and loss of libido? My whole sexual response cycle has changed since my surgery and chemotherapy. Part of the problem my partner and I are having is with my non-existent sex drive.

The first couple of months after I came home from the hospital, I would have this weird feeling when Jean would try to be close to me. It was like being on a bad drug trip or something. I felt as though my body was there with her but I wasn't. I felt nothing. My headspace was totally different from how it was before I got sick. I would lie there thinking, 'Oh my God, what's happening? Will I ever feel normal again? How many more opportunities will I have to be with Jean like this before I die? Why don't I feel what I used to feel?'

Cheryl: Well, for one thing, you were fighting for your life back then. That's bound to alter your perceptions a bit, wouldn't you say?

I had the same feelings when I was going through chemo. I remember wondering if there was a possibility of hurting myself if I resumed intercourse.

I was afraid of what might happen. I even thought what would happen if I died while having sex. I'll admit it, some of my fears were irrational, but that didn't make them any less real at the time.

Communicating these feelings to my partner was another hurdle to overcome. How could I tell him that I was no longer able to enjoy our sex life? Would he understand? Would this mean the end of all intimacy between us? Would the news affect his ability to perform sexually? I've seen how devastating this kind of information can be in the sex life of a couple.

In my practice over the years, I've had occasion to work with a number of men whose erectile dysfunction began at a similar moment in their life. A man's wife was sick, he attempted intercourse, and his wife cried out in pain and he lost his erection because he thought he hurt her. Even years later, after the wife's death, his guilt and shame would interfere with his ability to have an erection.

I didn't want this to happen to my partner. But I couldn't just pretend like nothing was wrong either. I knew we had to talk, but when? It couldn't be while we were being sexual, because that would appear like rejection. It had to be at a neutral time when I could speak freely without fear of being misunderstood.

Holly: Yeah, that's exactly how I'm feeling. What if I screw this up? What if this somehow scars Jean for the rest of her life? I don't what that to happen. I wouldn't be able to forgive myself. I'm afraid something bad might happen. That's why I feel frozen in place.

Cheryl: There is a way to overcome this stalemate. First, you need to reassure Jean that you are committed to working through this impasse with her. I think she needs some reassurance that you haven't given up. And in return you could ask her for her patience, because the process may be a slow one.

I suggest, however, that you give yourself a timeline; otherwise you may find yourself putting this off indefinitely. And that won't do.

I would then recommend that the two of you begin to explore what is possible now in your sex life together. Avoid comparing what you are able to do now with how it once was. Keep the exploration simple and open-ended. Don't create a goal to be achieved. You

remember what I told Mia about spoon breathing and sensual touch. Well, this would be a good place for the two of you to begin as well. Keep it playful and honor your limits.

Kevin: Are there male surrogates specifically trained to work with gay men?

Cheryl: There are, yes. Thank you for bringing that up.

Gay men in the age of HIV/AIDS have a unique set of sexual issues that need to be understood and addressed. Besides the obvious safe sex concerns, there are all the issues that arise with the death of a partner. Unresolved grief can cause sexual dysfunction.

When a relationship ends with the death of a partner, the surviving partner has an array of new concerns. How and when does he begin to date again? If he is sexual with someone new, does this violate the memory of his deceased partner?

I frequently hear the same complaint. 'I'm so lonely, but my grief is getting in the way of my having any kind of sexual feelings.'

The object for a therapist or surrogate partner is to help the surviving partner face these concerns as soon as possible. 'Listen, I'm sure your lover wouldn't want you to stop living. Choose life! It will be the best testament you could offer your deceased lover.'

If these concerns go unresolved for too long, the likelihood that they will develop into a full-blown dysfunction increases exponentially.

Robin: Hey, wait, I know a joke about this.

A wife says to her husband, "Dear, what would you do if I died?" "Why, I would be extremely upset," says the husband. "Why do you ask such a question?"

"Would you remarry?" asks the wife. "No, of course not," says the husband.

"But don't you like being married?" "Of course I do, dear."

"Then why wouldn't you remarry?" "Alright," says the husband, "I'd remarry."

"You would?" says the wife, looking vaguely hurt. "Yes, I would."

"Would you sleep with her in our bed?" asks the wife. After a long pause, the husband responds, "Well yes, I suppose I would."

"I see," says the wife indignantly. "And you would probably let her wear my clothes." "I suppose, if she wanted to."

"Really," says the wife icily. "And would you take down the pictures of me and replace them with pictures of her?" "Yes, I think that would be the correct thing to do."

"Is that so?" says the wife, leaping to her feet. "Then I suppose you'd let her play with my golf clubs, too." "Of course not, dear," says the husband. "She's left-handed!" (Everyone laughs.)

Cheryl: Kevin, you said in your check-in that you are looking for a partner, but that you are meeting men who are only interested in sex. Searching for a life partner isn't easy even under the best of circumstances. Looking for someone new after the death of a partner is even more difficult. There is always the tendency to compare the new love interest to the one who's died, and that can be disastrous.

Besides, where does one go to meet a potential partner? One thing's for sure, it's not likely that you'll find this person in a sex club or in a bar. I suggest that you look in a less seductive environment like a café or at the gym. An HIV support group might also be a good place to look.

Or perhaps you could try a common interest club, like the ones they have for line dancing or playing bridge. How about placing a personal ad? Or you could check out the many online sites that provide chat rooms for gay men.

Kevin: I've considered all those things and have tried most of them.

But what happens if I meet someone who is HIV negative? I don't want to get attached to guy who might reject me just because of my HIV status. That's why it's less of a gamble if I keep the connection more casual.

So you see, I'm in a double bind. I want the intimacy that comes from a long-term relationship, but I'm afraid of the rejection or, what would be worse, infecting him.

Besides, even though I'm doing okay now on the medications I'm taking, what if I get sick later? I don't want to put anyone through what I went through with Doug.

Cheryl: Everyone's gonna die sooner or later. So why not live until you die?

If I focus on the fact that lymphoma is one of the cancers that has a high reoccurrence rate, I wouldn't be able to live each day to the fullest. Just because a person is dying doesn't mean he or she should live without the intimacy that would enrich the end of their life.

Holly: I'm just sitting here wondering if some of what Kevin's talking about is happening in my relationship with Jean. It's hard not to think of myself as damaged goods. You were talking about that too, Robin.

Anyone else have those kinds of feelings? I mean, how can I make a gift of myself to someone if I'm not feeling much like I'm a treasure? I still have shame about losing my breasts. I'm not a whole person anymore.

Cheryl: And where did you lose your breasts, at the laundromat?

You forget, Holly, that I've done this group already. I've learned that it's not a good thing to talk like that. It's self-defeating.

You didn't *lose* your breasts. You had cancer. They were surgically removed to save your life. There's no shame in that! Besides, it doesn't sound like Jean thinks of you as damaged goods at all. Are you still attracted to her?

Well then, you're just gonna have to let your love for one another heal you of your shame and self-doubt. You are no less a woman without your breasts.

I wonder, have you taken the time to grieve the loss of your breasts? Could you go to Jean and ask her to hold you while you weep for what is no longer yours?

Your shame is getting in the way of reconnecting with Jean, just as you suggest. But Jean is your life partner and this is part of life. Share it with her. Don't try to carry this alone.

Clare: You're so lucky to have a partner who is willing to walk through this with you, Holly. I hope you'll find it in your heart to include her.

My problem is a little bit different. As I said in my check-in, I want to be more available to Charley for the closeness that is so important to each of us. But Charley doesn't know how to touch me anymore, so he keeps his distance. How can I change this, or do you think it's too late?

Cheryl: I was touched by the loving depiction you gave in your check-in of the intimate life you've had with your husband over the years. It can't be easy for either of you to see this wind down. However, the closeness and tenderness you've shared all this time need not stop now.

Do you sleep together in the same bed? Would you be comfortable initiating a little cuddling with Charley? The same technique of spoon breathing and sensual touch that I suggested to Mia and Holly would no doubt work for the two of you as well. You will, of course, need to take the lead role in this since, as you say, Charley no longer knows how to touch you.

Take his open hand in yours and guide it to where you want to be touched. Long, slow strokes, short strokes, soft strokes, whatever. Show him the kind of pressure you are comfortable with. Once you've established a simple routine of breathing and touching, give Charley permission to carry on even if you happen to fall asleep. Because this breathing and touching technique is so gentle and loving, it should be able to serve you even as you are actively dying. But you'll have to let Charley know that this is what you want. You could tell him that you would like to die in his arms. What an ideal way to bring your life together to a close. Do you think Charley will accept your invitation?

Clare: I couldn't say for sure, but I think if I suggested it to him in a way that lets him know that he would be doing it for me, it might work. I'm not sure about what I should say.

Cheryl: When words fail to communicate what is in your heart, you can always rely on touch. So maybe you will find that nothing needs to be said at all. Draw him close and keep him near you with touch. Something tells me Charley will find this irresistible. It could be the fondest of farewells. Something he'll always remember.

Speaking of farewells, I'd better make mine now. We're running overtime, and I want to let you go.

In parting, I'd like to leave you with these thoughts. You are entitled to intimacy and pleasure in your life, regardless of how your body looks or at what stage of life you are at. The fact that you are sick, elder, or dying need not cut you off from these precious life-enhancing things. Take the lead in defining what it is that you need, and then communicate that to those you love. Have confidence that this will be as enriching for them as it will be for you.

Thank you for being so open and honest during our time together. It's been an honor to be part of this process with you.

My Turn

Richard: Are your sexual and intimacy needs being met? If not, what concrete steps could you take to change this? Take all the time and space you need.

_____

_____

_____

_____

_____

_____

_____

_____

Richard: Thanks, Cheryl. You are amazing.

Next week we will return to the group format without a presentation. This will be a good time for us to do some reviewing. Because some of you have said that you've been overwhelmed with the information of the last three weeks of presentations, we'll also look at strategies for pacing ourselves.

Kevin and Clare will lead us in our memorial ritual for Max.

And of course there will be homework to go over. So we'll have loads of things to keep us busy.

Before we close, I want to set you up with this week's homework. I have prepared a fun exercise that you can do with friends. It's called: *Death and Dying Euphemisms.* There will be a prize for the person who comes up with the longest list.

Are there any final questions or comments before we conclude?

Clare: Thank you, Cheryl. This has been most enlightening.

AT-HOME WORK

Week 6 — Death and Dying Euphemisms

Brainstorm the euphemisms we use to talk about death and dying.

Make a list of all the euphemistic words/terms that you can think of that help us avoid using the words "death" and "dying" — for example, "croaked."

Try to determine their use and meaning. For example, why do we use phrases like "We lost him" or "She passed on"? What exactly are these phrases intended to communicate?

Look for the serious as well as the funny. Can you come up with any cross-cultural examples?

Be creative. Ask your family and friends for help.

Chapter Seven

Week 7:
Charting a Course

Checking In

Richard: Here we are at week 7 already. Can you believe it? Time is just flying by.

We have lots to do today so we had better get started. We have our check-in, of course, and we'll want to spend some time with last week's homework. I also want to give you an opportunity to review the presentations of the last three weeks. No doubt there will be things you'll want to revisit. And we'll save the last fifteen or twenty minutes for our ritual of remembrance for Max. Clare and Kevin will lead us in that.

Let's begin with our check-in. I'd appreciate it if you could bring us up to date on what's happening in your life. It's been more than three weeks since we've had the time to do an in-depth check-in like this.

Who would like to begin?

Mia: I'd like to start today, if that's okay. I've been on an emotional roller coaster the last few weeks. I'm having these wild mood swings. I can be really depressed and despondent at one moment and happy and confident the

next. I know I'm driving my family and my boyfriend crazy. I'm even beginning to scare myself.

One thing I know for sure. I'd be completely lost without this group.

I've been thinking about the last few weeks and how much this experience has meant to me. I've learned so much about myself and each of you has been so helpful. I've also been really impressed with the care and concern of the presenters. I've taken to heart much of what they've said and I can honestly say that I'm making some progress.

The week after Emmett and Steve were here, I had a long talk with my father about making out a will. At first he was shocked by the suggestion that I was preparing for my death. He didn't want to hear anything about it. It's bad luck to even mention death. But I reminded him of what he always taught me about doing business. He used to say, 'In order to be successful a businessman must be prepared.'

He would sit me on his knee and lecture me on the secret of his success. 'I can see farther than all my competitors.'

216

This used to make me laugh when I was a little girl because I thought he meant that literally. I didn't see how that was possible because my father is a small man with very poor eyesight.

I reminded him of this when we were having our talk about my will. 'Is there something wrong with your eyesight, father? How is it that now I can see farther than you?' He lowered his head for a moment and when he raised it again he was all business. He wrote down the name of his lawyer and told me to call him. 'Mr. Woo will assist you in any way you see fit.'

My father loves me. I am his only child. So I know that that was very hard for him. But at the same time I think he is also proud because he knows that his only daughter can see great distances, just like him.

I also had somewhat of a breakthrough after David's presentation on spirituality. I took to heart his suggestion that I begin to incorporate my meditation practice into my daily life. I was checking out the bulletin board at school one day while I was waiting for an elevator. I saw a notice for a class on meditation that was being held at the local Zen Center. So I decided to check it out. I was delighted to find that the Center is much more than a place to take classes. It's actually an established community with many components. I've been able to sit in on a number of the daily meditation sessions and it's really helped.

I was immediately attracted to a very elderly Japanese man who's one of the Center's founders, I think. I finally got an opportunity to speak with him briefly last week. I told him what I was seeking. He sat quietly and listened while I ranted and raved about how unfair I thought life was and how I was angry for being robbed of my life and my health. I must have gotten really worked up because I started to hyperventilate. He just sat there and watched. When I regained my composure and recovered my breath, I was just about to speak again when he signaled me to be silent. We sat in silence for what seemed like an eternity before he spoke. 'There is no wisdom in wanting what you cannot have.' That's all he said. Then he turned and walked away.

I haven't been able to get those words out of my mind since. Even though I'm Chinese myself, I can never figure out why Asians are so inscrutable all the time.

Raul: What does that mean? What ya just said about, ya know, Asians?

Mia: Oh, sorry. Inscrutable means mysterious. I thought he was being mysterious.

Raul: You thought he was being mysterious because he told you not to want stuff you can't have? Why is that mysterious? I think it makes a hell of a lotta sense.

I've had to do that all my life. It wasn't so easy when I was a kid, I didn't know better. But now, shit man, I just tell myself I don't really want stuff no more, because I know I can't have any of it. It don't hurt so much now like it used to.

Hey, guess what? Father Diego came to my house for dinner last week. Shit, man, it was so great. You shoulda seen my mother. She was cookin' and cleanin' for weeks before he got there. My madre, she's really somethin'.

Anyhow, so he shows up and everybody is bein' real nice and everything. He starts right in tellin' my mother that the house looks real pretty with the flowers and everything and that the food smells real good. He was makin'

some big points. I guess he figured he was gonna need them later. I kinda sat in the corner and shut up, because I knew what was comin'. So when we're eatin', Father Diego tells my mother how she's the best cook and all that shit. And she was sittin' there just eatin' it up. He was smooth, man. He was real smooth.

So then, after dinner, it's time for the fireworks. Man, they didn't even see it comin'. Me and Amelia kept lookin' at each other wonderin' what was gonna happen next. Shit, man, Father Diego just said it right out. He told my parents what him and me had been talking about for the last couple a weeks. He started talkin' about this group and everything. At first I don't think my parents got it. They kept looking at each other wonderin' what the hell he was talkin' about.

Then they started lookin' at me and Amelia. Oh shit! Look out now. So I had to tell them about what I've been doin', comin' here and everything. My mother starts cryin' and my father is lookin' all sad. Then me and Amelia start cryin' and Father Diego is just sittin' there lookin' at us like we're loco.

'Mi hijo, why? Don't you want to get better?' That's when I almost lost it.

'Shit, man, I ain't never gonna get better. Why the hell can't you see that?'

Father Diego tells us we should say a prayer for guidance and everything gets all quiet. He prays for me and my family. He asks God to open our hearts so that we can trust in His wisdom. And, like he was still prayin', he starts tellin' my parents that it's okay for me to quit doin' stuff that's just gonna prolong my life.

'God doesn't expect us to suffer for no good reason. You have been really good parents. This is not your fault. God is not punishing you. God loves us and wants us to have peace in our lives. Raul is a good son. He's doing everything he can to understand God's will, like doing this class. He told me he was afraid to tell you about it even though it has helped him a lot. Is that the kind of relationship you want with your son? The only way God can work in our lives is if we let all God's wisdom come to us. And each of us has a piece of that wisdom. God expects us to work together to have understanding. Amen.'

Nobody said nothin' for a long time, then my father says, 'I want dessert. Dolores, get everybody some of your delicious flan.' I knew the worst was over. Shit, man, Father Diego pulled

it off. It ain't over yet, but at least it's finally out in the open. I don't have to hide no more.

We are gonna go see Father Diego as a family once a week to talk about this some more. Things are better at home now. I love my family.

Clare: I am so proud of you Raul. I knew you were going to make this happen. Congratulations. What will you do now?

Raul: I don't know. I'm gonna just see how it goes. It's crazy, man, like now that I'm in charge of my life and that I don't have to hide no more, I don't want to die. I don't have so much pain either, so maybe that's part of it.

Clare: I'm making some headway with Charley too. He's a tough old bird, but I do love him.

I took Cheryl's advice and had a talk with him. I told him straight out that I wanted to die in his arms. 'I love you, Charley. You are everything to me. Hold me close, Charley, I'm so afraid. I'll only be able to do this with you by my side, just like always. It's you and me, we're still a team, right?' He couldn't say no. I went to hug him and he started to cry. 'I can't let you go. I won't let you go. I want to die, too.'

I said, 'Listen, my love, your turn will come soon enough, but now it's my turn. So you're gonna have to be strong for both of us.' We were holding one another real close, like the old days, when I told him I had to lie down because I wasn't feeling well. He broke the embrace as if I had slapped him. 'No, Charley, don't let go. Come lie down with me. I want to show you something.' I took him by the hand and led him to our bed. I was feeling very lightheaded but I wanted to tell him about spoon breathing. I don't think I got very far with the explanation before I passed out. But I remember thinking that it was so nice having him there with me. When I woke up about twenty minutes later, he was still there holding me. I took his hands in mine and brought them to my face. I kissed them both and whispered I love you again. There were tears in his eyes. 'You're my best gal. I'll never leave you.' Shortly after that I fell asleep again.

That's all I needed. Dear God, I hope it lasts.

Mike: You are such an inspiration, Clare. If only I could be more like you.

Clare: Thank you, Mike. You're so sweet. How are things with you and Maryanne?

Mike: I had an interesting week. I've actually been feeling a little bit better than I have lately. I have a little more energy and that's nice. Things are always better at home when I'm feeling better. I'm the world's worst patient. Maryanne can testify to that.

So, after group last week I started telling Maryanne about how Cheryl suggested I talk to my doctor about possibly talking one of the erectile dysfunction drugs on the market. I thought this would come as a surprise, but she already knew all about them. She told me she had been reading a lot about ED and MS lately. She said she wanted to tell me about what she read, but she said she was afraid to. 'Afraid, why?' 'Gee, I don't know, Mike. Let's see, what could it be? Are you serious? You've been such a bear when it comes to the topic of sex that I swore I would never mention it ever again. You think I like having my head bitten off?'

'I'm sorry, Maryanne. You're right, I'm an asshole.'

'Stop saying you're sorry all the time and do something about it.' And that's where the conversation ended.

Boy, I hate it when she does that to me. Of course, now I realize that she probably learned that from me. I do a lot more of that kind of thing to her than she does to me. She's picking up all my bad habits.

She was right, as usual. So without telling her, I made an appointment to see my doctor for an evaluation. I'll see him later this week. I've decided to be perfectly honest with him about my little problem. Maybe he'll be able to tell me if one or another of these drugs will work for me.

I also got a referral from Richard for a sex therapist in the East Bay. I know, I know, not a moment too soon. But hey, I'm a little slow sometimes. When I asked Maryanne if she wanted to go with me, she hesitated for a minute. 'I guess so, but only if you're serious. You are serious aren't you?'

I really love her. It takes so little to make her happy and yet I rarely make

the effort. I don't know how she stands it. I know I don't deserve her. Maybe one day I'll be able to make it up to her.

Raymond: I've been really swamped the last couple of weeks. Did I ever mention that Joann designated me as her executor? Well, she did, and since her death I've been running around taking care of all sorts of business. Boy, I am so glad I was here for Emmett and Steve's presentation. It's made all the difference in the world.

It's funny. When I was doing the homework exercises for that week's presentation, I was only thinking about the end of my life. For some reason, I completely blocked the fact that I would probably need this information for Joann's sake before I would need it for myself.

This was especially true with that one exercise, *Creating A Final Affairs Checklist.* That really came in handy. I'm glad we worked on that exercise together because I would have never been able to come up with all those things on my own.

Since I had the opportunity to rehearse all this stuff just a couple of weeks ago, I was feeling a whole lot more confident about getting through this in one piece. I really don't see how people manage all this after-death stuff without having the kind of help I got here. No wonder so many people feel abandoned when someone they love dies. I would be absolutely overwhelmed if I had to do all of this stuff cold.

Actually, I'm grateful to have all these distractions. I've been able to make myself so busy that I haven't had time to think about the fact that Joann is actually gone. I don't see how I'm gonna face my grief.

Intellectually I know that I'm just postponing the inevitable, but I don't think I have the courage now to do it right.

I mean, you should have seen me this past weekend. I had to box up the contents of Joann's closets. I had been warned that this is always a difficult task for a survivor, but I guess I didn't bargain on how difficult it was really going to be. I probably should have asked a friend for help, but I didn't. I was all alone in the room where she died. Her closets were filled with the most intimate reminders of how much she meant to me. I could still smell her scent on many of her clothes. I started bawling like a baby. It took me

three times as long as it should have. I kept blubbering all over the boxes.

It reminded me of how it was right after my mom died. As a kid, it didn't sink in that she wasn't ever gonna come back to us until my aunts started to box up her belongings. I remember being nearly hysterical as they took the boxes from the house.

See, even now, just talking about this makes me weepy. When am I gonna be able to pull it together?

Janice: I had to do the same thing after Albert died. I had to sort through all his things. Just like you, I was advised to have a friend help me box up his clothes, but I didn't listen either. I thought it was my responsibility alone. I was his wife after all and these were his private things. I actually thought that collecting his belongings and going through them would be a final act of love on my part. But it turned out to be more like some twisted, self-inflicted torture.

I was like a woman possessed. The more difficult it became, the more determined I was to get through it all by myself. I was a basket case for weeks afterward. It was like I needed to punish myself for something. It was my fault that Albert was dead and this is how I was to pay for my sins. Maybe I tried to do too much too soon after he died, I don't know. I cried my eyes out with each article of clothing I handled. I never want to have to do that kind of thing again.

It's funny that you mentioned Joann's scent on her clothing. The same was true with Albert's things. I've never told anyone this before, but for weeks after Albert died I slept with some of his clothing that I had squirreled away for myself. Just a couple of his old sweaters and an old hat he would wear sometime. I felt like a criminal doing this. What if anyone found out about it? Would they think I was crazy? It became an obsession and I remember being too embarrassed to tell anyone. I was so devastated by the loss and for some strange reason having his clothes in bed with me helped me sleep.

In time his scent disappeared from everything I had saved for myself and I was all alone once again. Dear me, this is still so upsetting and it's been nearly two years since Albert passed on.

I have something else I wanted to mention too, if that's okay. And I hope you don't think less of me after I tell you

this. I am ashamed to admit it, but I haven't done even one thing to better myself over the past seven weeks. I haven't followed through on even one of the fine suggestions I've received during our sessions. I'm still as alone and isolated as when I began this group. I've made no effort to contact a lawyer to complete a Do Not Resuscitate order. I haven't looked into joining a church. I haven't really tried to make friends with my neighbors, nor have I tried to do any of the things Cheryl suggested I do.

It's not like I'm ungrateful, because I'm not. I don't know what's wrong with me. You see, each week I arrive here eager for our next session to begin. I listen closely to the presentations. I take careful notes. I even make a list of things to do the following week. I'm full of the best intentions until I get home. Then they all vanish into thin air.

Everyone else seems to be making headway and having successes to report. Everyone, that is, except me. I feel like such a bad person for wasting this precious time.

Richard: I had no idea you were feeling this way. You're not a bad person, Jan; you're a good-for-nothing slacker, for sure, but not a bad person. (Everyone laughs.)

All kidding aside, this isn't a contest, you know. We're not here to compete with one other to see how much each of us can accomplish in ten weeks. The purpose of this group is to provide us an opportunity to free ourselves from the painful silence our culture imposes on death talk.

We certainly are not here to impose new strictures. Besides, since there is no one correct way to do this, who's to say that you're not doing it exactly the way you are supposed to at this time?

Perhaps it's just a question of timing, Jan. I'm just real happy that you are here each week and that you participate so readily and honestly.

Kevin: I'm sure glad you said that. I was beginning to wonder about this myself. Is there some hidden agenda for this group that I'm not picking up on? After all, there's has been so much great information and positive ideas exchanged. What would prevent there being expectations for achievement too?

I can see how Jan might feel pressured to perform. I know we talked about this our very first week together and you said

there would be no hidden agenda, but it probably bears repeating every few weeks or so.

I've seen it happen before. The expectation to conform or achieve can creep into a process like this and ruin the whole thing. I would hate to have our group turn into some kind of perfection script where we're being judged by how closely we measure up against some artificial model.

Mia: I feel the same way Kevin does. I wouldn't want that to happen here either. But luckily I'm not feeling any pressure like that. I wonder if anyone else is?

Kevin: Oh, I gotta finish my check-in.

Let's see, I've been feeling a bit disconnected and lethargic lately. Even work has been more taxing than usual and I really love teaching. I must have some kind of low-grade infection going on in my body. I've been achy and feverish a lot and I just feel out of it all the time. I called my doctor for an appointment to see him next week. It's probably nothing, just a touch of the flu, but it's enough to throw me off balance.

To be honest, every time something like this happens I always think that maybe this is the big one. Maybe this is what'll kill me. I've been so lucky for so long. I can't help but think that one day my luck will run out.

I was talking about this very thing with a friend over dinner yesterday. He's HIV+, too. And he lost his lover about the same time I lost Doug.

Richard: You guys lost your lovers? Where at?

Kevin: Touché.

What I meant to say is, our lovers died.

Damn, I've really been trying to be conscious about that too. I've even corrected other people when they've said lost instead of died. Bad habits are hard to break.

Where was I? Oh yeah, so my friend and I were having dinner and I was telling him about this group and all and he asked me if I thought it was working.

'Working? What do you mean working?' 'Like if you went to your doctor next week and he told you that you had six months to live, would you be able to handle it any better now that you are doing this group?'

I was quiet for a minute and finally I said that I couldn't say for sure. 'This group has really opened my eyes to new ways of thinking about death and dying and I'm glad that I'm doing it, but I'd probably still freak out if my doctor gave me six months.'

So now I'm confused about what this group is supposed to do. At the end of ten weeks am I supposed to be no longer afraid to die?

Richard: What was that you were saying a minute ago about unreal expectations?

I'd be satisfied to know that at the end of these ten weeks you could say with some confidence that you've confronted some of your fears and anxieties about death and dying.

This is just ten weeks out of your whole life. It couldn't possibly wipe away all the cultural conditioning that supports our denial and fear of death. I wonder, though, are other people feeling the same way?

Robin: I'm not, but I can only speak for myself. I'm not feeling any kind of pressure.

In fact, I think the opposite is true. Maybe it's just me, but I would like more structure. I haven't accomplished nearly as much as I probably could have, because no one has been on my case to do so. Like I admit it, I'm lazy. I need someone to push me.

I couldn't tell from what you said earlier, Jan, if you need more structure like me, or if you like things just the way they are.

Janice: Thank you for asking. Actually, I would very much like more structure. That's what I was trying to say in my check-in.

After I leave our group, I'm all alone. I have no one to prod me along or join me in doing the things I want to do. And I can't seem to generate the get-up-and-go I need to do these things on my own.

That was one of the best things about my marriage. Albert helped me get organized so that I could get things done. Going home to my empty little apartment after these wonderfully stimulating sessions just takes the wind out of my sails. I just sit there waiting for something to happen and it never does.

I need help.

Robin: Hey, if that's the case, maybe we should pair up and make it work for both of us. What do you say?

Janice: You mean you and I? Oh that would be lovely, dear, but I'm sure you don't want to be saddled with an old fuddy-duddy like me.

Robin: Don't talk like that. I don't let people talk that way about my friends. You are my friend, aren't you?

I asked you this once before. Maybe you don't remember or maybe you didn't think I was serious back then or maybe you think I'm some kind of freak. But hey, I'm dead serious about this. No pun intended. I think we'd be rad together.

Have you ever ridden on a motorcycle? Stick with me, Jan, and I can promise you that your life won't be dull.

Seriously, I need to hook up with someone as much as you do. I'm so goddamn lonely. And like Cheryl said last week, it's a crime to be lonely alone.

So what do you say? Two heads are better than one.

Janice: I remember you asked me to take a class with you when we first started this group, but I didn't think you were serious. I mean, look at me, I'm just an old lady. And you're so cool. I think that's the right word.

Oh, I would so love the company and I could make you dinner. I once was famous for my beef stew, you know. I'm a little rusty these days, dear. I haven't prepared that since before Albert passed on. But if you're willing to be a guinea pig....

Robin: You're on! We'll talk about setting a date when we get done here.

Well, that takes care of what I wanted to talk about in check-in. I think I just found myself a pal. Look out, San Francisco, we're gonna kick some ass.

Holly: I'm jealous! I love beef stew.

I've had a great week. No kidding. Jean and I are on cloud nine. It all started when I got home from group last week. No sooner did I get in the door when she's at me with her usual twenty questions. 'How did it go? What did you do in the group today? What did you talk about with Cheryl? Did you talk about me?' And so on and so on. She was following me around the house like a puppy.

I was afraid this was gonna happen. I was going over it in my head during the commute home. What am I going to tell Jean? I can't just blurt it out. Besides, what if she pitches a fit about me airing our dirty laundry in public? Maybe if I tell her I have a headache she'll leave me alone and I won't have to mix it up with her.

I did have a headache, a big one, but it was from all the anticipation. I had so much bottled up inside of me for so long, all that fear and shame, I didn't know how it was gonna come out or even if it would come out at all. And what if I say the wrong thing and make matters worse? I've done that more than once in our relationship.

When I got in the house, I headed straight for the bedroom but she cut me off at the kitchen. 'What's wrong, babe? Don't you want to talk about it?' I was shaking all over. My legs felt like rubber. I began to cry. I kind of fell in a swoon right into Jean's arms, just like in the movies, except I'm lots bigger than she is so she couldn't really catch me. I wound up slumped on the floor where my crying became a wail.

'Jesus, Holly, what is it? Talk to me. Are you sick? Say something, damnit.'

It was only then that I realized I hadn't yet said a word to Jean since I got home. I tried to speak, but nothing came out. I was like a madwoman curled up on the floor rocking back and forth sobbing like a motherless child.

Jean is getting pretty freaked out by this time. She had never seen me like this. She helped me to my feet and we stumbled to the bedroom and collapsed on the bed. Mind you, I'm still carrying on this whole time.

I started to undress. This generally is a signal for Jean to leave the room, because I haven't let her see me naked since the surgery. She was afraid to leave me alone like this, but she also didn't want to embarrass me any further. She got up to go. I could feel her anguish. Tears were streaming down her face. I reached for her hand and pulled her back down to the bed next to me. Still no words.

I began to undo the buttons of my top. My hands were shaking and I was moaning deep inside. I turned away from Jean and undid my bra and let it slip from my shoulders. I had gone this far, now all I had to do is turn and face her. But I couldn't raise my head. I was frozen in place.

I've never been so scared in all my life. Jean stroked my back with her fingers. Her touch was so gentle that it could hardly even be called a touch at all. But for some reason her caress calmed me. I took a couple of deep breaths and stood. Then I slowly turned toward Jean. I brought my hands to my face in shame and began to sob with even more intensity.

She stood and faced me, and her hands reached out until they came to rest on my scars. It was like her touch was both fire and ice, but I didn't pull away. There was no turning back. I was finally doing what I should have done two years ago.

When I was able to speak, the first words out of my mouth were, 'they're gone.' I took Jean in my arms and pulled her close and we kissed like lovers do for the first time in three years. (Everyone applauds.)

*K*evin: You go, girl!

Richard: Oh sure, I'll bet you expect me to follow that with my check-in. (Everyone laughs.)

Holly I'm so proud of you. Actually, I am very proud of each of you. What remarkable people you are.

I've had a good week too. I was invited to speak to a group of hospital chaplains last week and I think it went pretty well. It was an interfaith group of chaplains from a number of different hospitals in the area, so their experiences were quite varied. They get together on a regular basis to talk about their work and offer each other support.

I was invited to facilitate a discussion on the role of the hospital chaplain in end-of-life care. Most of the discussion revolved around the issue of how they could help their terminally ill patients achieve a good and dignified death for themselves in an institutional setting like a hospital or an extended care facility.

Interestingly enough, not one of the chaplains thought a hospital was a good place to die, and yet statistically more Americans die in a hospital than in any other setting.

Each chaplain had a horror story to tell about how impersonal hospitals can be. But despite the many obstacles, each was committed to changing the system for the betterment of all their patients.

Once they learned about what we do here at PARADIGM, they wanted to know if there was a way to condense this ten-week program into a weekend workshop. They thought it would a better schedule for healing and helping professionals, like themselves, who would otherwise be unable to attend a group like this. I told them that we're already working on that, and that hopefully by next year we would be offering a series of such workshops.

My Check-In

Richard: Take all the time and space you need for your check-in. This week, pay special attention to the accomplishments you've made these past few weeks. Are there still things that you wish to do? Do you need more structure like Robin and Jan? Where will you look for help? You might consider making a list of things you yet want to accomplish.

Here's a tip. Some people busy themselves making a long list of things to do and then they try to decide in what order to do them. This makes getting anything done nearly impossible. All the energy goes to prioritizing and none is left for getting things done.

Try this method instead. Make your list of what needs to be done. Look it over and choose the SINGLE most important thing for you to do right NOW. Lay the list aside and put all your energy into tackling that one task.

When you're done, or have gone as far as you can with it, go back to your list. Add anything you've thought of since you last worked on it and remove anything that's become unnecessary.

Now repeat the process. Again, choose the SINGLE most important thing for you to do right NOW. Lay the list aside and put all your energy into tackling that one task.

You may never get to everything, but you will have accomplished all the MOST important things on your list.

Group Process

Richard: Okay, great check-in this week. Thank you.

Let's turn our attention to last week's homework. By the way, this is my favorite exercise because it's so much fun. At the same time, it gets to the heart of our culture's denial and avoidance of death and dying.

Before we get to your lists, I'd like to know if anyone wants to comment on doing the exercise. Was anyone able to recruit friends or family to help brainstorm death and dying euphemisms?

Raymond: I had some friends to the house for dinner over the weekend and while we were having cocktails I decided to spring the exercise on them. The immediate and unanimous response was one of disgust.

'What a bummer. Jeez, Ray, this is sick. Has this got something to do with Joann's passing?' 'Hey, that's one. Passing.' 'This is so morbid. Wait a minute, I just thought of one. How about kicked the bucket?' Before you knew it, we were all hysterical with laughter and we came up with a mighty fine list to boot.

Robin: I had a similar response. Even my Goth, off-the-wall friends think I've got some kind of weird death fixation. They think Bobby's death really messed with my head. If they only knew.

Anyhow, once I got them past the initial 'that's sick' bullshit, it was fun. I never realized how many euphemisms there are.

Clare: I thought it prudent not to ask anyone in my family for help. I was afraid if I did I would only start a row. Everyone seems to have lost their sense of humor. So I was only able to come up with a few ideas on my own.

Richard: Okay, let's see if we can come up with a master list. Who would like to start?

Robin: Here are a few of mine.

These are euphemisms for death: 'passed away,' 'croaked,' 'threw in the towel,' 'stiff,' 'kicked off,' 'passed into the light,' 'gone fishing,' and 'six feet under.'

I only got a couple euphemisms for dying: 'coming to the finish line' and 'fade to black.'

Kevin: I was thinking about where we got some of these figures of speech. I never thought about it much until this exercise, but it appears that they come to us from lots of different segments of society and belong to many different eras.

Some are new and some are old fashioned. There are religious allusions, of course, like 'ascended,' 'Gabriel called,' 'home to Jesus,' 'sprouted wings,' 'in heaven,' and 'met his/her maker.'

Then there are the theatrical ones like 'doing Camille,' 'swan song,' 'curtains,' and 'the fat lady sang.'

There are farming allusions like 'bought the farm' and 'moved on to greener pastures.'

There are the New Age ones like 'transcended' and 'evolved into.'

I even thought of some nautical allusions like 'his ship came in,' 'shipped out,' 'sleeping with the fishes,' 'slipped the cable,' and walked the plank.'

Mia: This is great. I am a student of language and I love word games like this.

I must confess I had help with my list. I got a few of my classmates to help.

This is what we were able to come up with. 'Sleeping,' 'departed,' 'succumbed,' 'gone west,' 'kaput,' 'extinguished,' 'cash in (or out),' 'checked out,' 'conked out,' 'kicked off,' 'got a one-way ticket,' 'popped off,' 'snuffed,' 'bought a pine condo,' 'perished,' 'no longer with us,' and my favorite, 'ontologically challenged.'

You're just going to have to look that last one up.

For dying, I have 'racing against time,' 'won't last the winter,' 'his/her number's up' and 'one foot in the grave.'

Mike: I had some of the same ones that you guys had, but I also have these: 'bit the big one,' 'cashed in his/her chips,' 'cut down in his/her prime,' 'went to his/her final resting place,' 'gone to the big whatever in the sky,' and my favorites, 'worm food' and 'dirt nap.' (Everyone groans.)

Hey, give me a break, I didn't make these up, I'm just reporting them.

Clare: I was able come up with 'deceased,' 'asleep,' 'with the angels' and 'resting in peace' for death.

And for dying I have 'one foot in the grave,' 'a goner' and 'checking out.'

Raymond: I have a lot of the same ones you guys have, but I also have these for death: 'checked out,' 'done for,' 'extinct,' 'gone,' 'inanimate,' 'late,' 'perished,' 'crapped out,' 'pushing up daisies,' 'turned up toes,' and my favorite, 'assumed room temperature.'

For dying I have 'going downhill fast,' 'down for the count' and how about this one, 'circling the drain'? I got that one from an emergency room nurse. Apparently, this is nurse slang to describe someone who is actively dying. Isn't that a great one?

Holly: I guess people who are around death all the time, like nurses, would naturally come up with lots of euphemisms for death and dying.

I know they have polite ones they use when talking to lay people. Like when a friend of ours died in the hospital some years ago, we were told that she expired. Sounds like what happens to an old library card.

Let's see if I have any other ones that haven't been mentioned. Here's a couple: 'gone to the other side,' 'journeying home,' and 'dead as a doornail.'

I always wondered, what in the world is a doornail?

I also have 'breathed his/her last,' 'with the Father,' and the one I like best, 'went tits up.' I guess you know why I like that one. (Everyone laughs.)

I only have a couple for dying, 'crossing the river' and 'on the way out.'

Raul: This is hellacool.

I got some Spanish ones: 'finado (the end)', 'estirar la pata (gone stiff),' and 'pasó a mejor vida (gone to a better life.'

And how about, 'belly up,' 'dead meat,' 'snuffed out,' 'kicked the bucket,' 'burning in hell,' and 'bit the dust.'

like 'called home,' 'gave up the ghost,' 'resting in peace,' 'went to heaven,' 'laid to rest,' and 'passed on.'

Janice: I feel so embarrassed for laughing, but I can't help myself. I could only come up with real traditional ones,

Richard: What a great job. Congratulations! You guys knock me out.

My Turn

Richard: What was it like for you to do last week's homework? Did you find any euphemisms that weren't mentioned by the other group members? Were you able to recruit friends or family to help with this exercise? What was their reaction?

Richard: We have only 15 minutes left so I would like to turn this over to Kevin and Clare who will lead us in our Ritual of Remembrance for Max.

Kevin: Thanks to all your great input, Clare and I've been able to put together a little ceremony to celebrate Max's life. We've taken many of your suggestions and pieced them together to make a service that reflects all our needs as we say goodbye to Max. And if I have to say so myself, I think it hangs together pretty well as a whole.

Both Clare and I would like your feedback on this, since this is the first time either one of us has ever done anything like this.

Clare: As you can see, I've arranged this table at the center of our circle with a few simple things to help us focus our attention.

First and foremost is this wonderful picture of Max that Sylvia gave me. I understand it was taken a couple of years ago while they were on a holiday cruise to Alaska. Sylvia said it was the last vacation they took together. Max looks so happy. The picture captures what I remember most about him...his beaming, impish smile. I've lit these two candles and we'll be burning this sage incense. We also have this bowl of strawberries. Remember how much Max loved strawberries?

These three things – food, light and scent – are important parts of ritual in every tradition that I've researched. So I thought it would be nice for us to have these things too. We will also be using words and music and time for meditation to frame our service.

As we begin, I'd like to invite you to make yourself comfortable. Close your eyes, center yourself, and picture Max here with us, for no doubt he is close at hand.

I've chosen a lovely piece of music that will help us in our meditation. It's The Lark Ascending by Ralph Vaughn Williams.

Kevin: Let us pray.

God of timelessness and time, we thank you for this time and for those things that are yet possible and precious in it.

Thank you for the honesty that makes friends and makes laughter, for fierce gentleness, which dares us speak the truth in love.

Thank you for all the mysteries of loving, for one body close to another, for music and silence, for dreams and longing.

Thank you for calling us to commitment, to celebration, and to share our lives.

For calling us to welcome, to availability, and to oneness. Be with us now.* (Pause)

The Gardner
— Rabindranath Tagore

Peace my heart, let the time for the parting be sweet.

Let it not be a death but completeness.

Let love melt into memory and pain into songs.

Let the flight through the sky end in the folding of wings over the nest.

Let the last touch of your hand be gentle like the flower of the night.

Stand Still, O beautiful end, for a moment, and say your last words in silence.

I bow to you and hold up my lamp to light you on your way. (Pause.)

Ecclesiastes 3

For everything there is a season, a time for every matter under heaven:

A time to be born and a time to die;

A time to plant and a time to uproot what is planted;

A time to tear down and a time to build up;

A time to weep and a time to laugh;

A time to grieve and a time to dance;

A time to throw stones and a time to gather stones together;

A time to embrace and a time to refrain from embracing;

A time to seek and a time to lose;

A time to keep and a time to cast away;

A time to tear and a time to sew;

A time to keep silence and a time to speak.

(Pause)

Clare: Now it's our time for speaking or remaining silent if you would prefer.

I'm going to pass around this bowl of beautiful jumbo strawberries and invite each of you to take one. And as you are enjoying your berry, if you would like, you're welcome to speak a few words of remembrance of Max.

Raul: I hope you're happy Max, old dude. Find a nice spot for me. I'll see you soon.

Mike: Thanks for the laughs, Max. When I get all balled up in feeling sorry for myself, I hope I'll have the presence of mind to think of you and get over myself.

Holly: I found this poem called Friendship that I'd like to read, if that's okay.

Friendship
Anonymous

Friendship, the sun of the soul;

Revives me with its warmth

To the depths of the snows

With its flame.

And brings back to me,

The springtime of the heart.

So much so… that on my road

Will remain a few dear beings

Which like the trees will arch

And cover with green the winter's snow.

To those old friends who saw my beginning

My heart will never be closed.

Always old enough to remember

Always young enough to love.

*K*evin: Let us pray:

In your generous goodness, loving God, you shared Max with us. He, like us, is the finest work of your creation. Through him you renewed our confidence in humankind and our trust in the power of love. Therefore, we ask you in his name, to shower us with your bounty, sustain us, nurture us and give us peace. Amen.*

*Adapted from *Bread Blessed and Broken: Eucharistic Prayers and Fraction Rites* edited by John P. Mossi

My Turn

*R*ichard: If you were planning a Ritual of Remembrance for yourself, how would you structure it? What kinds of things would you include – music, readings, prayers, food, movement?

Mike: Hey, Kevin. You missed your calling. You should have been a priest.

Richard: That was beautiful, Clare and Kevin. Thank you.

Next week we will return to our presentation format. We will be considering life's Final Stages with our speaker, Dr. Brian Friedman, MD.

This is always a favorite presentation because participants get to ask all the questions they have about end-of-life care. For example: what should I expect as my body closes down? What do I need to have in place for a peaceful death? What is the role of pain medication in comfort care? In fact, we were thinking of renaming this presentation: *Everything You Ever Wanted to Know About the End-of-Life, but Were Afraid To Ask.*

In order to prepare you for next week's presentation, I want to set you up with this week's homework. I would like you to read this short primer I've written titled *Some Thoughts on The Dying Process: Dying Wisely and Well.* I invite you to take notes on what you read and come prepared to discuss final stages.

Are there any final questions or comments before we conclude?

Janice: I just want to say that this has been the best week yet.

AT-HOME WORK

Week 7 — Some Thoughts on The Dying Process: Dying Wisely and Well
Richard Wagner, Ph.D.*

Introduction

No doubt you will approach your death in your own way, bringing to the actively dying phase of life a uniqueness all your own. What follows are some personal thoughts on dying wisely and well.

I don't want to suggest that any of this is either conclusive or absolute. It is not. You may find that some of the things suggested below are present in sequence in your dying, or none may be. Your dying process may take months or just hours. What you can count on is that, short of a miracle, you will need to be the one to take the lead in all of this. Those who attend and survive you, even some of your physicians and other health care providers, will need a mentor, and the person best situated for that role is you.

I present this idealized scenario at some risk of being misunderstood. This is not about adjusting your deathbed pillows so that you can strike heroic poses for the edification of onlookers. Rather it is about achieving a good and wise death in the context of real dying, with all its unpredictability, disfigurement, pain, and sorrow.

I advise you not to think about your dying process in terms of a schedule, where one event follows naturally from the one before.

Your dying, like the rest of your life, will no doubt be full of surprises. However, there are benchmarks that you should know about just in case they occur as you die.

Start with the things listed below as a baseline. You may find that some of these changes may begin to occur as early as three months before you actually die. Or you may find that your actively dying stage may begin as late as a week or even days prior to your death. The most important thing will be for you to heed the promptings of your mind and body. Hopefully these will signal you to begin a movement from struggling against dying to one of acceptance and acquiescence.

Please do not confuse acceptance and acquiescence with resignation and succumbing. Resignation and succumbing are passive, as in 'something just overpowered me and I had no choice but to give up.' Resignation is based in self-pity, believing that 'in my dying I am powerless.'

Acceptance and acquiescence, on the other hand, are positive acts. 'I choose to let go, to relinquish control and to accept living and dying for what they are.' Wisdom comes in knowing when and where you are powerful and what the source of that power is.

One to Three Months Prior to Death – Turning Inward

By the time you realize you are actually dying, you will find that you have already begun to withdraw from the world around you. You will have less interest in the internet, newspapers or television, for example. You will invite fewer people to visit. In fact, you will probably have to practice saying, "Thank you, but I don't feel like company today."

You will find that even the people dearest to you will begin to figure less and less prominently in your scheme of things. This process of detachment is good. It is a necessary component of the dying process and is precisely what will help make the inevitable separation easier on everyone involved.

This is a time of turning inward and it can be a time of great insight for you. It will provide you an opportunity to sort things out, to evaluate yourself and the life you've lived. In other words, it can be a time to come to understanding about the meaning of your life and death.

Often this process is done with eyes closed, in a sort of meditation. It ought not to be confused with sleep, although your need for sleep will also increase at this time. You may add a morning nap to your usual afternoon nap. You may even be staying in bed all day and sleeping most of the time.

Those who attend you may not be attuned to the meaning of this inward turn and may become distressed. They may think it's a sign of depression. It's not. If you are able, try to reassure them that this is natural and that some quiet reflection on their part might bring them more into sync with you.

This inward turn will bring less of a need for verbal communication with others. Words are how living people communicate; touch and silence are how you will communicate as you die.

Rarely will you be able to count on those around you to understand this profound inward turn. Be patient with them. It's not ill will; they're just uninformed. An invitation for a loved one to embrace you can go a long way to calm both of you at this time.

Food and Nutrition

Food is fuel. You eat to live. As your body prepares to die, it needs less and less fuel. It is perfectly natural that your consumption of food will decrease and eventually stop. This is another very difficult concept for those who survive you to grasp. They will want you to eat, reasoning that eating will help you maintain your strength. You will need to help them understand that it is not food that will nourish you for what lies ahead, it is peace and serenity.

You will no doubt experience changes in your eating habits. Cravings will come and go. On some days nothing will taste good. On other days you may prefer liquids to solids. You will most likely eliminate hard-to-digest foods, like meat, from your diet first. Other foods will follow. And in time you will even choose to refuse soft foods.

It is okay not to eat. Eating just to please someone else will actually be counterproductive for you.

One to Two Weeks Prior to Death – Disorientation

Expect that you will be sleeping most of the time now. As you die, consciousness will be harder for you to maintain. Those who attend you will be able to arouse you from your slumber, but upon awakening you may experience a period of disorientation.

Those around you may find you confused at times. They may even report that while you slept you seemed to talk to people who were not there. Your sleep may appear to some as restless and fitful. This will most likely add to the agitation of those who witness it. They may misinterpret these events and imagine that you are in distress.

If you are not in distress, you can reassure them with confidence that this, too, is natural and that they should be at ease.

Breathing exercises like those practiced by expectant mothers, deep and paced, are helpful for all concerned.

Remember you are in charge of your dying environment. The anxiety of those who attend you, if left unchecked, can disturb your sense of well-being and cost you the serenity you seek.

Physical Changes

As you approach your death there will be discernible changes in your body. For example, you will lose weight. Your blood pressure will drop. Your pulse rate will either increase from its usual range to upwards of one hundred fifty beats per minute, or decrease to near zero.

Your body temperature may fluctuate wildly. At times you will feel feverish, at other times you will feel a chill. You will experience an increase in perspiration, and what some describe as clamminess.

Those who attend you should be prepared to deal with all these eventualities. Cold compresses and extra blankets should always be easily available.

Your skin color will change: flushing with fever at one minute, becoming bluish with cold at another. Often a pale yellowish pallor will appear. Your hands and feet will become pale or even bluish as your heart's ability to move sufficient blood through your body diminishes.

Expect your appendages and abdomen to swell and change color as bodily fluids begin to pool. This can also result in a change in your skin's texture.

Gentle massage with a light lotion is comforting for both you and the person doing the massage. Don't be afraid to ask for touch.

Your breathing will also begin to change. At times your respiration rate will increase from its usual range to forty breaths a minute or more. At other times your respiration rate will decrease to nine or even six breaths a minute.

You will want to prepare those who attend you for when you will stop rhythmic breathing altogether. This most often occurs during sleep.

Congestion in your lungs will cause a rattling sound in your lungs and upper throat, and may be accompanied by a dry cough. All of these changes will come and go.

Have those who attend you keep your mouth and lips moist. Ice chips on your tongue and glycerin swabs for your mouth and lips are ideal for this purpose.

One or Two Days to Just Hours Prior to Death

You may have a surge of energy just before death, particularly if you have recently discontinued all your medications, except those you take for pain control. (Many of the medications you consume to treat your illness can have unfortunate side effects. Eliminating them during your dying process often gives your body an opportunity to rebound, resulting in an energy surge.)

You may have periods of heightened alertness and clarity unlike what you have become used to. You may resume eating even though you may not have eaten anything for days.

You may even have a renewed interest in being with people. This is an ideal time for closure with those you love. Giving and receiving farewells and offering blessings, as well as ritualizing this most important passage can be uplifting and life affirming for all involved.

If you are afforded this effervescence, know that it will be short lived. Time is at its most precious now. Use it wisely.

Immediately following this small window of renewed vigor the signs of death's embrace will become more pronounced.

This can be a time of great distress for those who will survive you. They may have misinterpreted your rally of just days or even hours ago to mean that you are getting better. They should be reassured before this happens that all is on course and that your death is near.

There will be an increase in restlessness now as your body tries to compensate for a decrease in oxygen in the blood. Your breathing will become slower and more labored. It's not unusual for your breathing to stop for long periods before resuming. Sounds produced by the congestion in your lungs will become more audible.

Those who attend you can ease your labored breathing by changing your position in bed.

Don't expect to be present during much, if any, of this final stage. Your work is done. All you have to do now is let go. Nature will take care of the rest.

If you are registering any sensory input at all during this time it is most likely through your sense of hearing.

Those who attend you should be aware that they can be an enormous help to you at this time. To die peacefully with soft music playing in the background and with words of goodbye and thank you ringing in your ears will make all the difference in the world for both you and them.

Your eyes may be open or semi-open but you're not seeing anything. For all intents and purposes, you are no longer here. All that remains is for your body's mechanical systems to shut down.

Your eyes will have a glassy look to them or they will be tearing. Your hands and feet are now purplish, your extremities, back and buttocks are blotchy. Your dying is complete when you stop breathing.

However, what appears to be your last breath often is not. One or two long-spaced breaths at the last moments of life are not uncommon. When these finally subside, you are dead.

Your death, like most things in life, needs formal recognition. An official such as a doctor, hospice nurse or coroner must make that pronouncement.

Conclusion

Some final thoughts.

Throughout your dying process, those who survive and attend you will be looking to you for direction. They will expect and want you to express your needs and desires for as long as you are able. But even when you are no longer able to communicate in any form, crucial decisions continually need to be made. For example, when would you like life support systems such as oxygen removed, and by whom?

The wise person will have clearly and unambiguously addressed all such concerns both verbally and in writing. Durable Power documents and/or a Living Will are specifically designed for this purpose.

Remember there is no one particular way of dying well. In the final analysis, you will probably die the way you lived. However, if you wish to achieve an awareness, appreciation and acceptance of your own dying while participating in it, you can, but it will take work and commitment.

This kind of conscious dying won't eliminate the pain and poignancy of separation, but hopefully you will learn how to face these and live through them to the end.

Good luck.

*I'd like to acknowledge the pioneering work of Barbara Karnes, RN. She inspired this presentation.

Chapter Eight

Week 8:
Approaching The Exit

Checking In

Richard: Welcome back. Did you have a good week?

Let's get started. As you know, we resume our presentation format this week. Today we will be considering the final stages of life with my good friend and colleague, Dr. Brian Friedman, M.D.

As I said last week, this topic is always a favorite of our participants. And as you will soon see, there is no one better suited to provide us the information we are looking for than this remarkable person sitting next to me.

Brian will have an opportunity to introduce himself in a minute, but now I think we should get on with our weekly check-in. This week I like you to include your own end-of-life concerns so that Brian will be able to address them during our discussion. You might want to begin by responding to last week's homework.

Janice, I'm going to insist that you begin today. We're all dying to know what happened to you. Look at you. You look fantastic. What have you done to yourself?

Janice: Oh, Richard, how you do go on.

Oh my, you'll have to excuse me. I'm a little giddy this week. The most wonderful thing has happened. As you remember from last week, I invited Robin to dinner at my apartment so we could begin to support one another in reaching the goals we've set for ourselves as members of this group. I made my famous beef stew, which I must say turned out just fine. So I guess I still have the knack.

We were in the parlor having a cup of tea after dinner when out of the blue Robin says, 'Jan, let's do something with your hair.' Well, as you can imagine I was a bit shocked and embarrassed and I'm sure I turned red as a beet. I stammered for something to say, but before I could utter a word she was at my side pulling my hair this way and that.

'My goodness, what ever do you mean? Why, I've been wearing my hair like this for ages.' 'That's my point, honey. You got the best hair, not like mine. Mine's all raggy from years of abuse. But yours, wow, just look at it. It's so thick and healthy. Let me do a make-over on you, okay?'

'Oh dear, I don't know. You mean right here, right now?' All I could think of was how I might try and stall for time. This was all so sudden. What did she have in mind, I wondered? Did she want to make me look like a teenager? Well, no amount of protest was about to change her mind.

'I went to beauty school for a year, you know. I washed out because I was loaded all the time, but I think I still remember the fundamentals.'

My perfect evening with my new friend was turning into a nightmare. Before I could say another word, Robin was helping me into the bathroom so she could shampoo and cut my hair. I was in tears as I saw my hair falling to the floor around me. She was so engrossed in what she was doing she hardly noticed my reaction. 'Did I get some soap in your eyes, honey? Let me get you a towel.'

When she was finished she handed me a mirror. I took a deep breath and somehow found the courage to look. It was miraculous. I hardly recognized myself.

'This is just the beginning, honey. I want to do some color and maybe some make-up.'

Two days later she was back with a satchel full of beauty products. 'Where did you get all this? It must have cost a fortune.' 'Nope, these are all samples. I get them from a friend in the business.' By the time the leftover stew was reheated for dinner, I was as you see me today.

Isn't it wonderful? And I owe it all to Robin. I feel absolutely reborn. I have a whole new level of self-confidence. I've even found myself talking to my neighbors. It just comes spilling out of me. Goodness, I just never thought anything like this could happen to me. I am so happy.

Robin: Honey, it wasn't me. It's you. This beautiful woman was just locked up inside you all this time. All I did was open the door, that's all.

Jan, you are the same age as my mother. Poor thing, she doesn't have a proper daughter because I kept screwing up all the time. When I was with you for dinner last Saturday, and we were talking over tea, I realized just how much I need my mother. And last week's homework is what started the whole thing. I couldn't get the homework out of my mind.

While I was doing your hair I realized something very important. I'll never be able to die well if I'm estranged from my parents.

Now I understand why I was so adamant about connecting with you from the very beginning of this program. Hey, don't get me wrong, I really like you, but I see now that you're a mother figure for me.

Somewhere inside I must have thought that if I was able to establish a relationship with you, well then, maybe I'm finally mature enough to approach my real mother. Does that make sense? This is a big breakthrough for me and I have you to thank for it, Jan.

Raul: You mean that's it? Is that the end of the story? I mean, shit man, didn't you call you mother or nothin'?

Robin: No, not even nothing, sorry.

I know I'm a wuss, but I'm freakin'. What if she won't have me back? What if, after all these years, she refuses to talk to me? Like I wouldn't blame her if she didn't. I treated her real bad, and all

for what? She always did right by me. She tried her damndest; I was just a wild thing. Running off like I did must have broken her heart. I gotta do something to make this right, but I don't know what.

Janice: No mother could turn her back on someone as good as you, Robin. Take my advice and call her today. Tell her about this group and how it's gotten you to think about what's truly important in life. Tell her you love her and that you're sorry about the past. Ask her if she'd be willing to join you in making a new start. That's what I'd do.

You know what? I never finished my check-in. I was going to say that I really liked reading the homework. And I would like to ask our guest if he has any ideas on how I could make sure I won't die, like my husband Albert, in a hospital hooked up to a bunch of machines.

Clare: I just want to say how pretty you look, Jan. And, Robin, Jan's right. Reach out to your mother right away. You'll have no peace until you do.

I've spent most of my days in bed this past week. Charley finally admitted that it was time to call in hospice. That was a big step. Boy, am I glad that I took care of this when I did.

I think I told you that I started interviewing for the right hospice, months ago when I feeling much better than I am now. I wanted to be sure that the hospice I chose would be of the same mind as me about end-of-life care.

Of course my family scoffed back then. 'Shouldn't you be concentrating on living and getting better instead of dying?'

Now everyone's glad that I took care of this when I did. It was hard work interviewing the various hospices in the city. I know I wouldn't have the energy to do all of that now. Once I made my choice I got to meet some of the nurses and social workers. They were all very nice. It's important to me that I feel comfortable with the people who will be caring for me at the end.

After I completed all the necessary paperwork and coordinated it all with my oncologist's office, the only thing left to do was place the call to begin the service. And we did that on Monday.

I have a question regarding last week's homework that maybe you could help me with, Dr. Friedman. I have to combat my family, particularly my daughters, about eating. It says here in the pamphlet that Richard gave us that, "As your body prepares to die it needs less and less fuel. It is perfectly natural that your consumption of food will decrease and eventually stop." It goes on to say that, "This is a very difficult concept for those who survive you to grasp. They will want you to eat, reasoning that eating will help you maintain your strength."

Well, that's it in a nutshell, isn't it? I have no appetite. In fact, the smell of food cooking makes me nauseous. But every day there is a battle of the wills. 'Mother, you need to eat. Can't you see that you're just wasting away?' 'Thank you dear, but I just couldn't.' 'Try a little something. How about a little soup or maybe some pudding or Jell-O? I can make you Jell-O. You like Jell-O. Eat some for me.' And so on and so on and so on until they wear me down. Finally, I relent and have some of whatever they're pushing that day and I get sick afterwards.

All my resolve to stand my ground gets worn away. I haven't the strength to resist anymore. I'm embarrassed to say that sometimes it feels like abuse. I know they mean well, but it hurts, and I can't seem to make them see how it is for me. I hope we'll be able to touch on this a bit during our discussion.

Mia: I've been thinking about doing the same thing you did, Clare. I like the idea of interviewing for just the right hospice. I don't want just anyone attending me at the end. With a little luck I won't need hospice for a long time, but it's probably better to be prepared just in case it's sooner rather than later.

I was trying to put my finger on what it was about last week's homework that was so, how shall I say this, challenging. I did. I found it challenging.

One thing for sure, I never read anything quite like this before. But after thinking about it for a while, I began to wonder why I hadn't ever read such a thing? Why isn't there more of this kind of reading material available? I mean, why does everything associated with death have to be such a big mystery?

I'm sure that not knowing what to expect as one's body closes down only make matters worse.

But it wasn't just that the pamphlet was so explicit. I've come to expect that kind of thing in this group. There was something else too. I had to read over the homework a half a dozen times

before it dawned on me. I realized that the pamphlet was written as if it was addressed directly to me, the dying person. I mean, it couldn't have been more personal if the pamphlet began, "Dear Mia."

At first I didn't know how to respond. Did I really want to know everything there is to know about the mechanics of dying? Then I thought to myself, 'hey, wait a minute, are you pretending that if you keep yourself purposely uninformed about all this it won't happen to you?' You talk about the proverbial ostrich with its head in the sand.

As I said, reading the homework was challenging, but I'm real glad I have it.

Richard: I researched dozens of sources and spoke with numerous doctors and nurses before writing the pamphlet. Each source had pretty much the same information. I mean, it's not like there's a great deal of disagreement about what happens to a body as it closes down. It's all pretty straightforward. One or more of the body's major systems – respiratory, circulatory, renal, etc. – fails, and this triggers a shutdown of the entire system.

There also seems to be a general agreement about the signs of approaching death and what these physical manifestations mean in terms of the dying process.

So you're probably asking yourself, if everything is as cut and dried as you say, why did I bother to write a new presentation? Good question, and the answer is real simple. I wasn't satisfied with what was currently available.

The written materials fell into two distinct categories, the overly technical ones and the popularized versions written for a lay audience. And neither have as their intended audience the people who need this information the most, people who are dying.

I hear the same complaints over and over again. 'Why can't I get a straight answer about what will happen to my body as I die? It's the same old conspiracy of silence. Can't they see that this vacuum of information only adds to my anxiety level?'

Besides, I firmly believe that dying people need to take the lead in all of this. If dying people have access to clear, unambiguous information about the end of life, they will be better able to educate those who attend and survive them about what to expect as their life ebbs away. As it is now, it is more like the blind leading the blind, which only adds to the misery, confusion, and frustration.

Mia: Boy, isn't that the truth?

This really pisses me off. It does. It reminds me of the first time I was rushed to the hospital after I had my first episode of lung failure. I remember regaining consciousness in the emergency room. A team of doctors and nurses were frantically trying to save my life. A couple of days later, when the crisis was over, I tried to get a straight answer about my condition. You know, kind of get an idea of where I stood, or to be more precise, an idea where I lay. No one was willing to talk to me. It was amazing. I knew it had to be serious because I now had to use oxygen all the time, but I was being treated like a child. I was furious. I could have died right then and there and I would never have been afforded the opportunity to say good-bye to my parents.

Why do people think they have the right to rob someone of the opportunity to bring their life to closure with dignity?

I think this is one of the reasons that I have so little confidence in Western medicine. It is riddled with deception. Sorry, Dr. Friedman, I didn't mean to insult you. I sometimes get carried away. Maybe you could explain this kind of thinking to me, because I sure don't get it.

Raul: Yeah, why don't doctors say the truth? Maybe they think they're doin' us a favor by lyin' to us. That happens to me a lot too, Mia. I seen them whisperin' to my parents and then I see my mother cry. Shit, man, what do they think that I don't know?

So doc, you gonna be straight with me? I know that I'm dying and hey, it's okay. I mean, I've always been sick so who cares, right?

Anyhow, I wanna know how it's gonna be when I die. Am I gonna be in a lotta pain, or what? I mean, I can do it. I can put up with it if I know it's comin'. But I gotta know because the pain can be real bitchin', man and I gotta psych myself out for it.

Then I wanna know, how long is it gonna take to die? I read what you gave us to read last week and I thought it was cool, but I still have all these questions.

Mike: Jeez, I can't tell you how much this stuff gives me the creeps. I don't even know if I want to know about all this.

I had a hard time getting through the homework, that's for sure. I kept seeing myself lying there dying. I suppose that's the whole idea, but it about drove me nuts.

At the same time, I confess to having a morbid curiosity about the dying process. It's true. I've secretly wondered about many of these very things.

I noticed one serious omission in last week's homework though. It didn't address the little matter of, let's see, how can I put this, losing control over one's bowels. You know I have a thing about this. The idea of, and you will excuse me for saying it like this, but the idea of shitting the bed when I die is just too much. I've heard this happens all the time. Is this true, Brian?

There was something else I wanted to talk about too, and I'll just come right out and say it. I'm afraid that I'll panic at the end. I don't want to die and I'm afraid that I'll go out kicking and screaming just like my old man.

I mean, all this stuff about turning inward and contemplating one's life at the end sounds real good, but I'm not sure I'll be able to be that calm. I want to have a dignified death, but my anxiety level skyrockets just thinking about this. I need help. Is there anything that can be done for a person like me?

Raymond: I have similar concerns. Do you think that it's just a guy thing, or what?

I've been fiercely independent all of my life. I know this sounds like a real macho thing, but surrendering control will be real difficult.

On the other hand, like you pointed out some weeks ago, Richard, a lot of this control stuff is an illusion. I mean, if I was in control as much as I think I am, I wouldn't be the size I am. I would have

the discipline I need to slim down so as not to endanger my health any further. I'm confused about all of this.

If only I could be more like Joann. She was a real inspiration. She seemed to be able to just let it happen, and I don't know if I'll be able to do that. I am still so sad that she's gone.

As I was going through some of Joann's papers, I found this quote from one of Joann's favorite writers, Anne Lamott. She must have copied it from somewhere and saved it for herself. Apparently she read it many times because the paper is quite worn. Would you like me to read it? It's not very long.

"I remind myself nearly every day of something that a doctor told me six months before my friend Pammy died. This was a doctor who always gave me straight answers. When I called on this particular night, I was hoping she could put a positive slant on some distressing developments. She couldn't, but she said something that changed my life. 'Watch her carefully right now,' she said, 'because she's teaching you how to live.'

I remind myself of this when I can't get any work done; to live as if I am dying, because the truth is that we are all terminal on this bus. To live as if we are dying gives us a chance to experience some real presence. Time is full for people who are dying in a conscious way, full in a way that life is for children. They spend big, round hours. So instead of staring miserably at the computer screen trying to will my way into having a breakthrough, I say to myself, 'Okay, hmmm, let's see. Dying tomorrow. What should I do today?' Then I can decide to read Wallace Stevens for the rest of the morning or go to the beach or just really participate in ordinary life… I would want to keep whatever I did simple, I think. And I would want to be present."

— Anne Lamott

Holly: That's amazing. I'd like to get a copy of that for myself, if you wouldn't mind.

What a coincidence. This is just what I wanted to talk about in my check-in today. After my breakthrough with Jean last week, I've noticed that I have a renewed interest in living. I don't mean just going through the motions. I've done too much of that already. I want to live. I want to be present for whatever life holds for me and for as long as it is available to me. It also means being aware of my limits. When I'm tired or in pain I need to acknowledge that and rest. I'm not real good at taking care of myself in this way, but that's going to improve.

Last week's homework really made me think. First, because it had such a personal feeling to it. Like Mia said, it felt as though it was written especially for me. I had no problem picturing myself at the end of life. I know how it feels. I came very close to being dead once already. I remember it being kind of nice. All my worries seemed to melt away. I was amazingly calm. I wasn't frightened at all, that is, until the pain kicked in. I was having such intense pain that I couldn't think of anything else. It was awful. It robbed me of all that serenity.

This gets me to what I wanted to talk with you about, Brian. I want to talk about pain management.

I was just reading in the paper the other day that a new study of cancer patients concluded that many are experiencing an unnecessary amount of pain. The study said that there is adequate pain medication available, but doctors are hesitant to prescribe it, and so patients often go without. What could they be thinking? I don't want this to happen to me again. Once was enough.

Is it that doctors don't know about pain medications or are they afraid to prescribe them for fear of overmedication or addiction? How do I know that my doctor knows her stuff? Is there such a thing as a pain control specialist?

Oh yeah, there's one more thing too. Is it possible to be pain free and not be so dopey that I can't be present? I would hate to have to choose between pain and consciousness, if you know what I mean.

Kevin: My week was completely fucked. I went to my doctor to find out how come I've been feeling rundown all the time. You know how I thought it was just a touch of the flu? Well, it's not the flu. After a battery of blood tests and x-rays that took most of last week, I was diagnosed with lymphoma.

Oh shit! I told myself I wasn't gonna cry.

Holly: Honey, you just let those tears out, you hear. Don't be holding them inside. They'll make you sick. Take it from me, I know about these things.

Kevin: Thanks, Holly. I mean, what was I expecting? Did I think that I was

gonna get off scot free? I guess I'm still in shock. I started chemotherapy on Friday and radiation will follow. This sucks.

I guess I never thought it was gonna happen to me, you know, after all these years of dodging the AIDS bullet.

My doctor says there's hope. 'This new chemo is working wonders,' he tells me. Sure, and I have some swampland in Louisiana for sale too.

I think I secretly knew all the time. I mean, the increasing fatigue, the fevers, night sweats and this rash are not symptoms of the flu. Even I knew that. But oh my God, lymphoma! The biopsy showed that I have a real aggressive strain so there's no time to lose.

Funny thing, I think my doctor was even more shocked than I was. We go way back together. Alan was Doug's doctor. We've been through a lot together.

I was real proud of myself though. Alan sat me down in his office for the big talk. It felt strangely like being called to the principal's office. There was a mixture of anticipation and dread. After he dropped the C-bomb, we both started to cry. I'm glad he cried with me. It made me feel less like a leper.

'So how much time do you think I have?' 'Jesus, Kevin, we haven't even started the protocols yet and already you're talking about dying. Are you giving up? Is that what you're doing?'

'Wait a minute, wait a minute, Alan, I asked a simple question about a prognosis. I am not a child. I have important decisions to make and either you be straight with me or I'll find someone who will. This is not the first time you've seen this, so I want you to speak from experience. And I'm offended that you interpreted my question in terms of giving up. You know me better than that. All I'm asking you to do is give it your best shot. I want a best and worst case scenario. This will be a whole lot easier if I can see it coming.'

'Okay, this is how I see it. Your biopsy shows an aggressive strain of lymphoma. There's a 50-50 chance that the chemo and radiation will wipe it out. You're young and otherwise healthy, so I'm counting on a full remission.'

'And if it's the other 50%? What then?'

'We should know more in a couple of months. If we're not successful with the therapies, I'd say you might have a year.'

I can tell you, no matter how well prepared you are for that moment, hearing those words spoken aloud changes everything. I sat there in a daze. It was as if my life was flashing before my eyes. I know that sounds really trite, but it's true.

You want to hear something funny? I also felt a sense of relief. I wouldn't dare say this anywhere but here, but I did. I'm not sure what I was relieved of, but the feeling was very distinct. It's like the worst was over. There was a calm for a minute that was so beautiful. It didn't last long, but I'm hoping that I'll be able to tap into it again as I need it. It was so beautiful.

Doug used to talk about something similar to this when he was dying, but I didn't get it. Maybe there's something to it. I wonder if anyone else ever felt that way?

I know I'm rambling, but there is just one more thing I want to say. On my way home from Alan's office, I was thinking to myself how lucky I am to have each of you in my life. I have a greater sense of confidence that I'll be able to face whatever comes my way because of what this group has taught me. I hope to beat this and I think I will, but if this is the beginning of the end, I know now that I'll be able to handle that too.

This is so weird, but do you remember just two weeks ago I was telling you about having dinner with a friend who asked me if I thought this group was working? How he asked if I went to my doctor and found out that I had six months to live, would I be able to handle it any better now that I was doing this group? Just two weeks ago I said that I couldn't say for sure. Today I'm sure. And the answer is, yes I can. Now I hope I can sustain this feeling for when things really get rough, as no doubt they will.

Richard: And you can count on us to be here for you to help you through whatever lies ahead.

I've had a very full week myself. And your check-in, Kevin, has reminded me of an interesting coincidence that happened this past week. I have two individuals in my therapy practice at the moment who have caused me to think about the remarkable similarities different stages of life present us. My two clients couldn't be more different from one another, but I found myself giving the same advice to each of them. Let me explain.

Virginia is 16 years old, the only daughter of good friends of mine. I've known Virginia all her life. In fact, I

baptized her when she was an infant. Virginia has always been a favorite of mine, a real sweet kid, but one would have never accused her of being particularly attractive. She was more the quiet and unassuming type, an excellent student and a voracious reader, but not pretty in the conventional sense of that word. So I was surprised to receive a call from her mother asking me if I could make myself available to have a little chat with her daughter. She was at her wits end with Jean.

Apparently Virginia's been having some emotional problems since she began puberty a couple of years ago. I was able to make time available to see her the very next day. It had been almost a whole year since we had spent any real time together.

When she showed up at my door I was completely astonished. 'Virginia, is that you?' 'Hi, Richard. Yeah, it's me. Are you surprised?' Surprised? More like flabbergasted.

The proverbial ugly duckling had become a beautiful swan. But as it turned out, that was the problem. Virginia was completely unprepared for her radical transformation. The hormones raging through her body are triggering all manner of upset. 'What's happening to me, Richard? I don't know what's happening to me.'

We talked for a while about the natural process of puberty and Virginia confessed that she was having mixed emotions about growing up. 'There's some good stuff like, ya know, boys are like finally noticing that I'm alive, but it's all so confusing. I know that I'm driving my family crazy, but I just can't help it.

My mother bought me one of those tee shirts the other day, the one that says "Next Mood Swing in 20 Minutes." She's right. I want it to stop. I'm way over this, but I'm powerless. I wish things could go back to the way they were.'

Poor thing, she was on the verge of tears throughout our entire conversation.

'Listen, Jean, here's how I see it. Puberty is going to have its way with you, like it or not. There's no turning back the clock. You simply haven't got an option on this one. However, that does not mean that you're powerless. On the contrary, it's completely up to you how you will respond to the changes happening in your body. You have the option of embracing them, learning their lessons and maturing with grace and dignity, or you can choose to resist while puberty drags you, kicking and screaming, into adulthood. It's completely up to you.

And ya know what else I think? I think it's probably a good thing that you learn how to do this now, when you are young, because you will be asked to relinquish your youth and beauty someday to the aging process and you'll be expected to do that with grace and dignity too.'

Joseph, my other client, is 56 years old and is in, as he says, the prime of his life, but has just been diagnosed with an inoperable brain tumor. The medication he takes to keep the swelling down in his head has completely destabilized him. He's furious over the fact that he will die soon.

'Why is this happening to me, Richard? Am I being punished for something?' It was as if Joseph and I were having the same conversation I had with Virginia a couple of days before.

'You haven't been singled out, everyone will die. How and when one dies, it is merely the luck of the draw.'

'If only God would reverse this, I'd do anything he wanted.' He pounded his legs in frustration and his eyes brimmed with tears. 'This is so unfair. Why can't everything go back to the way it was?'

'Listen, Joseph, it looks like the cancer is going to have its way with you, like it or not. There's no turning back the clock. You simply haven't got an option on this one. However, that doesn't mean that you're powerless. On the contrary, it's completely up to you how will you respond to what is happening in your body. Will you embrace your mortality, learn its lessons and die with grace and dignity, or will it take you out kicking and screaming?'

The similarities between the two conversations were uncanny. Here were two different people in completely different circumstances. Both were experiencing the same emotional turmoil over similar, naturally occurring, and irreversible conditions of life. Life is leading both Virginia and Joseph into new, uncharted territory for each of them and I have no idea how they will respond to the challenge. Both, I believe, will make peace with their lot in life in their own way and on their own terms. I'm just real glad that I was able to be with them as they faced the future.

My Check-In

Richard: Take all the time and space you need for your check-in. This week I'd like you to include your own end-of-life concerns. Begin by responding to last week's homework.

_____

_____

_____

_____

_____

_____

_____

_____

_____

Group Process

Richard: Brian, it's all yours. Would you take a few minutes to introduce yourself, and then you could direct us in our discussion.

Brian: Hello, my name is Brian Friedman. I'm the director of the Emergency Department of Davies Medical Center here in San Francisco. My training is in Family and Community Medicine and I had a private practice for a number of years prior to my decision to specialize in Emergency medicine. As you can imagine, I've had plenty of experience with death and dying in my career and so it was an interesting coincidence when I met Richard at the gym one day and he told me about PARADIGM.

What was so fascinating about our chance meeting was that despite our different backgrounds and training, both Richard and I had come to the same conclusion about dying in America. Simply put, it's often deplorable for many, many people.

For example, there is nowhere near the attention paid to those exiting this world as is afforded those entering it, and yet both are critical moments in the life of each individual.

I asked Richard to send me more information about his project and after looking over the material, I concluded that the concept was sound and that I wanted to join forces with PARADIGM in one fashion or another. So I agreed to serve on the Advisory Board and we've had this happy association ever since.

It's always a great pleasure to address a group like this because this kind of interaction is precisely what medicine is all about. It's the human dimension of being a physician that makes this work so rewarding.

Unfortunately, that sometimes gets lost in our overly mechanized health care delivery system. Don't get me wrong, I'm all in favor of the advances modern medicine has made over the years. It's just that sometimes the relentless march of progress actually interferes with the essential person-to-person element that makes medicine not only a science but also an art form.

Okay, let's make this happen.

I was really impressed by your check-in statements. It's clear to me that you guys have really done your homework. Allow me to refer to my notes here a bit and I'll see if I can respond to each of the thoughtful issues you've raised.

I'd like to start with you, Jan, because your questions get right to the heart of what we're talking about. By the way, I really like your hairstyle. It's very attractive.

Janice: Why, thank you, doctor. How nice of you to comment.

As you know, I'm concerned about dying in the same way my husband died, in a coma in the hospital and on life support.

Brian: As far as I can see, this is entirely avoidable, but a patient must be prepared for this possible scenario. That's where advance directives, like the Durable Power of Attorney for Health Care, come in.

You've all been through the presentation on legal concerns so I'm sure you already know a lot about these important documents. You may have even completed one yourself.

Well, this is your first line of defense against anything happening to you in the health care system that would contradict your wishes. Advance directives like the Durable Power and the Do Not Resuscitate Order are becomingly increasing popular tools for patients to communicate their wishes about end-of-life care to their care providers.

You can tailor these documents to fit your specific needs, so if you don't want any artificial means keeping you alive, you can spell that out.

In the same way, if there are particular medical procedures that you would like under specific conditions, you need to make those things clear too. For example, if I'm involved in an accident and brought to the emergency room, I may want a more aggressive medical intervention than if I arrive at the hospital as a terminally ill patient.

Years ago people had to fight for the authority to participate in their health care decisions. Now, at least in California, hospitals are required to ask each incoming patient if they have any advance directives. And if the answer is no, the patient is invited to speak with the hospital social worker so she or he can receive further information on them.

The second line of defense in my estimation is hospice care. As you know, hospice is a specific philosophy about end-of-life care. It differs from, let's say a hospital, in as much as it is focused exclusively on palliative comfort care and not on diagnostics or treatments.

Hospice is the perfect choice for someone in the final stages of his or her life, which by definition means a prognosis of six months to a year.

However, before the need for hospice arises there may be a great deal of gray area that needs to be addressed. For example, I may want certain diagnostic tests if my condition is considered reversible, but not if it would only postpone the inevitable. That's why I suggest that one cover all his or her bases beginning with the advance directives right through hospice care.

Robin: I have issues that revolve around being in control of my dying. I mean, I know everybody has these issues to one degree or another, but I'm trying to look at the whole picture. I want to have an active role in every aspect of my dying from setting up the environment to possibly even choosing assisted dying. Have you any thought about that, Brian?

Brian: As I was saying to Janice, advance preparation is key. It's no good waiting for a crisis to occur.

There are lots of things you could do beyond completing the advance directives I just spoke about. I would suggest that you begin by trying to script out a few possible end-stage scenarios, like if I should happen to become bedridden; this is how I would like us to respond. Or if I'm having a great deal of pain, this is how I would like us to handle that.

Then of course you would need to communicate this to all those who will attend you, everyone from your doctors and hospice team to your friends and family. This takes a bit of coordination, but I think it's worth the effort.

You mentioned something interesting in your check-in that I'd like to comment on. You said you were just beginning to realize how much you need your mother and that you didn't think you'd be able to die well estranged from your parents. What an important insight. And it ties in nicely with what we've been talking about.

I think that managing one's dying environment is a very important component to dying well. And I don't mean just arranging the furniture.

Few people give much thought to who will be on the scene in their dying days. And yet a miscalculation in this area can cause a great deal of disruption.

It's been my experience that people facing imminent death often jettison the social graces that would otherwise hold sway in their life. I've seen dying people change their priorities on a dime. What would have been a tolerable situation when one was well suddenly becomes intolerable as they are dying. The stereotype of the long-suffering dying person indulging all manner of craziness from those who will survive him or her is just that, a stereotype.

More and more people are discovering that if they want to die in peace, they will have to carve out a peaceful environment for themselves, and that may mean restricting access to friends and even family members whose behaviors are disruptive.

Richard: That's been my experience as well. That's why I wrote what I did in the pamphlet I gave you for last week's homework. "Remember you are in charge of your dying environment. The anxiety of those who attend you, if left unchecked, can disturb your sense of well-being and cost you the serenity you seek."

Some people haven't the personal strength to monitor their environment and so it's important that they delegate this task to someone who will be able to maintain the kind of environment they desire.

For example, I always think it's a good idea to delegate someone to answer the phone, someone who will take messages for you instead of automatically handing the phone to you. Screening calls in this manner will afford you the opportunity to decide if and when you would like to return the call. This person may also need to run interference for you with troublesome or disruptive individuals who may wish to visit. 'I'm sorry, Richard is unable to receive visitors at this time. May I call you when he's feeling a little better? I'll be sure to tell Richard of your call and your concern.'

Clare: What an excellent idea. I hadn't thought of that. I've been feeling obligated to answer each and every phone call and to see each visitor even if I don't much feel up to it, and at times it's been very difficult for me.

I'm afraid that I may even have to limit access to some of my children, because even though I love them dearly, they can be very disruptive.

Dear Lord, I hope they'll understand and not hold this against me.

I have only to remind you of the concern I raised in my check-in to make my point. My well-meaning daughters are forcing me to eat when I have neither the desire for food nor the capacity to digest it. Have you any suggestions on how I might be able to handle this situation, Brian?

Brian: You raise a very delicate issue, Clare, especially for families who have traditionally expressed their love for one another with food. Your daughters are probably feeling helpless and frustrated and I wouldn't be a bit surprised if your children are actually redoubling their efforts to get you to eat, thinking as they must that this will be good for you. I'm sure that they simply don't know how else to respond. I think that it's probably the only way they know how to cope.

The only remedy for this is to educate your family about the need for nutrition at the end of life. I suggest that you give them Richard's pamphlet to read.

Highlight the section about eating and request that they honor your wishes in this regard. If this fails, you may need to have your hospice team run interference for you with them. Request your hospice social worker or nurse to have a talk with your family. Sometimes the added weight of a professional opinion will carry the day.

There is one other point I'd like to make on this topic. While solid food consumption may not be necessary and can even be detrimental in the last weeks of life, hydration on the other hand is essential because dehydration is a very painful, weakening and debilitating condition.

So you may find that this is an area where you could make a happy compromise with your family. You could ask them to always make sure there are a variety of liquids available for you to consume, as you desire them. Chilled water, warm broth, ice chips, Popsicles and the like all fit the bill. Just be aware that frequent sips of one thing or another are more beneficial than a full glass or bowl of something at any given time.

Mia: Can I change the subject?

As I said in my check-in, I have an overpowering fear that my dying days will be a nightmare of distress over being able to find my next breath. Is there anything that you can tell me that would diminish my fears?

Brian: Yes. I would first want to try to get a handle on how much of the distress you report is associated with a panic attack and how much has to do with your worsening lung condition. I realize this may sound suspiciously like the proverbial chicken or the egg question, but I would want to know if you are having difficulty breathing because of your panic, or are you panicked because you are unable to breathe.

Deciphering this puzzle will be the first step in finding the appropriate intervention you'll need at the end of your life.

When the human body is starving for oxygen, the normal response is anxiety. Everyone has experienced this in one form or another. Just imagine having that split-second anxiety associated with, let's say, staying under water a bit too long last for minutes or even hours.

Mia: Tell me about it. That's just how it is for me even now. So you understand my concern.

Brian: I do, and that's why we need to investigate this further. In your dying days you will find that your mobile oxygen unit will continue to help alleviate some of your distress.

On top of that there is an array of anti-anxiety drugs, not pain medications necessarily, but specific drugs to block out the adrenaline surges that cause the panic. I suggest that you begin to review, with your doctor, all the current pharmaceutical options available to you. Because if you discover what works for you now, you'll have more peace of mind knowing you've already determined the best solution to your problem later.

Richard: Mia also brought up another interesting concern in her check-in. It's a perception that many people have about the health care industry in general and their doctors in particular. It's the patronizing and even paternalizing we sometimes encounter when we interact with our health care providers. Can you speak to this and maybe give us a couple of pointers on how we could address this if we encounter it?

Brian: Doctors are human first and medical professionals second. All the psychological foibles inherent in the human condition can also be at play in the psychology of any particular doctor. This is not an apology, just a statement of fact.

One thing I can say for sure is that every doctor begins his or her career with the intent of healing people, saving people's lives, and if they err, it is generally on the side of doing too much rather than too little. Therefore, it shouldn't come as a great surprise that most doctors interpret death as a defeat in one sense or another. After all, they are only reflecting the prevailing sentiment of the culture. One need only look at the obituary page of any newspaper for confirmation of this fact.

I'm always reading things like: 'She lost her battle with cancer.' What kind of message is being conveyed there? Who among us wants to be seen as a loser? And what doctor wants to be seen as the one responsible for that defeat?

Now if you are finding that you've come to an impasse with your doctor, that you are no longer seeing eye-to-eye about a treatment protocol or end-of-life issues, I believe it is vital that you speak your mind.

This is a particularly vexing dilemma for elders and seniors, because they can remember a time when it was never appropriate to question the judgment of one's physician. Luckily those days are over, and even though some doctors still behave in an authoritarian manner, they are in the minority. Most of the doctors I know invite their patients to be forthcoming about the issues that concern them and engage them in that manner.

Mia: If I'm having a problem with my physician, how do I go about talking to her about it? If I feel as though my doctor is treating me like a child, how do I confront her about this without making matters worse?

Brian: Like all interpersonal relationships, skillful communication is the key. And perhaps the best way one can become adept at this is to begin by jotting down your thoughts so that at your next appointment you will bring up your concerns in a confident, adult manner.

Or you might try writing your doctor a letter outlining your concerns. You could then present the letter to her at your next appointment.

Or if you're not particularly confident about your writing skills, you might want to ask a friend, family member, or the person you've selected to be your durable power to join you at your next consultation. This person could serve as your advocate and help facilitate a clearing of the air.

No doctor I know wants to be at odds with his or her patients. Good medicine is dependent on a healthy, interactive relationship between patient and doctor. If your relationship with your doctor isn't like this, then there's work to be done or a new relationship with another doctor needs to be established.

Raul: Like I was sayin' when we started today, I want some straight answers about how it's gonna be for me when I die. How long is it gonna take? If there's gonna be a lot a pain, I need to know upfront so I can psych myself out, know what I mean?

Brian: I'm not familiar with the particulars of your personal medical history but I can say with some confidence that if the cause of your death is kidney failure, you're in luck. A uremic coma is a very peaceful, relatively painless way to die. If I had a choice for my own dying, this is what I'd choose.

When one's kidneys fail, there is a slow build-up of toxins in the body that over time, a week at most, will lull you into a stupor, which then becomes a uremic coma. Death comes swiftly thereafter.

Raul: So like you're saying you think it'll be okay? That's cool. How long do you think it'll take, like if I quit dialysis tomorrow?

Brian: If you're in total renal failure, I'd suspect that you'd be dead in a manner of days, certainly within a week. You'll simply lose consciousness and die.

Mike: Lucky break for you, Raul. I mean, not that you should die or anything, but kidney failure sounds, you know, like an okay way to go.

Jesus, what the hell am I saying? This is so crazy. This is my eighth week in this program and I'm still flabbergasted at what I find coming out of my mouth while I'm here.

I don't know. I mean, I appreciate all the straight talk, but I just can't figure out how I feel about it. There's this whiplash thing going on in my head and it continues to keep me off balance. I gotta do something to clear my head.

Okay, okay! You want to know what's bothering me? Don't laugh but I have some, how shall I put this, control issues, if you know what I mean.

Brian: You're concerned that you will soil your bed as you die, right?

Mike: Well, yeah. I suppose you could put it that way.

Brian: No need to worry, Mike. You're laboring under one of the more common misconceptions about dying.

It's easy to see how a mythology like this gets started. It is true that a violent or traumatic death can and often does trigger a sudden relaxing of the muscles that regulate the voiding of bodily waste,

but it's not true in a more protracted death.

As we've already talked about, dying people don't consume all that much food and so waste production is practically nil.

My experience, interestingly enough, tells me that dying people are more apt to complain about the opposite concern. Many of the most commonly used pain medications have the unfortunate side effect of producing constipation. This is a much more real concern to dying people than loose bowels.

If I may, I'd like to address the other concern you raised in your check-in, Mike, the issue of not wanting to die as your father died, kicking and screaming. You said that you were afraid you might panic at the end and ruin everything.

On this point too you can ease your mind. It has been my experience that most dying people are too weak, too tired or too medicated to freak out as they die.

Think about it, Mike, the very fact that you are doing this group proves that you have a much better handle on dying than your father ever did. But if your concern lingers, you should know that there are now many effective anti-anxiety drugs available to treat panic attacks that were unavailable to your father.

Raymond: Thank you for that, Brian. I needed to hear that too. It's funny how these misconceptions arise out of nowhere and yet they can plague folks right to the end.

Brian: That's so true. But there is an antidote to these unsettling feelings. That quote you read from Anne Lamott sums it up. How did it go? Oh yes, 'To live as if we are dying gives us a chance to experience some real presence. Time is full for people who are dying in a conscious way, full in a way that life is for children.'

Holly: Brian, could you talk some about pain control? Is there such a thing as a pain management specialist that a patient could consult?

Oh yeah, one more thing. What's the difference between pain control and comfort care?

Brian: Let me start with your last question first. Yes, there is a difference

between pain control and comfort care. Comfort care is a specific type of pain management. Pain control, which simply means medicating the patient to a point where he or she feels no pain, is relatively easy. Comfort care, on the other hand, is considerably more challenging. It attempts to balance the other needs a patient might have with his or her need to be comfortable. And that's precisely where things get tricky.

Every patient defines the word comfort in a slightly different way. For example, one patient may have very little tolerance for pain. 'I want to be as pain free as possible even if it means being in a coma-like state.' While another patient may have different priorities. 'I want to be conscious and awake and I'm willing to tolerate some pain knowing that I will be able function clearly right up to the end.' So as you can see, different priorities call for different pain relief strategies.

Comfort care is an art form. It attempts to balance the amazing array of pain medications available today with an effort to accommodate the priorities of each patient. All of this takes exceptional skill. And while there are physicians who are more adept at handling end-of-life pain concerns than others, there's not really a clinical specialty per se.

There are palliative care *doctors*, but no pain-ologists in the same way as there are oncologists or cardiologists. But who knows, maybe some day this area of study will branch off as a clinical specialty all its own.

Actually, I think we're moving in that direction because there are more and more pain management centers springing up around the country. These centers employ an interdisciplinary approach to pain control and while they currently focus on chronic pain rather than end-of-life pain, I could see where in the future these two different pain issues could meld into one.

In the meantime, the key to unlocking good comfort care is communication. Begin by clearly stating your specific priorities to your physician or hospice team. This will ensure that you get the kind of pain management you want.

Remember that this is a collaborative effort that is dependent on your feedback. You must keep those who attend you informed on what's working and what's not.

Holly: Is this where the notion of self-administered pain relief comes in?

Brian: That's right. The PCA (Patient Controlled Analgesia) pump is an integral part of this strategy.

This device connects directly into your IV system. Your doctor sets a baseline dose of medication that is constantly and automatically being infused, so that you'll avoid the roller coaster effect that comes from massive doses of pain medication at less frequent intervals. The PCA pump allows you to increase the amount of medication you are receiving. So in the event that you are experiencing discomfort, you can self-administer an extra preset dose of medication by simply pressing a button. It's completely computerized with built-in parameters to safeguard against an accidental overdose. Many patients appreciate the sense of control this device offers them.

Richard: Perhaps this is an academic question, but is there any reason nowadays for someone to die in pain?

Brian: No, not unless they want to. There are plenty of different pain medications and even more pain relieving modalities available, so there is absolutely no reason for anyone to die in pain.

However, the particular needs or specific circumstances of a patient may demand a bit more creativity on the part of the physician in alleviating that individual's pain, but it can be done.

Kevin: That leaves me, I guess.

As I mentioned in my check-in, I just got some bad news. I have lymphoma. And I have a feeling I won't be able to tolerate the chemo and radiation very well, so that doesn't bode well for the future. But I'm trying to stay as upbeat as possible.

One thing I can tell you is that I plan to be proactive in my dying. I don't plan to hang around for the bitter end. I've already spoken to my doctor and he said that he wouldn't abandon me when the time comes.

I know we're going to talk more about assisted dying next week, but can I ask you for your thoughts on the matter?

I hope I'm not putting you on the spot here.

Brian: I don't mind talking to you about this at all, and I appreciate the sensitive way you asked your question.

Primarily there are legal constraints that keep physicians from being more involved in their patient's end-of-life choices than perhaps they would like to be. But the harsh reality is that any physician who is upfront and vocal about his or her efforts to assist patients to die will be consumed in the legal and political firestorm that will follow.

So the prudent physician maintains a very low profile in this regard. That's not to say that physicians aren't assisting their patients. They are, but they're doing so by nudging nature along, assisting the natural dying process of their terminally ill patients.

This is less of an ethical minefield for most doctors than assisting a patient to die who is not terminal, but who has a chronic debilitating disease that has robbed him or her of any quality of life. This would be considered assisted suicide, where the first instance would be assisted dying.

I know that to some this might sound like splitting hairs, but this is a very important distinction that must be made. An assisted suicide is by definition the altering of the course of the disease process by ending the life of a person. This is fundamentally different from a physician who is comfort-controlling symptoms in a terminally ill patient, because the death trajectory is not doctor induced. The doctor is just assisting the natural progression of the disease.

Doctors can and do assist patients in other ways too, by evaluating the risks involved in, let's say, taking a certain medication in the final stage of life that will unquestionably lead to death. Or helping a patient evaluate the risks involved in stopping a certain procedure like dialysis, when the outcome again will unquestionably be certain death. This is a legitimate role for a physician.

Kevin: It's been my experience that people who are dying die a better death knowing that they have their little stash of lethal medication squirreled away in their bedside drawer just in case. It's a control issue, plain and simple. It's like carrying an umbrella so it won't rain.

Brian: I certainly understand that psychology.

So if keeping a bottle of a possibly lethal dose of medication around the house for what we'll refer to as emergency use only, if that diminishes the anxiety of an actively dying person, then I'm all in favor of it. It's been my experience that these medications are rarely used to hasten death, but as you say, Kevin, the simple fact that they are there can make dying easier.

In the final analysis, if you are expecting your physician to aid you in your dying, either to consult with, to acquiesce in your decisions, or to be actively involved, you must communicate your wishes clearly and unambiguously.

I advise you not to imagine that your doctor can read your mind.

And if for some reason the channels of communication are blocked or muddled, as I was telling Mia, it's incumbent upon you to remedy this in some way or find another doctor you can talk to.

Health care, especially at the end of life, is best when it is a partnership. It is your right to collaborate fully in all aspects of your care if you so choose.

And on that note I'll say goodbye.

My Turn

Richard: How would you evaluate your relationships with your health care providers? Are you able to communicate your wishes to your doctors or hospice team? Are you an active partner in your health care? If not, what needs to change for these relationships to become collaborative?

_____

_____

_____

_____

_____

_____

_____

_____

_____

_____

Richard: Thanks, Brian, that was outstanding as usual.

Next week is our last presentation. It concerns the topic of assisted dying and I'll be leading that discussion myself.

As you know, this is a very controversial topic. We will naturally be considering the issue of physician aid in dying, but I hope to broaden our discussion to include all aspects of death midwifery.

I think you will be surprised to find that next week's topic includes much more than the idea of hastening one's death. We will be keeping this topic, like all the other topics we've discussed, open-ended and in a proper context – the context of enhancing life near death.

We'll be looking at a wide range of concerns, like designing our last weeks, days and hours, the power of forgiveness, and the art of giving and receiving blessings.

But before we close, I want to set you up with this week's homework. I've saved the most difficult exercise for last, but I think you're up to it. It's called: *Strategic Planning for the End Game.*

This exercise will provide you an opportunity to consider what your final six weeks of life might look like. It will help you bring together all the things you've learned these past weeks, but you'll also need to concern yourself with timing, pacing and prioritizing.

Are there any final questions or comments before we conclude?

Clare: I just want to tell you, Brian, what a joy it's been to have you with us today. I really appreciated your thoughtfulness and candor. I couldn't have asked for more. Thank you.

AT-HOME WORK

Week 8 — Strategic Planning for the End Game

You've just been given a six-week prognosis. You have only 6 weeks in which to bring your life to a close. Five of the six weeks you will be as you find yourself now. However, you need to keep in mind that your energy level will decrease each week, so plan accordingly.

The sixth week you will be confined to your bed. How will you use this time? What will your priorities be? What will you need to have in place for your ideal, managed, peaceful, good death?

Pay special attention to your last day. What will it be like? Who will be with you?

This exercise investigates the concepts of timing, pacing and prioritizing.

Week 1

_____

_____

_____

_____

Week 2

_____

_____

_____

_____

Week 3

_____

_____

_____

_____

Week 4

_____

_____

_____

Week 5

_____

_____

_____

Week 6

_____

_____

_____

Your Final Day

_____

_____

_____

> "**Boris:** You get used to the taste of death.
>
> **Alexi:** What does it taste like?
>
> **Boris:** Like liver."

Woody Allen, Love and Death

Chapter Nine

Week 9:
With a Little Help From My Friends

Checking In

Richard: Hey there! Welcome back. We're coming down to the wire here. I hope you can feel the momentum. Imagine, only one more week to go. Hard to believe isn't it?

Today we wind up our series of presentations with this week's topic: Assisted Dying. And as you know, I will be your guide.

But before we get to that, we've got our check-in to do.

This week I'd like you to review your responses to the *Strategic Planning for the End Game* exercise that you got for homework last week. Because this is such an important exercise, I want to give you as much time as you need before we move on to the presentation. So let's begin.

Who would like to be first?

Clare: I'd be happy to begin today, if that's all right.

I wish I had been given this exercise to do when I first began this group. I understand, of course, why that didn't happen, but it's too late for me now. I'm

sure I haven't six more weeks in me. I'd be surprised to find that I have more than two or three weeks left. I've been so tired these past days. This is the first time I've ventured out of my bedroom, let alone out of the house, since last week's session.

That's why I chuckled to myself when I read the instructions for the homework. It says here that only the last of the six weeks would I be confined to my bed. Well, that's not what's happening to me. I don't want to disrupt the process of the assignment, so I decided to use last week as if it were week 1 and go from there. So here is what I came up with.

Week 1. I haven't much energy left these days, but that's okay since most all my work is done now anyway. There's just a lot of time for dozing and dreaming.

Very little of the outside world is of interest to me anymore. Surprisingly, even news of my grandchildren no longer holds my interest.

I'm taking in very little food. My children and their families continue to visit on a regular basis. There is a lot of life in the house even as my life ebbs away. That's just the way I want it. My son Stan is helping me with my final correspondence. I'm writing letters of farewell to friends and relatives. I plan to do a couple each week.

Charley and I have our time together in the mornings. He's being a real trouper.

Week 2. Much the same as week one. I'm listening to music, especially Mozart, and I'm enjoying watching nature programming. Over the years Charley and I have made quite a collection of our favorite programs on DVD, now I can watch them when I want. It's important to me to stay connected to nature even though I'm no longer able to get out into it on my own.

I find I want a lot of quiet time these days. I probably sleep most of it away, but that's okay. I'm preparing a small memento for each of my friends in my PARADIGM group. This is our last week together and I want to thank them for their kindness.

Week 3. A tearful farewell to my fellow group members. I'm going to miss my new friends. I've asked young Raul from group to be with me as the time for my death approaches. I've become

very fond of him; he is like one of my own grandchildren.

There are a few phone calls I have yet to make, to neighbors mostly, thanking them for their friendship and many kindnesses. Charley helps me into the garden in the afternoon to sit a spell and listen to the birds and feel the sun on my head.

Week 4. I do one last review of my final paperwork and estate plan with my lawyer and my son Stan. They are sure we've taken care of everything. This gives me a great sense of relief. I won't think of this again. We've had to increase the pain medication and so I'm sleeping most of the day.

When I'm awake I find myself staring about my room looking at all the old familiar things that are there. I try to remember the history associated with some of the objects – an antique paperweight, a chest of drawers that belonged to my mother, a painting that Charlie and I bought shortly after we were married – so many fond memories.

Week 5. I want to spend an hour or so with each of my children and grandchildren over the next two weeks. I have something to say to each of them, a mother's final instructions, I guess.

I know this is difficult for them, but they'll just have to adjust. This is what life is all about.

When I am conscious, I watch all the life that continues around me with an air of detachment and bemusement. I still have a certain interest, but I'm no longer engaged. I continue to watch my nature programs and listen to music when I feel up to it.

Week 6. These are my last days. There is very little life force left in me.

I am away from here most of the time now. I'm not sure where it is I go, but it must be a nice place because I return anxiety free. I want Charley to be near me as much as possible. We look through some old photographs together. There are some smiles amid the tears. I am so thankful for my rich and full life. I wish I could spare him this.

Young Raul comes by for an hour. He tells me of his family and Father Diego. We wonder how the other group members are doing and then we say goodbye. Both of us know that we will be together again very soon.

My Final Day. I want to die in the morning, at dawn, when it's quiet and the day is just beginning. I want to slip away quietly. Actually, I think it will be more like not returning from one of my absences rather then slipping away.

The pull from the other side is much too hard to resist anymore. I belong there now, not here. When Charley awakes he will find me. He has instructions on what to do next. All he has to do is call the children and the hospice nurse. My daughters will wash and dress me in a fresh linen gown that I've set aside. The rest will take care of itself.

Raul: You went and told 'em about our secret plan. That's cool, I guess. Me and Clare made a promise to be with each other at the end. Even if she dies first, I know that she'll be there when I need her. She said she would and I believe her.

So do you wanna hear my thing? Okay, here goes.

Week 1. I want to party with my friends, go dancing. I don't dance but I like to watch. I want to go to some movies too.

Week 2. I want to go to Disneyland. I was only there once when I was a kid. I want to go on all the big rides this time.

Week 3. My mother has to make me her special mole. I want lots of ice cream too.

Week 4. Oh yeah, I better make sure that my will is done and everything.

Week 5. Go off dialysis, stop doin' all my medicine, except for pain.

Week 6. Things should go pretty fast. I want to say goodbye to my friends and brothers and sisters. I want to be at home in my bed.

My Final Day. I want lots of little candles burning, like they have in church. I want my mother to hold me and to sing to me. And I want my father to tell me a story about when he was a kid in Mexico. Father Diego has to be there too. Like it has to be all real peaceful. Then Clare, you come and get me, okay? And that's it.

Mia: Wow, this is so incredibly powerful.

I don't know what to say. I didn't take this exercise as seriously as I should have. I guess I was afraid of what I might uncover. I can't believe I'm such a coward. And of course this triggers my feelings of inadequacy.

I wonder why am I resisting this so much? I'm ashamed of myself, especially after hearing what you wrote, Clare. It was so poignant.

Anyhow, here's what I decided I would do. I would travel throughout Europe one last time for the first four of the six weeks. I would stay at the best hotels, eat at the best restaurants, and go to the most exclusive spas to be waited on hand and foot. Once I had indulged every hedonistic desire I could think of, I would return home completely spent.

Then I decided that I would need to repent for acting like the spoiled little rich girl, because that kind of self-indulgence really gags me.

Isn't this just like me to be full of ambivalence and contradictions even in my last days?

Damnit! This is all so very discouraging. I expected to be much farther along by this time. I feel like I failed.

Week 5. Leave my apartment. Give everything away to whoever wanted it. Empty my checking and savings accounts. Give all the money to charity. Get a room at the Zen Center, that is, if they'd have me.

Week 6. Meditation and chanting. Try to come to some kind of understanding about what this all means.

My Final Day. I would like my parents, grandparents and my boyfriend Troy to be with me on my last day.

That's it. That's all I could come up with.

Is this too lame, or what?

Richard: Darlin', what is your trip?

Why all of this negativity? Don't you find that self-defeating? If this is your idea of how you will make your exit, then own it. No need to editorialize or apologize, at least not for our sake. Right, gang?

I thought that what you came up with was totally in character. In fact, had you come up with something more like Clare's, I would have thought you were being dishonest.

You are who you are. You're not Clare. You have very powerful emotions, ambivalent and contradictory as they may be. It's your essence, your crucible. Deny them at your own peril. Besides, I find your honest personal struggle to be extraordinarily compelling and completely disarming.

Some people have the fantasy that at the end of their life everything is supposed to come together like a jigsaw puzzle, that all the little pieces will magically fall into place and there will be satisfaction all around. It simply doesn't happen that way. Sorry!

In more than thirty years of being present at hundreds of death scenes, not one was without the drama of conflicting emotions. Even the most saintly people have their share of ambivalence. I've come to chalk this up to being human which makes what we're trying to do here all the more remarkable.

So please, cut yourself some slack and just be your own wonderful, less-than-perfect self.

Kevin: Ditto to what Richard just said.

Mia, I thought your response to the exercise was right-on. Believe me, if I had your resources, I'd do the same damn thing. Fuck 'em if they can't take a joke. Know what I mean? What's that saying? 'Living well is the best revenge.' Go for it, girl! Maybe you do swing wildly from one extreme to the other, but there's an overall balance to it. That's what I admire, the balance. How many poor suckers will go to their graves without ever having lived? Like Auntie Mame said to Agnes Gooch, 'Live, Agnes, live! Life is a banquet, and most poor suckers are starving to death.'

I'm feeling like shit. This chemo is kicking my butt big time. I'm nauseous all the time and my hair is beginning to fall out. I was laying in bed yesterday, sick as a dog, thinking to myself, is all of this worth it? And my God, what if it gets worse? So I haven't been in the best of moods to be doing the homework, especially this assignment, and I think it shows in what I wrote.

I decided that everything will be dependent upon how I'm feeling. I should probably say upfront that I plan to be really proactive in my dying. I have stockpiled enough lethal medication to put myself away when the time comes. I don't plan to wait around for nature to take her own sweet time, I can tell you that. Anyway, I decided that the first couple of weeks I would travel back east to see friends and family. Unlike Princess Mia, I'll have to fly coach and stay in a Motel 6. (Everyone laughs.)

Week 3. I want to have a big party at the house while I'm still able to enjoy it. Everyone will be invited. It'll be sort of like a wake, only the corpse, me, will still be walking around. I never much liked the idea of folks having a big party after the guest of honor is six feet under.

Week 4. Time to get serious. I think I'd like to go on a retreat of some kind. I want to make sure that I'm clean with God. I mean, I think I am, but I just want to make sure. Because I don't wanna show up at the pearly gates and have the old man look at me like leftover doodoo.

Week 5. Just because I can, I'm gonna cheat death by one week. Now I realize that all of this is wild speculation, but if I actually could say with certainty that I had ten days left, I'd take my leave today. I guess I want to feel like I'm in charge. More about this when we have our discussion later on.

My Final Day. A last supper with Rich, Reggie and Derik, they're gonna be my angels. We've gone over everything – the cocktail, the pills, and the morphine. Each person knows his role. It will be an evening of sweet blues and cool jazz and, of course, John Coltrane.

For some reason I want to die sitting up and so that's how I've planned it. I want it simple and elegant, well, as simple and elegant as a death can be.

Janice: Robin and I worked on this exercise together. It's true what they say; two heads are better than one.

We started with the premise that our last six weeks of life started last week when you gave us the assignment. We decided that it would be easier to visualize the clock ticking down now as opposed to some vague time in the future. Besides, it was a good way to review what we've learned in this group.

Robin: That's right. We wanted to start with the most practical things first. So we started by going over that Final Affairs checklist that we put together as a group a few weeks ago. That was real helpful.

Janice: We both decided that six weeks is simply not enough time. (Everyone laughs.)

No, I mean it. Even if we only paid attention to the big things there was hardly any time to spare. For example:

Week 1. Find a lawyer to help me create a will and execute a Do Not Resuscitate Order. Make an inventory of household items, furniture, and the like. Make an inventory of personal possessions, jewelry, and the like.

Robin: Since both of us are without family, at least in the immediate area, and neither one of us is married, we would have to manage all of this on our own. This exercise really brought home to me what Jan's been saying all along. Dying alone would be a perfectly awful way to go.

Since both of us started about the same place, our first couple of weeks look remarkably similar.

Week 1. Get computer software needed to create a will and complete all advanced directives. Make a list of assets and liabilities. Make a list of immediate people to be notified at the time of my death. Have a garage sale.

Janice: Don't laugh. One of the things both Robin and I discovered doing this exercise is that each of us is too poor to die. (Everyone laughs.)

You think I'm kidding. Look, we talked about what each of us wanted with regards to the disposition of our remains. I want to be buried next to Albert, but even a cut-rate funeral service isn't cheap.

Robin: And I want to be cremated. But that too can be an expensive proposition. I checked around a little and found that there is a huge difference in prices for what appears to me to be the very same freakin' service.

Janice: Both of us want to die at home, or at least not in a hospital, so that would mean getting hospice involved.

Week 2. Find just the right hospice. Make a visit back home to see the few surviving relatives I have in Illinois.

Robin: Yeah, after all the talk last week about final stages, I want to make sure that I got that covered, so hospice it is.

Week 2. Set up hospice care. Take the bus back to Minnesota to see my parents.

Week 3. Work on putting together a memorial service. I don't want what happened to Bobby to happen to me.

I was thinking of borrowing a video camera from a friend so I could make a video that could be played after I die. It'll be cool, like talking from the grave. You don't think that's too dramatic, do you?

I was also thinking of selecting some music and reading for the service itself.

Jeez, this sounds pretty controlling, doesn't it? I can just hear my friends now, 'Leave it to Robin to dominate her own funeral.'

Shit, who cares? It's better than having it be a disaster like Bobby's.

Janice: I don't think it sounds controlling. I think your friends would appreciate all the care you've taken to help them through their grieving. I know I would.

Week 3. Take some quiet time for myself. Seek spiritual guidance. Call David Pettee for an appointment.

Robin: This is where Jan and I have a difference of opinion. I intend to end my life on my own terms and on my own schedule.

Janice: And I simply can't do that.

As long as I'm not in excruciating pain and I have adequate care and maybe a friend or two who will be with me, I'd just as soon let nature take its course.

Robin: Yeah, right. That's a mighty tall order, pain-free, adequate care and surrounded by friends. What's the likelihood of that happening?

I don't know, do you think I'm just being cynical? I mean, I look at my track record in life so far and think, sure, count on it. I always seem to come up short in the luck department, so I'd just as soon not take any chances and be prepared for every eventuality.

Janice: When Robin and I began talking about this the other day, I told her that I had very strong reservations about even discussing the topic of euthanasia. 'I don't feel comfortable talking about this. I just don't think it's right. What if they find a cure?'

Robin: Hey, I'm not planning on doing this tomorrow. I just think that terminally ill people should have the right to choose. That's all I'm saying.

We're gonna talk more about this later, right? Good, because I want to finish talking about my homework.

Week 4. Prepare to make final exit.

I've read up on how to do it. I'll need to get all the necessary medications somehow. I've even sent away for a book on making my own helium hood kit in the

event that I'll need it. I'd prefer to have someone help me, just in case there's a slip-up, but I'm determined to do it alone if I have to.

Janice: Robin has many very persuasive arguments. We talked long into the night about this. I told her that I'd be there for her and I'd help her if she needed me, but I'm not interested in that option for myself.

Week 4. Enjoy my music and my books on tape. Continue with my journal. I think I'd like to tape messages of farewell to a few friends back east. Oh, and I need to find a good home for my cat, Muffin.

Week 5. Go to the park one last time. I hope this is in the spring, because I would love to see the roses in bloom.

Week 6. Nothing left to do but die. I would want my last days to be quiet and serene.

My Final Day. I would like Robin to be with me as I die, and Muffin has to be there too. Maybe Robin could fix my hair one last time. I would want her to hold my hand to give me strength. I'd like her to read me some of my favorite poetry.

Oh yes, and I would like to have my room full of cut flowers. Wouldn't that be nice? Roses, mums and lilies, big sprays of them, how I do love flowers. And then I'll just close my eyes and be gone.

Robin: I'd just as soon not off myself, I'd prefer to slip away quietly, just like Jan, but I just don't see that happening.

In fact, this whole exercise is nothing more than a big fiction. These idyllic deathbed scenes are nothing like any I've ever seen. I don't want to sound like some old bitter cynic, but more likely than not, there'll be lots of pain, anxiety, disorientation, discomfort, distress and even dementia. If I get the option to short-circuit that, I will, so help me God.

My Final Day. I would eat a light lunch with a friend. Jan? (I'd want music playing, but haven't figured out what kind.) Take some Compazine. Swallow my 25 barbiturate caps slowly and methodically along with some brandy. If I'm alone, I'll use the plastic bag. If I have company, maybe that won't be necessary. If everything goes as planned and there are no problems, I'll be out of here in a matter of a few hours.

Mike: Is it my turn? That's what I thought. I just want to say from the onset that this was a very humbling experience for me. I was able to see the prospect of going with some dignity and grace for the first time. It was amazing. I tried to be attentive to what I know are my limits, because that's generally where things fall apart. When I overdo it, I get frustrated and angry and ruin the whole thing. Okay, here goes.

Week 1. I want to go to the Grand Canyon one last time. Maryanne and Kyle will go with me.

I don't travel very well anymore, but this is real important for me so maybe it would be doable. I figure Maryanne could drive the van and I could just relax. I just don't want it to turn into a fiasco. Sometimes I bite off more than I can chew and this always turns the whole mess into more of a problem than what it's worth. I don't want to do anything that is going to cause friction. I want my last weeks to be as trouble-free as possible.

Week 2. Clean up all the loose ends at the office. Make sure all legal and financial concerns are in order.

By necessity over the years, Maryanne has had to become more and more involved in the business end of our marriage. In fact, she probably knows more about many things than I do, but I want to make sure that when I die the transition will be flawless. So I want to go over the trust, insurance policies, financial records, that kind of stuff.

I have some private papers at the office that I'd like to clean up. Leaving the office for good will hurt. It's been such a big part of my life for so long.

Week 3. Make a video for my son.

Since I won't be around as he grows up and becomes a man, I thought I'd make a video of all the things I would want to tell him as he matured, simple everyday things that a father would tell his son. I'd teach him the secrets of shaving, the fine points of football, the art of romance, you know, the little secrets I've learned about women, that kind of stuff.

This would break my heart, but I want my son to remember me as a nice guy.

Week 4. Say goodbye to friends.

This is real important to me. I've got a load of friends that I would want to say goodbye to, but I'm not sure how I would go about doing this. I'm not much of a letter writer and an email or even a phone call seems so impersonal. I don't have enough time to have lunch with each one, so I'm stumped. Maybe I

should start doing this long before week 4. I guess I have some rearranging to do.

Week 5. This week is for Maryanne.

How do you make amends for years of being such a hard ass? How do you bring a marriage to a close? How do you say I love you in a way that will last forever?

I really do want her to get on with the rest of her life, but how do I tell her that? She's still young and beautiful, she should find herself another guy, but it has to be the right guy, someone who will treat her well. Not a lawyer... listen to me trying to control things. This is just what I don't want to have happen. She hates it when I do that. God, I hope I don't fuck this up.

Week 6. Have Father Joe over for a drink and the last rites.

I got stuff I need to get off my chest and I want to do this before I die. Father Joe is the only person I'd trust with my secrets. He's a good guy. We've been through a lot together. I just hope that the rest of the week goes by fast and that I won't be in too much pain.

My Final Day. I wanted to ask you, Richard, if you'd be there for me. I know you wouldn't let me get away with any shit. Besides, just seeing you there with Maryanne and Kyle would give me the courage I need to let go and, God knows, I'll need that.

Raymond: I need to say upfront that I am diametrically opposed to assisted suicide of any kind, including physician assistance. There's just too much room for abuse. I can't help but think about how things would be if we started eliminating the people we think are no longer productive. You could be sure that old and disabled people would be the first to get the ax.

These people are our most vulnerable and I would like to think most valuable citizens, but I'm afraid the tide of this culture's prejudice against age and infirmity would overwhelm them. It's such a slippery slope that I don't think we ought to venture out onto it.

That being said, I can move on to my homework.

I don't think I was particularly successful in projecting myself to the last six weeks of my life. I don't know why that is, exactly. I guess I just don't see the urgency or maybe, now that Joann is gone, I have no one to count on to be there for me and I can't face that.

I know this is a fool's paradise and this pretense won't help matters, but I just can't run out and get myself a new best friend. And everything from the legal implications of my dying to my last day depends upon having a best friend, at least it does for me.

Okay, this is what I came up with.

Week 1. Update will (or trust). Make sure all advance directives are executed and operative. Begin hospice.

Week 2. Finalize after-death care plans.

Week 3 through *Week 5.* Spend quality time with my children. Talk to them about my impending death.

Week 6. Marathon viewing of *I love Lucy* reruns. I'd prefer to die at home, but maybe it would be more realistic to assume that I will die in a hospice somewhere. See, I'm completely lost.

My Final Day. ????

It's not like I didn't try. I'm just real disoriented at the moment. All I can tell you is that I don't want to die alone.

Holly: I had just the opposite experience as you, Ray. I really got into the exercise. My problem was being realistic about what I could and couldn't do. So I decided that I would make a fantasy 6 weeks and a more realistic 6 weeks.

Week 1. In my fantasy I would travel to Europe for the first three weeks. I would do all the things that I've always wanted to do, which mostly would involve going to the Alps. I love the mountains, maybe because I'm from costal Georgia and we don't have mountains back home. Or because being in the mountains is as close as ya'll can get to being in heaven. I think I'd spend most of my time wondering about God, taking in all the clean fresh air, and purifying myself for the big day.

A more realistic scenario is that I spend a week at Tahoe. What the heck, a mountain is a mountain, right? Oh yeah, call hospice if it's not already in place.

Week 2. Review all end-of-life paperwork, trust and advance directives, and finalize after-death care plans. Close down my business.

Week 3. Go through personal effects. Prepare final gifts for friends. Farewell party with friends.

Week 4 through *Week 6.* Family time. Time for sitting in the garden and contemplating all the beauty.

My Final Day. Jean, Annie and the women from my church will be there. I wasn't sure what else I wanted to say about my last day. I kind of figure that if I have the people I love there with me, the rest will take care of itself.

Richard: I had a good week. An acquaintance of mine, actually a mutual friend of my good friend Kim, called me out of the blue last week. She asked me if I would be available to consult with her and her husband about his dying.

I didn't know Rebecca or James very well, but I was happy to accept their invitation. When I arrived at their home, I found James very close to death. The scene was calm and, at first glance, everything seemed to be in order, but the tranquility was deceptive.

Rebecca began by telling me that she thought something was wrong. 'What do you mean, wrong?'

'I don't know. I can't put my finger on it exactly. James has been actively dying for weeks. Why is it taking so long? We've prepared for the end in the best way that each of us knows how, both psychologically and physically. Everyone has been extremely helpful. Hospice has been wonderful. But we never thought it would turn out to be such a marathon. We've been waiting and waiting for what seems like forever for the end and it doesn't happen.'

'Don't misunderstand, I'm not impatient for James to die, but there's something unnerving about all of this that has us both on edge. It's like standing at the airport fully packed for a long trip waiting to board a flight that never arrives. It's been exhausting for the both of us. I can't help but think we've overlooked something. I've quizzed James about it, but he doesn't know what it could be either.'

'That's when Kim suggested we talk to you. We're both afraid that our impatience and anxiety is gonna disrupt the tranquility we've worked so hard to achieve. Can you help us?'

James confirmed what Rebecca told me. 'Look at me! There's nothing left that works, I can barely see anymore. It's pathetic. I should have been dead by now. Even my doctors are surprised that I'm lingering. I think I've been extremely patient so far, but this is ridiculous. I want this to be over, damnit. I don't know how much more of this I can take.'

There was a blockage, no doubt about it. I could feel it all around me. Had they overlooked something important? I thought I'd better try and find out.

'James, is there anything left undone? Did your restaurant sell?'

'Yeah, months ago. I'm satisfied that we've taken care of every last legal detail. I've even had two different lawyers sign off on the deal.'

'How about family? Any unfinished business there?'

'No, my parents are here, sisters and brothers have all been through here at one time or another. I'm feeling real good about all of my relationships.'

I was stumped. They appeared to have thought of everything. Nothing seemed out of place. So why did we all feel on edge? We sat quietly for a while and then I said, 'James, maybe it's something metaphysical.'

'You mean like God and heaven and that sort of thing?'

'Yeah, in a roundabout sort of way. I was just sitting here thinking about what would be on my mind if I were in your place, facing my imminent death. I suppose I would be thinking about immortality, not in any conventional sense of that word, but more in terms of my legacy. I guess I'm self-conscious enough or maybe it's vanity, I don't know, but I think I'd be wondering about my contribution to this wounded world.

Since I think about this a lot and I'm not sick, I'm sure that I'd be concerned about it as I lay dying. We're not such different people, you and I. Do you ever wonder about the impact you've had on your world? Is any of this even making any sense?'

Silence. Then tears pooled in his eyes.

'I've been a foodie all my life. I came to the Bay Area thirty years ago because it's the center of the food world. All the world's greatest cuisines come together here. It's the culinary Mecca. This town really appreciates the creativity and art involved in cooking. I've had the good fortune to work with the best chefs in the world and, in turn, they've shared my table. I was good. I was real good. And now that I'm dying, no one has asked me for my recipes. Was it all for nothing?'

We were stunned by what we were hearing. Rebecca spoke first.

'Sweetheart, your friends would never think to ask you for your recipes. They all secretly covet them, of course, but asking for them would be out of the question.

It would be kind of ghoulish, don't you think? Like vultures hovering, waiting to pick over a carcass. And you have to admit that you haven't been particularly forthcoming about any of this yourself.'

'Yeah, I know, but I'm dying. It's different now. It's my legacy, just like Richard said.'

Two days later a simple but elegant ritual had been prepared. Champagne was chilled, a couple of friends were called, and James directed Rebecca to fetch his treasure. Choking back tears of gratitude, he blessed us all.

'Thanks for making this such a great ride, you guys.'

As he said this, he handed each of us a computer disk, which held the booty. James entrusted us with his cookbook manuscript in the hopes that we would have it published after his death. He insisted that the title be: 'Food to Die For.' We promised that we would do our best and thanked him for his trust and friendship. I guess that took care of that, because seven hours later James was dead.

My Check-In

Richard: Take all the time and space you need for your check-in. And this week I'd like you to review your response to the *Strategic Planning for the End Game* exercise. Were there things mentioned by the other group members in their responses that you would like to include in yours?

_____

_____

_____

_____

_____

_____

_____

_____

_____

_____

_____

_____

Group Process

Richard: Good work, you guys, on a very difficult exercise. It was interesting to see how each of you dealt with the challenge of projecting yourself to your last weeks and days.

As is often the case, some of you had highly scripted scenarios while others had no more than a sketch of what that timeframe might look like. Interestingly enough, there was one common denominator in each of your responses. Did you notice what it was?

No one wanted to die alone.

This doesn't come as a big surprise. Most everyone expresses a desire to have company in their dying days. And given the option, most everyone would prefer the company of friends and family to that of strangers. Very few of us have the personal strength to walk this unfamiliar territory alone. We're social beings, after all, and there's nothing about dying that changes that.

I'd like you to keep this in mind as we begin today's discussion on assisted dying, because it's this social dimension of the dying process that gives us the best context for understanding this delicate issue.

I believe that we should keep our discussion as open-ended as possible so we're not tempted to reduce the whole affair to the single issue of assisted suicide, because that will do nothing but polarize the debate.

A case in point – I thought it curious, Ray, that you took the time to mention in your check-in that you are opposed to assisted suicide of any kind, including physician assisted suicide. Is that all you thought we were gonna talk about?

Raymond: Well, yeah, that's exactly what I thought. Isn't that what assisted dying means?

Richard: Nope, not the way I understand it.

It's true, acting to hasten death in the final stages of a terminal illness falls under the general heading of assisted dying, but I don't think it defines the concept. In fact, I believe that reducing the concept of assisted dying to a single issue would be a mistake for two reasons. First and foremost, it discounts all the other more common modes of assistance regularly being given to dying people across the board.

And second, this more extraordinary form of assistance is relatively uncommon. So you can see why I'm so adamant about keeping the discussion inclusive. It just wouldn't be balanced otherwise.

Besides, dealing with the issue of proactive dying can become sensationalized, distorted, and even freakish if this option is not presented as an integral part of the entire spectrum of end of life care.

A really good metaphor for what I'm talking about is the midwife. Like a birth midwife, a death midwife assists and attends in a myriad of ways. A midwife is the one who is most present and available to the dying person, the one who listens, comforts, and consoles.

But a midwife may also bring an array of other basic skills, like expertise in the care of the body such as bathing, waste control, adjusting the person's position in bed, changing the bedclothes, mopping the brow, or keeping the person's eyes and mouth lubricated.

A midwife may also be proficient in holistic pain management and comfort care such as massage, breath work, visualization, aromatherapy, relaxation, and meditation.

A midwife may take responsibility for maintaining a tranquil and pleasing dying environment. Often this means arranging the person's home or room, not only in terms of the practical considerations, but also in terms of the aesthetic as well. This may include arranging flowers and art, reading aloud or playing music softly.

A death midwife, like a birth midwife takes the lead role in the caring for and comforting the one who is dying. Without this kind of compassionate presence, few people would have the opportunity to achieve a good death.

*K*evin: That's all fine and good, but I was hoping that we were gonna talk about, you know, the more proactive aspects of assisted dying. I mean, I know I'm gonna want help in bringing my life to a close when the time comes and no amount of breathing exercises and adjusting pillows is gonna cut it. Am I making myself clear?

Richard: I understand what you are saying. You want some practical advice on how to end your life if the need arises. I can assure you that we'll be getting to that in a minute. I just wanted to make sure that we all appreciate the context of our discussion.

Clare: I'm glad that you're taking the time to help us frame the debate in this way, Richard, because I'm confused. I have the same reservations as Ray, but now I'm not sure my concerns are warranted. Maybe I need more time to figure out what it is we're talking about when you say, 'proactive dying.' Is it euthanasia, assisted suicide, self-deliverance, what? And why so many different terms?

Richard: You make a very good point, Clare.

Unfortunately, there is no agreement, even among experts, about a common vocabulary for this debate. And thus the public discourse often generates a whole lot more heat than light. And the topic of proactive dying will continue to be a hot-button issue until we can come to a consensus about the parameters of the debate, and that seems like a long way off.

Personally, I have trouble with each of the three terms you mentioned. Euthanasia is much too technical. Did you know that at one time this word meant an easy, good death? Now, unfortunately, it is defined as mercy killing, a classic example of how language can be corrupted.

I also try to avoid using the term 'assisted suicide' when talking about someone hastening his or her death in the final stages of a terminal illness. The word suicide is inappropriate in this instance, because suicide usually denotes a desperate cry for help, which is rarely if ever the case for those facing the imminent end of life.

I don't much like the term self-deliverance either. It's just one of those vague, contemporary euphemisms that does nothing to clear the air. In fact, when polled, most people haven't a clue about what self-deliverance means. I prefer the simpler, more straightforward terms 'proactive dying' or 'aid in dying.'

Maybe this would be a good time for us to stop and assess what expectations each of you has about the direction of this discussion.

Mike: I'm open to talking about the whole spectrum of ideas, because I haven't really formed an opinion about any of this yet. And I think you're right, Richard, to suggest that we ought to begin with a mutually agreed upon vocabulary. It would be too confusing otherwise. We started this discussion using the term assisted dying, so I vote that we stick with that.

Robin: I second that. I know that this is controversial and all, but like Kevin, I hope that we're not gonna wimp out and sidestep the big issue of a person's right to choose. I want to get a handle on the practical considerations should I ever want to end my life on my own terms.

I hope no one thinks that just because I want to talk about proactive dying that I'm advocating for it.

Janice: I'm having a hard time with this too. I mean, it's all so confusing and there are so many subtleties to consider. I guess I'd have to say that I'm not particularly comfortable with the notion of assisted suicide or, as you call it, aid in dying. But I wonder if I'd feel differently if I were in unbearable pain.

And what about a situation like my poor Albert? I was the one who had to beg the doctors to take him off life support. I just couldn't bear to see him like that. So I suppose, technically speaking, that was assisting Albert to die.

Where do we draw the line between what is acceptable and what isn't? And who is going to make that determination? I have more questions than I have answers.

Raul: Yeah, that's right. Who's supposed to decide all of this? I mean, shit man, what if somebody was to say to me I couldn't stop doin' dialysis when I want to quit? Ain't that my decision? Now that I kinda got my family seein' things right, I don't wanna go through all this crap again with somebody who don't give a shit about me. No way!

Mia: I agree with Raul. I think the choice should remain with the dying person.

Raymond: But Mia, what if the dying person is just depressed?

Mia: You say that like depression was some minor complication that, quick as a wink, could be remedied.

Listen, Ray, I know from my own experience that psychological or emotional anguish is often more debilitating than any physical pain. Let's face it, managing serious and chronic pain is as difficult as managing serious and chronic depression.

And there's another thing too. The first couple of weeks after I got out of the hospital after nearly dying, when I finally realized I'd never be able to resume my previous lifestyle, I was pretty wrecked. My Western doctors wanted to put me on an antidepressant. Just like them to push pills at a problem that they simply didn't understand.

I wasn't depressed, I was grieving. I know the difference. These are two very different things.

I can't see the logic in medicating a grieving person like there was something wrong with her. And yet it happens all the time. You go to the doctor with symptoms of profound grief and you get an antidepressant. We need to walk through our grief, not medicate it and shove it under the carpet like it wasn't there.

Wow! Where did all that come from? I guess I have stronger feelings about this than I thought. All I really wanted to say in response to your question, Ray, is that the depression argument is a red herring from my point of view. Let's just say someone is depressed because his or her life is over, then what?

I just hate all the condescension.

Clare: I'd have to agree with you about how most doctors respond to death. Very few of the ones I've ever had the pleasure of knowing handled it very well. They acted as if death were some personal affront. I've even heard a doctor say that she had failed because one of her very senior patients died.

I remember what Doctor Friedman said about doctors last week. Most perceive death as the enemy. I worry that any discussion about proactive dying that begins from that kind of starting point will end in an impasse. Sometimes I wonder if doctors and their dying patients aren't talking past each other on this.

Kevin: I'm so glad that I have the doctor that I do. Alan is different from most. He even told me once when Doug was dying that seeing as much death as he had made him rethink all that death-as-failure bullshit.

When I told you about the talk I had with Alan after he gave me my lymphoma diagnosis a couple of weeks ago, I didn't mention the part of the conversation where he said he'd help me kick off when the time came.

I began that part of our conversation in a real matter of fact way. He's a friend, after all.

'Will you help me when the time comes? Jesus, I don't want to be a veg. If you're gonna be squeamish about this, Alan, I what to know right now so I'll have the time to look around for someone else.'

'No need for that. You aren't the first to ask me this and you won't be the last. I promise that I will walk through this with you, regardless of what happens.'

You know what I resent? I resent having to keep this a secret. Alan didn't have to remind me that there are laws against physician aid in dying. Alan's entire career could be in jeopardy if anything was to come out about this. This pisses me off! This clandestine nonsense is ridiculous. It's not like any of this is unheard of, but for some God-forsaken reason this compassionate practice continues to be locked in the closet.

You know what I think? I think we need a death liberation movement! Closets are for clothes, not for people or ideas. What kind of culture do we live in anyway? We have physician assisted capital punishment but not physician aid in dying for terminally ill people. I don't know, I just don't get it.

Holly: Right on, Kevin. A society that has capital punishment but not physician aid in dying is a society that believes that death is a punishment.

I'm sorry, but after being sick and nearly dying myself, I don't see it that way. I don't see how we'll ever bridge the gap between the two mind-sets, punishment on the one hand and compassion on the other. It's like talking about apples and oranges, there's no common ground!

Raymond: I believe that if we are going to err, we ought to err on the side of caution.

I have sympathy for someone who, at the end of his or her life, can't find relief from pain, but I still firmly believe that it is better for that one person to suffer than for the society as a whole to embrace mercy killing. It's a slippery slope, I tell you.

Before you know it, no one will be safe.

Kevin: I can't believe that you could say such a thing. How could you be so heartless?

Richard: Okay, okay. I'd better jump in here before things get said that we'll regret later.

Do you see what I mean when I said that the public discourse on this topic often generates more heat than light? It'll continue to be a hot-button issue until we can come to a consensus about the parameters of the debate.

I appreciate the fact that each of you has very strong feelings about this issue and I believe that's a real good thing. After all, we're talking about the sanctity of life, but I also suspect that there is a great deal more common ground shared by both sides of this debate than either side is willing to admit.

It's the impassioned rhetoric that always seems to get in the way, so until

cooler heads prevail I think we'd better move on.

Robin: Could we please spend what little time we have left in talking about the practical considerations of proactive dying? I don't want this opportunity to slip by without so much as a nod in that direction.

Richard: Thanks, Robin. That's exactly the direction in which I want to move our discussion. And I'd like to begin by reiterating the proviso you made a few minutes ago.

Just because we're talking about the specifics of proactive dying, our discussion should not to be construed as an endorsement.

I'd like to begin this final segment of our discussion with the stories of two very different death scenes. I was invited to be a consultant on both occasions.

Jeffery was dying of AIDS. He and Alex, his lover of nearly twenty years, were preparing for his imminent death. Jeffery had a fear that he was beginning to slide into dementia, which was his worst nightmare. He wanted to short-circuit this final indignity and wanted to know if I would help them plan a strategy for proactively ending his life. I told them that I would be happy to offer them whatever information I had.

On this first visit with them I tried to assess the situation, to get a feel for the level of commitment that each person was bringing to this endeavor. There was no doubt about it, Jeffery was actively dying, his doctor confirmed the dementia diagnosis, and so time was of the essence.

'Have you guys done your homework?'

'If you mean, have we squirreled away enough medications to do the trick, the answer is no. We never gave this eventuality a thought until recently and now there's not enough time to do that.'

'Will your doctor assist you with a prescription for a lethal dose of, let's say, a barbiturate?'

'Doubt it. We've never talked to her about this. I don't even know where she stands on the issue.'

'Well, then, how were you going to make this happen?'

'We were thinking about using street drugs, you know, coke and heroin. I also have some oral morphine left over from a friend who died last year.'

'That's it? That's your plan? What if you mess up on the dosage or something else goes wrong? I've seen it happen. You could be in worse shape than you are now and still not be dead. Do you have a Plan B?'

'We've talked about it some, Alex and I, and Alex promised that he wouldn't let me suffer.'

'What does that mean? Alex, do you know what it is you are promising?'

The three of us talked for hours about their half-baked scheme. I tried to get them to see how implausible their plan was and how serious the consequences if there was a miscalculation.

They would have none of it. Their love for each other and Alex's blind commitment to Jeffery to preserve him from any more suffering was all there was to know. Alex would be as resourceful as necessary, even if it meant he had to suffocate Jeffery in the end.

Ten days later I was called to their home again. I didn't realize it at first, but earlier that day they had set their plan in motion. Alex had scored some cocaine, freebased it, and watched as Jeffery shot up. Both of these guys had had a long history with intravenous drug use so all of this was familiar territory.

Unfortunately, Jeffery's history with drug use complicated matters considerably. He had built up a tolerance to the drug and even though he was nothing more than skin and bones, the dose was not lethal.

This is the situation as I found it. Jeffery was comatose and appeared near death, and Alex was at his wit's end.

'He's been like that for hours. I thought for sure he'd be dead by now. I think we've screwed up. What am I gonna do now?'

'I'm afraid I can't advise you. I can only help you weigh your options.'

As I saw it, Alex had two options. He could call the paramedics and have them try to revive Jeffery with all the trauma that would involve, or he could honor the commitment he made to Jeffery and complete the plan they rehearsed.

Then there was Earl and his wife Christina. Earl was in the final stages of lung cancer. He was a hard, difficult man, plagued by many personal demons. Even when he was well, people used to say that he was an acquired taste, and if you ask me, that was being generous.

The sicker he got, the more difficult he became. He alienated just about everyone – his sons, his friends, even the people from hospice. No one could tolerate his fury. In the end there was only Christina.

Some weeks before he died, Earl demanded that Christina call me over for a visit. I wasn't inclined to accept the summons because I hated to see how he treated her, but Christina sounded so defeated on the phone that I relented and made plans to stop by the following day.

Nothing had changed in the 8 months since my last visit. Despite being a mere shadow of his former self, Earl was as abusive as ever. How had Christina been able to stand it all this time, I wondered?

'I want to die! I want this to be over now. I can't get decent care. All these fucking doctors and nurses make me sick. They don't know what fuck they're doing. I sit here day after day in my own shit waiting for someone to help me.'

'He doesn't mean that, Richard. He gets good care.'

'Pipe down! I'm doing the talking. What the fuck does she know anyway? She don't know nothin' about what it's like for me.

Listen, Richard, I want to die. I want to end it right now, but I need help. I'm sick of this shit.'

'What kind of help do you need?' I asked.

'I read *Final Exit,* you know. I know how to do it. I got all these pills I can take.' Earl pointed to the cache of pill bottles in the nightstand drawer. 'But I don't want any slip-ups. I need someone to help me with the plastic bag at the right time, and she won't help me.' He nodded in the direction of his long-suffering wife.

It was true. Christina absolutely refused to help. When I asked her why, she could only sheepishly shrug her shoulders. There was much more to this than what was on the surface.

Earl then turned his attention to me. 'You got to help me. You're the only one left.'

'Earl, I won't and can't. It's not that your request is out of line. It's because I'm a stranger here. In all the years that we've known each other, you've never once invited even the most casual of friendships to form between us. You've always kept me out. You can't ask me to overlook that now. You're asking me to participate in one of the most intimate experiences two people can have in life and, I'm afraid, there just isn't any foundation for that here. I'm sorry.'

'You're a fuckin' coward, just like everybody else. So you can just get the fuck out and leave me alone.'

I hated to leave Christina alone with him, but I did as he demanded. Christina showed me to the door.

'Why won't you help him?' I asked when we were alone. 'It would be the end of your misery.'

'That's exactly why I won't. After all these years, I couldn't be sure that helping him die would be an act of compassion which would end his suffering, or an act of violence which would end mine.'

These two scenarios provide you with a blueprint of what not to do if you are seriously considering having someone assist you to die.

Robin: Okay, I get the picture. So what do I have to do if this is the way I want to go out?

Richard: First, if you expect heroics from the people who attend you, even if it doesn't include hastening your death, you'd be well advised to treat your attendants as heroes. Mutual respect and consideration, honor and compassion should be the hallmarks of your relationship with them.

Kevin: You also have to have a well-thought out plan.

Richard: And a Plan B. There's no substitute for meticulous attention to detail. Who, what, when, where, and how. Do your homework.

A good place to start is with the primer, *Final Exit* by Derek Humphry. Everything you need to know is right there.

Ideally, you'll have the assistance of your physician, at least in terms of providing you with a prescription for a lethal dose of medication. This is not as uncommon an occurrence as you might think. Unfortunately, even though recent polls show that 69% of respondents support the right of terminally ill patients to receive help from physicians to end their lives, and 72% say they oppose federal legislation that would prohibit physicians from prescribing lethal doses of medications like barbiturates to their terminally ill patients, doctors continue to be at risk because current law does not reflect the majority opinion.

It's wise to establish the kind of relationship with one's doctor, as Brian Friedman pointed out last week, which would allow your physician to have a clear conscience when prescribing a lethal dose of medication. Don't expect this kind of assistance from a doctor who is a stranger.

I also recommend that you begin a frank dialogue about the topic of assisted dying with your physician long before you need to make that kind of request. The more history you have with your doctor in this regard, the less likely he or she will interpret your request, when made, as an indication of depression.

You'd also be well advised to make your case as dispassionately as you can. An intelligent, well thought out argument for your right to die with dignity will get a better reception than if your presentation appears to be whimsical or hot-blooded.

Remember, if you make your case in terms of compassion, it's not a particularly difficult case to make under the correct circumstances.

Holly: And if a doctor's assistance is not available, what then?

Richard: Then stockpiling a lethal dose of appropriate medications may be the answer. This, of course, takes long-range planning. But then again, I believe this prospect demands this kind of serious consideration and personal resolve.

Remember, you'll also need an anti-nausea drug like Compazine. This medication will make it less likely that you will vomit up the lethal drugs you will be taking.

Mike: How do I go about finding out who would be willing to help me?

Richard: By asking.

I would begin by interviewing those I love, to see who may have psychological, emotional, or moral reservations to assisting me in this fashion.

I would never ask anyone to violate their ethical code regardless of how much I need help.

I would continue my search until I found the right person or persons to help me. I would insist that they read *Final Exit*, so that they would know exactly what I expected of them.

I would want to be sure that the person I choose to assist me could be trusted to complete the task if necessary.

Without belaboring the point, I would check in with this person regularly to see if their level of commitment remains high, and I would excuse anyone who had developed the least reservations about helping me.

It's well advised to keep the number of people involved to the smallest number possible. One or two people at the most is my recommendation. Confidentiality and coordination of effort is essential and large groups make that virtually impossible.

Mia: That leaves the questions of when and where?

Richard: Let's consider the question of where first.

Proactive dying is best accomplished in the privacy of your own home. There is no wisdom in trying to do this in an institutional setting like a hospital or extended care facility for all the reasons that I just mentioned.

With regard to the question of when, there's a real simple answer, possibly never.

As I said at the beginning of this discussion, proactive dying is a relatively rare occurrence. It's been my experience that even people who are completely prepared to end their life don't, because they always find a reason to live another day. The indomitable human spirit generally triumphs. People tend to live their deaths until nature takes its course.

People are forever drawing lines in the sand, so to speak. I'm often told by sick, elder and dying people that they have every intention to end their life when such and such occurs – when I can't walk, when I can't see, when I'm no longer able to take care of myself, etc. But when that time actually comes, most people discover that life is still precious and worthy of living at least another day.

The real reason so many people are so passionate about their right to choose how and when they die is so they will have a sense of continuity in their life.

People have confidence that, while they are well, they have control over their living. This may be an illusion, but most people believe they are the masters of their own fate.

So it comes as no big surprise that they would want to be as confident about controlling their dying.

I guess that's why dying people tell me so often that having their cache of pills in their bedside drawer makes all the difference in the world. 'I don't intend to use them, at least not now. But I know that they're there and that makes me feel more in control of my own destiny.'

No wonder so many Americans support the notion of assisted dying. That's the kind of people we are. We like to have choices. It makes us feel powerful and in control.

I'm afraid that's all we have time for today. I want to thank you for helping me make this presentation possible. Your open-mindedness has been truly refreshing.

My Turn

Richard: Have you given any thought to proactive dying? Where do you stand on the issue?

_____

_____

_____

_____

_____

_____

_____

_____

_____

_____

Richard: Next week is our final week together. We have a bunch of things we need to take care of, not least of which is the evaluation process. In order to prepare you for that, I want to set you up with this week's homework.

I would like you to complete these evaluation forms. One will help you to evaluate the five presentations and the other will help you to assess the program in general.

This is a very important part of the process. We depend on your critique to keep the program fresh and up-to-date. So please take all the time you need to thoughtfully complete these forms and we'll go over your comments next week.

Are there any final questions or comments before we conclude?

Mia: Oh, I almost forgot. I have a joke. My father told me this one, if you can believe that.

You know how when a Chinese family opens a new restaurant, all their friends and relatives send flowers or a potted plant to wish them good fortune? Well...

A Chinese family had just opened a new restaurant and friends decided to send flowers for the occasion.

The flowers arrived at the restaurant, but when the family read the card, it said, 'Rest in Peace.'

The father of the family was indignant. Was this some kind of bad joke? Surely the suggestion of death at this auspicious occasion would only bring bad luck. He called the florist immediately to complain. The florist, realizing his mistake, apologized profusely.

'Sir, I'm really very sorry for the mix-up, but if you think you have reason to be angry try to imagine this – somewhere there is a funeral taking place today, and they have flowers with a note saying, 'Congratulations on your new location.' (Everyone laughs.)

AT-HOME WORK

Week 9 — Evaluations

Please take the time to complete one of these evaluation forms for each of the six presenters. The Final Evaluation form that follows will assist you in critiquing the entire program.

Evaluation

Title of Presentation: _____

Presenter: _____

Your responses and comments will help us evaluate the services we offer. Please indicate with a check which response most accurately reflects your opinion regarding the following statement.

	Strongly Agree	Agree	Disagree	Strongly Disagree
The purpose and objectives were clearly stated.				
My expectations were met.				
The presenter was sufficiently organized and qualified.				
I felt safe and supported in my sharing.				
The homework for this presentation was helpful.				

The <u>most</u> helpful things I learned were:

_____

_____

_____

The <u>least</u> helpful aspects were:

_____

_____

_____

Comments/suggestions:

_____

_____

_____

Final Evaluation

What were the most important things that you learned from this program?

_____

_____

_____

_____

What did you like best about the sessions?

_____

_____

_____

_____

How would you rate the experience of the facilitator?

_____

_____

_____

_____

What did you like least about the sessions?

_____

_____

_____

_____

If you were to improve 3 things about the group, what would they be, and how would you improve them?

_____

_____

_____

_____

Please comment on your experience of this group's format:

Information: _____ Enough   _____ Too much   _____ Not enough

Sharing time: _____ Enough   _____ Too much   _____ Not enough

Would you recommend this program to a friend or family member?

_____

_____

_____

Please add any further questions and/or comments.

_____

_____

_____

_____

Chapter Ten

Week 10:
Closing the Circle

Checking In

Richard: Welcome back, everyone. Here we are at the end of our ten weeks and you're still here. Congratulations!

Today we'll begin with our check-in. As usual, we'll spend some time with last week's homework and since this is our last week together, we'll also be looking to the future before we bring our group to a close.

So let's begin. During your check-in this week, besides providing us with an update on what's been happening in your life, I'd appreciate it if you could speak briefly about how your attitudes towards death and dying may have changed over the past ten weeks.

How about you, Raul, will you start us off today?

Raul: Okay, sure.

Shit, man, I can't believe that this thing is over already. It's been hellacool. I learned a lotta stuff and you helped me find a good way to talk to my family, so I'm happy. I don't know what I woulda done if it wasn't for you guys.

See, me and my parents are good now, we're still goin' to see Father Diego every week. He's so cool, man, he really knows how to talk to my mother real good. And I'm not so worried anymore like I used to be, so that's great.

Richard: What about the future?

Raul: Oh yeah, I graduate from high school pretty soon, so that's cool. Then I think I'll just hang out for the summer. I was thinkin' maybe I could come by here and help you do stuff. I could answer the phone and shit like that. You don't even have to pay me or nothin' unless you want to.

Richard: Thanks Raul, I'd like that very much. I could use the help and the company.

But I'm curious, what about ending all your treatments? You said when we began this group that you wanted to quit dialysis and let nature take its course. What's happening with that?

Raul: I don't know, it's not so bad like it used to be. Not the dialysis, but the way things are at home. I guess mostly I was tired of havin' to fake it for my parents. They're not pushin' me anymore like they used to and I like that. I got some new pain meds too, so that's helpin'. Things are okay for now, so I thought I'd stick around. Besides, I gotta help you run this whole thing, right?

Holly: Raul, when I first met you, I just couldn't believe that you wanted to die. I remember going home and telling Jean that there was this sweet young guy in the group who wants to die. I told her that even though you'd been sick since you were a little kid and that you weren't looking so good now, I couldn't get over the fact that you actually wanted to end it all. I just wanted to take you and shake you and yell, 'hey, don't give up!'

What I discovered over these past ten weeks was I was just projecting all my own death anxiety on you back then. I didn't pick up on what was really going on with you until later. Like it was only a few weeks ago that I realized that you weren't giving up at all, but that you knew you were going to die and had made peace with the fact long before I met you.

I guess I was being just like your family, huh? If only I had paid closer attention to what you were saying back then, I would have seen how wrong I was about you. But I've got to say that I wasn't doing this on purpose. You see I couldn't hear your story back then because I had too much screaming going on in my own head to hear anything from anyone else. In fact, I think I missed most of the first couple of weeks of this group because I was too busy paying attention to Holly.

This group helped me turn down the volume inside my head a little bit so that I could begin to hear what was going on for ya'll. Boy, I wish I could turn right around and start this whole group all over again. I know I'd get a lot more out of it a second time around.

Mike: I hear ya, Holly. I feel the same way. What an ornery cuss I was.

Raymond: What do you mean, 'was?' (Everyone laughs.)

Mike: Hey, watch that.

Okay, okay, so this ten weeks didn't turn me into a saint, but you have to admit I made some progress, and I haven't even told you the best of it. I'm on the little blue pill.

Clare: What little blue pill?

Mike: *Viagra!*

Robin: Get outta here! I knew something like that was up. I was afraid that I was going to have to come over there and slap that grin off your face.

From the looks of it, I'd say that you're finally gettin' some.

Mike: Finally is right! This is a frigging miracle drug. It's so amazing! No kidding!

I'll spare you the graphic details, because you know how shy I am.

Robin: Yeah, right!

Mike: Let's just say it works. I'm happy. Maryanne's happy that I'm happy. The whole goddamn world's happy that I'm happy. (Everyone groans.)

No, you've got to understand what a big thing this is for me.

Raymond: No pun intended.

Mike: Would you crackers let me finish? I mean it! This medication has changed my life.

Cheryl's little tidbit of information a couple of weeks ago changed my life. So I'd like to repay the favor. What about this Mentor Training Program you keep talking about, Richard? I think I want to plug into that. I think that I could really make a contribution to the next generation of folks coming through this program.

What I'm trying to say is I want to stay connected.

Richard: I think you'd make a great mentor, Mike. I was hoping you'd want to continue with the program. I'll talk more about this next step in the process a bit later, but right now I'd like to continue with our check-in.

Mia: I'm having a lot of the same feelings that Holly's having. I missed a lot of the first few weeks of this group because I was all balled up with my own stuff. It wasn't until Max died that I realized this wasn't just about me. I feel bad about that, because I let my own anger and frustration get in the way of learning all I could from each of you.

Oh well, no use in crying over spilled milk. Besides, it wasn't intentional.

I suppose if I went over some of the homework that we had those first few weeks I could recapture some of what I lost, but it wouldn't really be the same as doing it with all of you. So I want to stay connected too.

Clare: Well, I'm just glad that I made it through the whole course without missing any of the meetings. I honestly didn't think I was going to be able to make it. Even though I'll miss you all terribly, I'm glad this is coming to an end. I haven't the strength to make it to even one more session.

What was that euphemism for dying? Oh yes, circling the drain. I know that I'm circling the drain now. I will die very soon. I know that. And frankly, it couldn't come too soon. I am that tired.

Charley and the kids are exhausted too. No one will admit it, of course, but I can see it in their eyes.

I'd like to ask each of you to remember me as someone who wanted to die with dignity and grace. I believe I've accomplished that and I have each of you to thank for helping me make that a reality in my life. You'll probably never know how much this group has meant to me.

But in an effort to show my gratitude for what you've done for me, I have a little gift for each of you, a small memento to help you remember me by. I hope you will accept my gift in the spirit it is given, with heartfelt appreciation for the many gifts you've given me these past ten weeks. Thank you, everyone.

Raymond: No, it is I who must thank you. It has been such a privilege to be with you these past ten weeks. I feel as though I've been in the presence of a saint. You've taught me so much, and your words of encouragement and support when Joann was dying made all the difference in the world. I'm really going to miss you, Clare.

This group has been a godsend. You've inspired me to take a good, hard look at my life and quit being such a slug.

So I have a little surprise for you, it's my way of giving each of you a gift. It's not like something you can hang on your wall or anything, but I hope you'll understand that my gift to you is only possible because of your many gifts to me.

So here it is. I've made a commitment to turn my life around.

Richard, you said something to me the second week we were together. You said, 'Ray, why not choose life?' Those words have echoed in head throughout this course. Two weeks ago I made this promise to myself and now I make it to each of you. I pledge to always choose life. No more running and hiding. No more taking the path of least resistance. And just so you know that I really mean it, here's a sample of what I'm already doing.

I joined a gym. Can you stand it? Me at a gym! I even got myself a personal trainer, who's been busting my hump big time. I ache in places I didn't even know I had places. But, you know what? It's a good ache. It's the kind of ache that makes me feel alive. And here's the

corker, my trainer's put me on a diet. It's a no carbohydrate diet. Well, low carbohydrates anyhow. I said to him. 'Are you crazy? You expect me to give up bread and potatoes and pasta? I'll die! Why not just shoot me in the head now and be done with it?'

Well, I'm two weeks into the diet and besides the rather severe carbohydrate withdrawal I've been experiencing, the diet's working. I've already lost fifteen pounds. My trainer says that the cravings will disappear in time. God, I hope so, because I'm even having pasta dreams at night. Mmmmm, pasta! So you've got to know that I'm serious about choosing life if I'm willing to make this kind of sacrifice.

Which brings me to one final thing that I need to say. Kevin, I owe you an apology. I was such a bear last week. It was probably the carbohydrate withdrawal, but whatever it was, I was way out of line during our discussion on assisted dying. You'll have to forgive me I just wasn't myself last week.

Kevin: That's funny, I was just going to apologize to you for my behavior last week. I haven't been myself either. The chemo is killing me, but not the lymphoma. After three weeks of this shit, there's no discernable change in the cancer, so I've decided to quit the treatment altogether.

My doctor thinks I'm being premature in making the decision to stop, but I just couldn't stand it anymore. And for what, some vain hope that a miracle will happen? And what about my life in the meantime? I have zero quality of life.

No! Forget it. I've been so sick that I've only been able to make it to school once this whole week. We have a big end-of-the-year concert coming up in just three weeks and I'm way behind in getting that together.

You know what breaks me up? I mean, other than having to shave my head because my hair was falling out in clumps. I never got to Europe. I was going to go this summer, remember? Just bum around the whole time, but that's not gonna happen now. Why did I wait so long?

Please, you guys, take a tip from me. Things deferred turn quickly into things denied. Don't let this happen to you. Get out there and do all the stuff you've been putting off until another time, because, darlings, there's no guarantee there'll be another time.

Janice: So what are you going to do?

Kevin: I don't know. I guess I'm just going to let it all wind down. I mean, what else can I do? Alan, my doctor, says that I should regain some of my strength and vitality once all this chemo clears my system, but after that there will be a gradual decline till the end. I figure I got six months tops.

Richard: How are you feeling about that?

Kevin: I guess I'm trying to be philosophical about it all. I figure I've been living on borrowed time all these years since my HIV diagnosis anyhow.

One thing I can say for sure is I'm much better off having done this group. I feel like I've been able to look death in the face these past ten weeks and I didn't flinch. So maybe, just maybe, death is not so foreboding after all. I'm beginning to see what you meant, Richard, when you recalled your own death revelation. You said that you began to see death like St. Francis did when he called her, 'Sister Death.' I guess you'll just have to check with me in a few months to see what I have to say then.

One final thing. You guys have all been so terrific. I don't know what I'd do without you. So maybe I won't try. I want to continue with the program too. There's still a hell of a lot more that I need to figure out about this dying business and I don't know a better place to find the answers than right here. So you ain't gonna be rid of me yet.

Robin: I'm sure glad to hear that, because I'm not going anywhere either. I'm just getting the hang of this.

I don't have anything else to report, so I'll save my comments about the process for when we do the evaluations, if that's okay.

Janice: I guess that leaves me. I went to church on Sunday. Did I tell you I joined my local Presbyterian Church? Well I did, join, I mean. It is very nice and the people have been exceptionally friendly. Two ladies even asked me about my hair. I just smiled and said a friend did my hair for me. I think they were jealous.

There's a bake sale next week and I told the pastor that I'd be happy to do some baking and to help out at the sale itself. Goodness, it's so nice to be getting involved again, and I have all of you to thank for that, especially you, Robin. I just don't see how I would have been able to do it without you. Your friendship means a great deal to me. Thank you.

And thanks to each of you for providing me this opportunity to come back to life and start to grow again.

Richard: I had a pretty good week. I did a memorial service for my friend Kenny who died a couple of days ago. That was an adventure.

Kenny and I had been friends for nearly twenty years. He and his lover Matt used to have some of the best parties in town. Over the years they built up a very interesting group of friends. One could always expect to encounter fascinating people and stimulating conversation when visiting their comfortable home.

Kenny used to refer to his friends as his San Francisco family. It was a way of distinguishing us from his blood family who live in Kansas, but it was also a term of endearment that described the close bond of affection that he formed with his friends.

In the last weeks and days of Kenny's life, friction began to develop between his blood family and his San Francisco family. I watched with sheer amazement as a rivalry began to form. Friends and family were jockeying for position. Who was the most important to Kenny, who had the most profound grief? Kenny was actively dying so he couldn't put an end to this nonsense. And the strangest thing was that somehow I got caught in the middle of the feud. You see, I had real close ties to both sides. Each family began to claim me as the champion of their cause. I found out that each side in this increasingly divisive contest was using me against the other.

'Richard said this...'

'Well, that's impossible, because when I talked to Richard he told me this...'

Fortunately, Kenny died oblivious to the unhappy drama unfolding around him, but unfortunately his death only increased the tension.

I should probably add here that there was absolutely no reason for any of this nuttiness. Kenny's two families had always been close to one another. He worked real hard to integrate both families into his life and he never showed any favoritism. But grief is a powerful emotion and it can distort realities and drive otherwise sane people to do and say completely insane things.

On the day of the memorial service I showed up at the mortuary to find the two families sitting like armed camps on either side of the of the chapel. I went to the front of the room to begin the service and looked out on the two families lost in their independent grief. I thought to myself that this wasn't how it was supposed to be.

I began with a prayer as usual, but then I couldn't continue.

'I've come here to grieve the death of my friend and to celebrate his life and I can't continue, I won't continue, until we bring some kind of resolution to the animosity that has developed between Kenny's two families. You do dishonor to the memory of your son and brother, lover and friend if you let this foolishness continue. This is shameful and I'm not going to be part of this. I won't let this happen, not here, not today.'

So I just sat down and waited to see what would happen next. There were a few moments of stunned silence. Then Kenny's mother, Julia, mopping the tears from her eyes, stood up and crossed the aisle. She went directly to Matt who was also sobbing and reached out to embrace him. He stood to receive her embrace and then walked her back to her seat on the other side of the aisle where he took his rightful place beside Julia, his arm around her.

This tender act of reconciliation broke open the entire service. It was as if a cloud had lifted, and I'm sure that it was Kenny's doing. Once we all regained our composure, I was able to stand before all of my friends and lead them in the celebration of a life well lived.

My Check-In

Richard: During your check-in this week, besides providing an update on what's been happening in your life, I'd appreciate it if you could address how your attitudes towards death and dying may have changed over the past ten weeks.

_____

_____

_____

_____

_____

_____

_____

_____

_____

_____

_____

_____

Group Process

Richard: Okay, let's turn our attention to the evaluation process. I can't overstate the importance of your input at this point. It's imperative that this program stay vibrant and that can only happen if we pay careful attention to the feedback we get from each participant of every group. For example, this program has expanded over the years from a one-hour a week, eight-week commitment to the current two-hour a week, ten-week commitment that you are now completing.

Thanks to the thoughtful critiques of our participants, we are constantly fine-tuning this cutting edge experience so it will continue to be the valuable resource it is.

I'd like to begin this portion of our time together by taking a look at your evaluations of the presentations. Our first presentation was on legal issues with Steve Susoyev and Emmett Giurlani.

Mike: This was the best presentation, to my mind. These guys really knew their stuff. I like working with a pro,

especially when it comes to the law, and these guys were pros with a capital 'P.'

I appreciated the way both Steve and Emmett paid attention to detail without getting lost in the minutiae of the law. I put down on my evaluation form that I strongly agreed with all the five statements regarding this presentation. The objectives were clear, my expectations were met, the presenters were organized and qualified, I felt safe and supported, and the homework was helpful. I gave them both an A+.

Raymond: I thought so too. And what was so great about it was I was able to use the information I received almost immediately when Joann died.

I liked the fact that both Emmett and Steve had a sense of humor and that they were so easy to talk to. They sure were different from the two or three other lawyers I've had to deal with in my time. These other guys were so impatient and condescending.

Janice: I have to confess, I was dreading the Legal Concerns presentation. I even found the homework overwhelming. But I was pleasantly surprised to find that both Steve and Emmett were warm and inviting and easy to talk to. I learned a lot about wills and advance directives.

Richard: Anyone else? Any dissenting opinions?

Mia: This is not a dissenting opinion exactly. In fact, it's not really a comment about their presentations at all. I just wanted to say that this is one of the weeks that I was so caught up with myself, so full of self-pity, that I missed a lot of their very important information. I remember Steve and Emmett being very kind to me, but I still feel as though I could use a refresher course.

I wonder if there's a way I could sit in on this presentation at another time, maybe with the next group?

Richard: Good question. Yes, anyone who's completed this ten-week program is welcome to sit in on any or all of the presentations with another group. That's one of the perks of being an alumnus.

Okay, our next presentation was spirituality with David Pettee.

Robin: I liked David a lot and I thought he did a fine job with a real difficult subject.

I was happy to discover that there are plenty of ways to define spirituality that doesn't get all messed up with religious dogma. I felt really comfortable sharing my spiritual journey with him.

Holly: I did too. I thought David was well organized and extremely qualified. He was also very supportive. I liked his low-key, friendly manner.

Kevin: This presentation got me to do some serious thinking about my own personal spiritual journey and that has been really helpful to me. I only wish we had had more time to dig even deeper then we did.

Clare: I thought the homework for that week was well thought out. I too wish we'd had more time to get into some of the different notions of spirituality, like nature religion.

Richard: Anyone else? Any dissenting opinions?

Raul: I thought he was cool. He reminded me a lot of Father Diego.

Richard: Okay, our next presentation was sexuality and intimacy with Cheryl Cohen-Greene.

Mia: This was my favorite presentation. Cheryl was outstanding. I think what made her presentation so special was the fact that she had cancer and that she'd gone through one of these groups herself. She really knew what we were dealing with.

Holly: I agree. Cheryl was excellent. And her presentation had so many practical applications. As you know, she helped me make a major breakthrough with my body image stuff and for that I am eternally grateful. I wish I could thank her in person.

Richard: You can, Holly. I'll give you Cheryl's email address and phone number before you leave today. I encourage you to contact her directly and tell her what you've just told us. I'm sure it would make her day.

Anyone else? Any dissenting opinions?

Raul: She sure was nice to me and she wasn't, like ya know, scared to talk about all that sex stuff. She's the only lady I ever met who could talk like that.

Mike: As you know, that week was sheer torture for me. I would have rather had a root canal. But Cheryl's information paid off big time. I'm sure glad I stuck it out.

Raul: I'm glad you stuck it out too. Because shit, man, now you can have it stick out all the time. (Everyone laughs.)

Richard: See how you are, Raulito? Don't worry, Mike, all this ribbing is a sign of our affection.

Our next presentation was final stages with Brian Friedman.

Kevin: This was my favorite presentation. And Brian is such a hunk, hubba, hubba, hubba! I thought the homework was extremely helpful, too.

Clare: Yes, I really enjoyed Brian's presentation too. It was filled with so many practical suggestions on how to talk to my doctor. Living my death, having my life ebb away as it is, has been less intimidating thanks to Brian. His information on what to expect as my body shuts down has been very important for both my family and me.

Janice: I also gave this presentation high marks. I was particularly impressed with Brian's discussion of comfort care.

Richard: Anyone else? Any dissenting opinions?

Okay, our final seminar was my presentation on assisted dying.

Robin: Hated it.

Kevin: Me too.

Raul: Me three.

Mike: Yeah, I should've stayed home.

Richard: Okay, you guys. What's gotten in to you today? You're as squirrelly as a bunch of fourth graders on the last day of school.

Robin: Sorry, couldn't help myself.

Richard, I'm sure glad you did that presentation yourself. And I'm glad that you took the time to frame the discussion in the way that you did. Now when I look at the question of assisted dying, I'll do so with a more open mind.

Kevin: Like I said earlier, I feel like I was being a bully last week. At first I thought you were just going to be politically correct and avoid the whole issue of proactive dying. It was only at the end of our sometimes-heated debate that I understood what you were trying to do.

Now I know why you tried to make the discussion as inclusive as you did. So if you think I was being a jerk last week, you're probably right.

Mike: I thought that you handled the topic with great finesse. The issue of assisted dying is a moral and legal minefield. I'm just glad I wasn't responsible for that presentation. I wouldn't have known where to begin. I think it's courageous of you to even include this topic on the list of seminars for this group.

Richard: Anyone else? Any dissenting opinions?

Raymond: After I realized what a hard-ass I was being last week, I could see that all my comments were doing was polarizing the debate. Thanks for being so patient with me...with all of us.

My Turn

Richard: What are your comments regarding the presentations? What were the most helpful things you learned? What were the least helpful aspects? Please refer to last week's homework.

Richard: Alrighty then. Let's turn our attention to the evaluation of the program itself.

Mike: Richard, this has been the best thing that's happened to me in a long time. I know I came here with a chip on my shoulder the size of Cleveland and I know that I have a long way to go yet, but I can honestly say I'm glad I did this course. And I want to thank each of you for being so patient with me. I know it wasn't always easy. So I owe you all big time on this one.

My only suggestion is that I would like to see the program extended by a week or two and maybe each session could be three hours instead of two. And yes, I would absolutely recommend this program to a friend.

I think Maryanne would really benefit from doing this course. Any chance someone who's not sick or dying could participate?

Richard: Sure, she'd be welcome to join us at any time. This program is designed for anyone who wants to face his or her mortality; you don't have to be sick to do that.

I'd also like to make a brief comment about your suggestion that we extend the course beyond the current ten-week, two-hour a week commitment.

I just don't think it's feasible. Just imagine if, when you started the group ten weeks ago, Mike, you had to look forward to three hours a week for twelve weeks. You would've never stayed the course. Remember how you couldn't wait to get out of here the first couple of weeks? I appreciate the fact that you didn't have enough time to accomplish everything you wanted to, but remember this is only the beginning.

My philosophy is: leave your audience wanting more.

Janice: This is so sad, having the group coming to the end like this. I'm not very good at saying goodbye, especially since this group has meant so very much to me.

The thing I liked most about this group was the weekly sharing. As you know, when I started this program I was awfully isolated, living by myself and all after Albert passed on. This group has helped me break out of that isolation and start living again.

Richard, you've been wonderful. Your thoughtfulness, generosity, and wonderful sense of humor made this program very special. I thought you were masterful as our facilitator. And yes, I would recommend this program to a friend or family member.

Thank you, everyone. It has been a pleasure to be with you these past ten weeks.

Robin: Ditto.

Hey, I'm no good at saying goodbye either. All I can say is that it's been great. There's nothing I didn't like and plenty that I thought was fantastic, especially you, Jan. Richard, you were marvelous too. And I'm looking forward to becoming a mentor.

Raul: Man, this thing changed my whole life around. Ya remember what a scared little shit I was when we first started? Bein' here made me not so scared, not just about dyin' but about livin' and talkin' to my family and all that shit.

Father Diego wants to meet you, Richard. He says he thinks you could help him talk to some of the other sick people at church. And my parents want you to come to dinner too. Is that okay?

You guys are the bomb. Thanks for helpin' me with everything.

Mia: I'd like to thank everyone for being so supportive. That's been the best thing about being here with each of you. I've learned so much about myself and how I've been letting my fears of dying get in the way of my living.

I think I've also been able to get a handle on my anger. The meditation I'm doing at the Zen Center is helping, but mostly I owe each of you a debt of gratitude for being so patient in helping me see that I had a problem.

The only thing I'd change is the amount of time we had for our group sharing. There never seemed to be enough time to address all the issues that came up on any particular week.

I think your point about extending either the amount of time for each week's meeting or the number of weeks involved in the commitment, Richard, is well taken, but I still wish there would have been more time for us to just talk among ourselves. That's the real value of this program, isn't it? I mean, I suppose one could find all the information that we got during the presentations somewhere else, but where could one find a group like this, where everyone is dealing with his or her mortality?

Raymond: That's interesting. I have just the opposite opinion.

I really liked the group part of this program for sure, but I thought the presentations were the best part. In fact, I would like to have had even more presentations. The reason I say that is because I thought the presentations were the very thing that kept us focused. Without them we probably would have suffered the fate of all the other support groups I've ever been in. After a while, the reason for being together begins to blur and the group loses its direction, and it turns into nothing more than a bitch session.

That didn't happen here and I'm glad. Besides, where else would a person go to find all the practical and personalized information we received from our speakers?

Holly: I agree with Ray. I thought the presentations were the heart and soul of the program. There was something about the presentations that made them special, but for the life of me I couldn't come up with what it was until it finally dawned on me.

You know how most folks talk about death in the abstract? Well, not one of the speakers did that. Each presenter talked to us like death is a reality and that was really refreshing.

I should probably say that I found this a little intimidating at first, because I wanted to hide out and pretend that

none of this applied to me. Boy, I'm sure glad they kept up the pressure by being so upfront about it all, because I'd probably still be playing hide and seek.

You know what else I really liked? I liked how you made each of us all feel welcome, Richard.

Even though we all came from such different backgrounds and lifestyles, you made us all feel right at home. That's kind of amazing, because when we first started I said to myself, 'Honey, this ain't never gonna work. Just look around, I don't have anything in common with anyone else.' I was so very wrong. We had our mortality in common and that's all that was needed.

So thanks, ya'll. This has really been something.

Kevin: I can't get over how this group appeared just at the right moment for me. I firmly believe that there aren't any accidents in life. I really believe this was meant to happen. Maybe it was fate or God, I don't know, but whatever it was, it's uncanny.

What this group did for me was help me uncover the reserve of personal resourcefulness I've been building up since Doug died. This has been like a refresher course for me.

I'm glad that some of us will be continuing on to do the mentor training together, because now that I know that my time is limited, I want to make the most of it. And what better way is there than helping other people to tap into their own reserves of resourcefulness?

Clare: I'm so proud of you, Kevin. I wish I could join you in that noble endeavor, but alas I won't be here. No, that's not true. I'll be here, all right, but you'll have to look to your own hearts to find me. I promise I'll never be farther away than that.

The best thing about this group for me was having the opportunity to speak my mind about my own dying without having it discounted as a bunch of hokum. You don't know how wonderful that was for me.

This has been the only place I've been able to talk about the concerns I have without being told not to talk like that. This group helped me strengthen my resolve to die with dignity and grace, something I surely wouldn't have been able to do without the group.

The presentations were wonderful, of course. All the practical advice was so helpful. The weekly homework exercises were thought provoking and kept my mind focused throughout the week.

But there's nothing that compares to the friendships I made here. I found you each a kindred spirit, a fellow traveler on this unfamiliar road, and that's been the greatest gift of all.

Kudos to you, Richard, for making this all possible. I have a much greater sense of peace as I approach my death because of this wonderful program.

I should probably also tell you that I'm trying to get Charley to enroll in this program because I think it will help him with his grieving process. Do you think that's a good idea?

Richard: I think that's an excellent idea. I believe that the grieving process is all about learning to put death in its proper perspective. That is, despite the sense of loss one experiences, one must learn to embrace the fact that death is a natural and essential part of life. And what better way to do that than to face one's own mortality head on?

Yes, I believe Charley will find a home here, if for no other reason than this is the place where you came to celebrate your own mortality and as you've just said, you'll never be very far away from those of us who made that possible.

My Turn

Richard: What are your comments regarding the program itself? What did you like best? What did you like least? What things need improving? Please refer to last week's homework.

Richard: So now it's my turn to evaluate you.

Over the years I've facilitated dozens of these groups and each one has had a unique personality. Some groups have been difficult, and others seemed to run effortlessly, almost on their own. Your group has been extraordinary in that I felt, even from the beginning, a deep connection to each of you. It's been an honor and a pleasure to spend these past ten weeks with you as you made this journey of discovery.

I want to thank you for your kind remarks earlier about my skill as a facilitator. I appreciate them all the more since they come from people I hold in such high esteem.

I know you think that I took the lead these past weeks, and in some sense of that word I suppose you'd probably be right. But the truth of the matter is, and I speak from experience here, we walked together, side-by-side, supporting and encouraging one another when one or another of us faltered.

And you should know that there were many times that I felt as though I was being led by you. Your honesty and openness, your willingness to be vulnerable, has been an enormous inspiration to me. Thank you.

I look forward to working with those of you who wish to train as mentors. And I suppose this is as good a time as any to tell you a bit more about that process.

As you know, PARADIGM operates on a generational model. Now that you've completed this ten-week program you are considered a PARADIGM Associate. If you wish to continue with us, you will be paired with a mentor, someone who is just a few steps ahead of you in the program.

Your mentor will serve as your confidante and a personal guide to the rest of the program. You will then join your mentor in The Mentor Training Program. This is a more open-ended experience than the one you are just completing. It consists of a series of specialized workshops and seminars covering the major issues and techniques of enhancing life near death.

You will be invited to begin a video chronicle of your personal journey. Your mentor will help you get started and share his or her videos with you.

Your video chronicle will provide you with an opportunity to evaluate your progress toward fulfilling your own personal goals in dying. And in turn your videos, along with those already created by people who have gone before you, form our unique library of the developmental histories of men and women just like you who have committed themselves to dying wisely and well.

You will also be able to choose from an array of other resources including massage and bodywork, exercise and nutrition programs, meditation, journal work, and art therapy. As you become more familiar with other aspects of the dying process, and acquire some experience in assisting others, you will in turn become a mentor to someone new. And the circle will be complete.

As we close, I'd like to invite you to join me in one last group hug. I am so grateful for all the wonderful things that happened to us these past weeks, for friendships formed, for wisdom shared, for all the grace, tolerance and generosity that seemed to pour from each of you. And I'm thankful for the gift of our friend Max, who brought us so much joy and laughter.

You've just spent ten weeks pioneering a new standard of a good death so you are in a unique position now to help the rest of society desensitize death and dying. I hope you'll take every opportunity to share what you've learned here with all those who might benefit, because as you know, there are a whole lot of amateurs out there.

Stay in touch. I love you.

About the Author

Richard Wagner, Ph.D., ACS

He is psychotherapist/clinical sexologist in private practice since 1981. He is the founder and executive director, of PARADIGM Programs, Inc., a nonprofit organization with the mission of enhancing the end of life.

He has been working with terminally ill, chronically ill, elder and dying people in hospital, hospice, and home settings for over 30 years. He facilitates support groups for care-providers and clinical personnel, and provides grief counseling for survivors both individually and in group settings.

He designs, develops, and produces long and short term in-service training seminars and workshops for helping and healing professionals.

He often speaks in the public forum on policy issues related to religion, human sexuality, aging, death and dying, surviving chronic illness, and moral development.

For more information: www.theamateursguide.com.

26065143R00199

Made in the USA
Charleston, SC
22 January 2014